THE
ULTIMATE
Choice

by
Ken Gingrich

Kenny and Judy Gingrich

The Ultimate Choice

Library of Congress Number: 2013939150

International Standard Book Number: 978-1-60126-382-7

Printed 2013 by
Masthof Press
219 Mill Road
Morgantown, PA 19543-9516

Dedication

I would like to dedicate this book to my wife Judy, and to my son, Kenny and his wife Michelle, and our grandson Brady. They all have been a great influence and joy in my life.

Acknowledgements

I would like to extend my thanks and appreciation to the following people. My wife, Judy, for her part in typing the stories from my recordings, for her valuable input and for the many long hours she put into this book. To Don Shaw, who helped me in the writing of the hunting portion of this book. As well as to my sister, Susie, for her dedication and helpful ideas as she helped format the non-hunting chapters in *The Ultimate Choice*. We strove to finish this book in a six-month-time period.

Table of Contents

Introduction

Ken Gingrich was born in Lancaster County, Pennsylvania, and grew up in a Mennonite home with many guidelines. He received his education in a two-room schoolhouse, living the lifestyle of a country boy among the Amish and Mennonites. At an early age he chose to live life his way, going in a different direction from his simple beginnings.

His speech impediment led him down a path, looking for acceptance and approval. He became a troublemaker finding trouble at every turn. He thought he found what he was looking for in motorcycle racing. This led to outlaw motorcycle clubs and other unlawful activities.

In pursuit of adventure he became an avid hunter in North America, breaking President Teddy Roosevelt's record for harvesting the most mountain lions. He became a guide in Canada for over 40 years, guiding bear and caribou hunts. Looking for greater adventure, he traveled to the African Plains many times to have experiences of a lifetime.

You will read about the many times his life could have ended. Through the twists and turns of his life, he is here to share his life's story with you. He shares his perspective on the many changes he has experienced over his lifetime.

In conclusion, you will learn about the Ultimate Choice leading him to find the fulfillment and acceptance he was always searching for. You will find this a quick moving story, filled with action and adventure.

Simple Beginning

In a small town, called Goodville, I made my entrance into the world. Goodville is nestled in Lancaster County, Pennsylvania, which is known for its many religious groups, including the Amish. Today the Amish continue to use horse and buggies for their transportation and resist the changes of the world around them. I was raised in a Mennonite home with my parents pointing me in the right path, but I chose to take my own path. I was always looking for the next thrill and wanted to see what the world had to offer. As a youth, that path included alcohol, partying, girls, and motorcycle gangs. As an adult, my quest for adventure was satisfied through adventurous hunting. The first 30 years of my life included many choices taking me far away from the "good" in the name of the town where I was born and raised.

I was one of seven children. My brother Carl is 1½ years older than me, and my brother Irvie, is 6½ years younger. I have two older sisters, Millie and Lorraine, and two younger sisters, Lois Ann and Susan. I always remember feeling I was different from my brothers, sisters, and friends. As an infant I was accidentally dropped by a nurse onto a hard floor. This was the first of many hard knocks I experienced as a child. As far back as I can remember I had a speech impediment,

1

Gingrich Family 1956, sitting: Edna, Susan, Irvin Sr., Standing: Carl, Lorraine, Lois Ann, Ken, Mildred, Irvin Jr.

causing me to stutter and stammer. This became a daily hindrance for me, resulting in a lot of teasing. My parents tried to help me overcome this speech defect by sending me to various doctors and programs but nothing seemed to help. Every time I opened my mouth to talk I was faced with the possibility of embarrassment. I had this hanging over me all my life and starting at a young age I went about finding ways to compensate for my weakness. I went about to prove to myself and others I could do something well, and that seemed to be, getting into trouble.

My life was tumultuous and could have ended many times. I believe there is a purpose and reason why I am still here, to share my autobiography with you. Many of these stories have been difficult for me to revisit. My desire is not to glorify sin, or to expose others, or to bring attention to myself. Life is relational and it has been a challenge to know how to tell my story, as it involves many others' lives as well. I hope you will be able to see how my choices, made in my younger

Goodville School, where I attended grades 1 through 8th grade.

years, took me on a path of destruction. I am grateful for the opportunity I was given to make the Ultimate Choice and head in a different direction. More about this later.

I attended 1st through 8th grades at Goodville School. The house I lived in as a child was across the road from the school. The school was a two-story building, housing first through eighth grade. Elementary students were downstairs taught by one teacher and the older students were upstairs. The good part of living by the school was skipping the packed lunches and walking home to a good lunch that mom had prepared for us to enjoy. The bad part was having to gather all the eggs. We had a one-hour break, so we would quickly eat lunch, gather the eggs, then rush back to school for the tail end of the baseball game before the bell rang to end recess.

Carl and Kenny gathering eggs.

Every evening my father had work scheduled for us following our day at school. We had thousands of chickens and needed to gather the eggs twice a day. As a seven year old, I would have preferred playing, but work came first. We helped my mother and sisters pull weeds in our large garden and pick the ripe vegetables. Mother froze the vegetables and canned bushels of peaches, pears, and cherries for the winter months. We had a large lawn to mow, without a powered lawn mower. My brother and I mowed the yard together—one of us would push and the other one pulled the push mower with a rope.

We helped our horse-and-buggy Mennonite neighbors thresh their wheat the old-fashioned way. My first job as a youngster was to sit on the horse and direct him around the loft. The horse trampled on the straw, packing it down. After threshing the wheat, the straw mound was piled up as high as 20 feet. It was always exciting to get the horse down from that high elevation. They tied a rope to the horse's halter and a couple of guys would get behind the horse and push him off the pile. At the end of the day, I was relieved to be off the horse and the horse was relieved to be back on solid ground.

At a young age I was labeled as the troublemaker, the one who took chances, got into fights, and would do anything crazy others dared me to do. I was seeking attention and approval, trying to help me feel good about myself in spite of my stuttering and poor academic performance. This is not meant to be an excuse for my inappropriate behavior, but one exposure to pornography definitely had a negative influence on my life. One day while walking along the road, I picked up a *Playboy* magazine someone carelessly tossed aside. As a young boy I was exposed to material that warped my mind. I hid this magazine in the chicken house, using it to continue to pollute my mind. Knowing the effect this one magazine had on my life causes me great concern for our present society. Today our young people have access to the internet, which could allow them to view pornography on a daily basis.

At nine years old, while in third grade, I remember committing what I thought to be my first big sin. My friend had a younger sister and we offered her five cents if she would undress and show us her private parts. At our schoolhouses, we didn't have indoor plumbing so we had outhouses for our bathrooms. The boys would open up the trap door while the girls were going to the bathroom to, "see what we could see." During recess the boys and girls played tag with our own rules. To add excitement to the game, our goal was to tag each other in inappropriate places. Initially, I felt guilty and would confess my inappropriate behavior to my mother. As I progressed in age, I trained my God-given conscience to ignore its plea to change my course.

I stopped trying to succeed in school because my efforts only seemed to result in defeat. I flunked third grade and was held back while my friends moved on to fourth grade. Back in that day, there was no special help provided for a struggling student. With one teacher for four grades, they certainly didn't have time to give me individual attention. I created many ways to cheat, hoping to increase my chance of receiving a decent report card. Each time I was caught I had to figure out a bigger and better way to try to beat the system. Reading and spelling were my worst subjects. I experienced desperation as I trailed far behind and couldn't see any way of catching up. Art class was one of my better subjects, but even this strength was used in a wrong way. In sixth grade I drew pictures of people involved in sex acts and passed them around for my classmates to see. The teacher caught me and called my parents to show them the pictures. My parents did the best they could to bring correction and direction to me but they didn't know what more to do. I was very strong willed and insisted on doing things my way.

Wanting to take good care of me, my mother made a dentist appointment for me, with a dentist located in Lancaster City. Going to the city was a rare trip and I was extremely scared and didn't want to get on the dentist chair. I planned a way of escape, and asked my mother if I could go outside for some fresh air as I awaited my turn. Once outside the office, I took off for downtown. I never did come back to take my turn and my embarrassed mother was left alone to apologize for her absentee son. She became the scared one as she drove around the city looking for her ten-year-old son. We eventually found each other, but that was the last trip to any dentist until I was twenty-two years old. My fear and stubbornness caught up with me and this time I was willing to go to the dentist to get rid of the severe toothaches I was experiencing. I found a dentist that obliged my request to have all my teeth pulled and to walk out the same day with dentures.

I had another memorable and unplanned trip to Lancaster. My parents were taking my sisters shopping and my brother and I were given a list of chores to complete while they were gone. We made a quick decision to jump into the trunk of the car and go along for the ride. We kept the trunk lid slightly open for air and off we went. The shopping trip to the nearby town of New Holland was unsuccessful so they decided to drive to the city of Lancaster. We pulled into a parking garage, where an attendant parked the car for you. The attendant told my dad about unusual noises coming from the trunk. My dad assured him nothing was in the trunk, but when they checked, much to everyone's surprise, they found us. We were in our old, dirty work clothes, in no condition to enter the fancy city stores. My father stayed with us in the car, while the women shopped. I will spare you the details but I will tell you, the women had a more enjoyable trip to Lancaster than we did.

I wasn't excited about taking more shopping trips, but I was very excited when my father introduced me to my first hunting experience at ten years old. He took my older brother and me hunting for pheasants, rabbits, and squirrels in our neighbor's fields. Neither my father nor I had any idea this was the beginning of many more hunting adventures to come. My brother and I would hunt in our backyard with pretend homemade guns. We crafted our guns from tobacco lathe with a nail inserted as the trigger. We walked the fields after school looking for, and collecting shotgun shells. As we grew older, my brother and I hunted on our own. My mother would add to our fulfillment of having a successful hunt by making potpie with whatever the harvest of the day happened to be. My father didn't have much time for hunting but worked long and hard and took seriously his responsibility to provide for his family. I only recall one time when my dad took me deer hunting.

I knew my dad was opposed to having a radio in our home but I thought it was worth a try. At twelve years old, a neighbor sold me a radio that didn't work, the only sound it produced was a loud hum. My hope was to repair the radio and keep it in my bedroom, so my brothers and I could listen to the Philadelphia Phillies baseball games. When I brought it into the house, my father was very upset with my purchase. He informed me he would not allow a radio in his house. The radio was ousted, but I found another way to do what I wanted.

When my older brother purchased his first car, it came with a radio. My younger brother and I would sit in the car parked in the garage, and listen to the ballgames. On Saturday nights we enjoyed listening to the music of the Grand Ole Opry from Nashville, Tennessee.

One of the privileges of being a 7/8th grader, was getting a day off to attend a public farm auction happening in our neighborhood. There was an ongoing rival among the boys of the liberal Mennonites and the conservative horse-and-buggy Mennonite boys. We looked forward to these sales as a time and place to fight with our rivals. We started the day by gathering eggs from the chicken houses and ears of corn from the corn crib. The eggs and corn soon became flying objects to hurt and arouse anger among the opposing sides. We found this a successful method to insure the big fight we were looking for.

At one sale, I decided to attack a group of boys and girls standing on the barn floor. I climbed up into the hay loft, and found a 70-pound bale of hay as my weapon of attack. I dropped it from 25 feet and watched as it landed on top of them and they collapsed onto the floor. My foolish act could have easily broken their necks but fortunately for them and for me, no one was seriously hurt. It was payback time for me at the next sale. I was standing on the barn floor, when they took the two ends of a thick tug-of-war rope and ran around opposite ways intentionally getting me caught in the rope. They pulled me over to a post, continuing to encircle me with the rope. I could no longer breathe as the rope tightly wrapped around my body. I passed out and when they realized the seriousness of their actions, they quickly untangled the rope, just in time for me to catch my breath. We played other competitive games like broom sock, jump rope, and tug-of-war with pulls between the rival Mennonite boys. While the adults were busy making their bids on cattle and tractors, their children were busy keeping the opposition alive.

My mother's parents were members of the conservative Mennonite church that used horse and buggies for their transportation. A few years later her father decided to leave this church and go to a more liberal Mennonite church which allowed its members to own cars. My mother's oldest sister stayed in the conservative church and she and her husband had twenty-one children. This meant I had cousins who were on the opposing side. It wasn't right, but I was fighting with my own first cousins at these barn sales. One of my cousins who was older and bigger than me, came after me to set me straight. I climbed up the barn rafters, to the peak of the barn. He caught up with me and could have knocked me off the rafters, to take a huge fall to the barn floor. Thankfully, he let me off easy, giving me a good scare. Our mothers didn't have a clue of the day's event, but as sisters they would have been dismayed at their sons' rivalry.

At the barn fights, my aggression often landed me on top of the pile; while in the school room, I found myself at the bottom of the pile. I had no idea how life was going to work out for me when I felt like a failure in so many areas. I was no longer required to take tests or participate in school work. At the end of each school year I was merely passed on to the next grade. The teachers probably wanted to get rid of me as much as I wanted to get rid of this humiliating time of my life. I never did get a report card at the end of eighth grade and that was the end of my formal education. At the age of fifteen, the Pennsylvania law allowed students to discontinue their formal education if they found a job, usually farm related. I saw this as my way out. I quit school and entered the work world as a hired man, for a neighboring farmer.

I continued to hear the words of my teachers telling me I would never amount to anything. With those words spoken over me, I wanted nothing more then to prove them wrong. Thirty years later I drove to my grade school teacher's home in my company pick-up truck. I knocked on her front door and introduced myself as the boy who would never amount to anything. I stepped aside and told her to take a look at my truck which had my company's name on it. She said, "Well good for you Kenny." It would have been nice to hear those words of encouragement while in school, I'll admit, my behavior didn't warrant it. Looking back, I realize God did bless me with the gift I needed to be successful in the business world. I had a natural ability in math, a skill I needed the most, for the various business opportunities that came my way.

I continued working on a neighbor's dairy farm for two years. I learned a lot about cows but even more about the reality of long hours and the hard work of a working man. We farmed tobacco which is especially labor intensive. During the summer months we put in many 18-hour days. The hot humid days of summer consisted of hoeing weeds in the tobacco fields. Late summer was spent harvesting the tobacco by cutting the stalks, spearing them onto a lathe and hanging the tobacco in the barn to dry. Over the winter months we took the tobacco down from the rafters and brought it into the stripping room. Here we stripped the leaves off the stalks, and baled it into 100-lb. bales.

The church allowed its members to farm tobacco, which was an exceptionally profitable cash crop. Many of the Mennonite men would smoke cigars and cigarettes. I remember my father farming tobacco and smoking. This all changed for my dad and many other Mennonite farmers when a traveling evangelist came and revival broke out. Our family went to nightly meetings under a huge tent for weeks. My dad and others were convicted about growing tobacco and smoking. Some farmers went home and immediately disked under their tobacco crop. My dad finished out his crop but never planted another crop of tobacco. My dad also stopped smoking and replaced it with the habit of chewing gum, which continued until the day he got his dentures. I didn't share my dad's conviction and started to smoke at the young age of eleven. My age stopped me from buying cigarettes, however that didn't stop me from picking up cigarette butts I found along the road. I looked forward to lighting them and drawing the few puffs that remained.

The word disk, triggers another memory from my farming days. The farmer I worked for planted potatoes. One day it was time for me to learn how to operate a tractor and hook up a disk. He instructed me to go to the field at the far end of his property and disk the field. I was disking for quite some time when I saw him running down the field, waving his hands and yelling. I stopped the tractor to hear him telling me that I had just disked up his newly planted potatoes. I was in the wrong field. He probably wondered if he had hired the wrong man.

The local tomato and potato farmers would hire town boys to harvest their crops. We picked the produce by hand and were paid by the basket. It was a back-breaking job in the middle of hot summer days. We tried to break up the boredom and have some fun. We had many tomato fights, using the rotten tomatoes as our weapon. This was the sport of the day, mixing work and play just to survive the day. Another way I earned money was to catch wild pigeons roosting on barn rafters and silos. We went to the neighbors' farms at night and caught the unsuspecting pigeons. We were lucky enough to never have a serious fall, as some of the silos were 50 feet high. The risk was worth the reward when we received our money from selling them at the local farmers' market. We also set traps in nearby fields to capture possums, skunks, and muskrats. At dawn we walked to our traps with anticipation of seeing what we caught, with thoughts of how to spend the money we would earn. We reset the traps in hope that the next morning we would receive our reward for getting up at the break of day.

Twice a week, 10-15 boys and girls worked for a business, providing services for local chicken farmers. This job needed to be done during the night. The company bought a black hearse to get us to the job site. On our way to and from the job we watched for hitch-hikers or some unassuming person walking along the road. We pulled up to them, opened up the doors and yelled for them to jump in. You can only imagine the expression on their faces as they took off running.

Our job was to inject the chickens with a hormone and de-beak them to prevent them from pecking each other. We needed to chase the chickens into a small fenced off area to catch them. Sometimes they would pile up and smother each other. The contract only allowed a small amount of dead chickens each night. To stay below our quota we would throw dead chickens into the hearse and throw them out the windows on our way home. The farmer never really knew the number of chickens he lost. We also found inappropriate ways to relieve our boredom. We held the chickens like footballs and saw how far we could kick them. In these chicken houses there were huge fans used for ventilation. We would throw the chickens into the fans, and when they came out the other side, they were in pieces. If we were pecked by a chicken we were debeaking we cut their top beak off for revenge, making it difficult for them to eat. The chicken houses were always dark, so the boys and girls used this as an opportunity to mess around with each other. We were paid for the time we put in, but some of the activities were definitely not in our job description.

Work and church were a huge part of our life. I was in church every Sunday morning and on Sunday nights. Twice a year there were special evangelistic meetings, called revival meetings. They would be held for one or two weeks, with a guest preacher. It was customary for young people to accept Christ and become a member of the church around the ages of 14-15 years old during these revival meetings. This was the first step in beginning the Christian life. This step included repenting of your sins, making a commitment to follow Jesus, water baptism and becoming a member of the church. My parents made sure I was there every night. I sat through many revival meetings and fought off strong convictions to stand up and acknowledge I was a sinner and needed Jesus as my Savior. I was scared of going to hell and wanted a way of escape, but wasn't ready to make the changes inwardly or outwardly. I was confused with the life giving choice of having a relationship with Jesus, mixed with having to follow the rules and guidelines of the church. In spite of my rebellion, confusion, and questions, at the age of fifteen I decided to do what was expected of me. The preacher offered an invitation at the end of his sermon for anyone to make a decision to ask Jesus to forgive their sins and to commit their lives to Him. As a token of this decision to publicly confess Christ, you were asked to stand during the singing of a hymn. I don't remember the exact song, typically it would be "I Surrender All," "Just As I Am," "Amazing Grace" or "Where Will You Spend Eternity." During the singing of the hymn I stood to my feet and made a public confession of what should have been a major change in my life. I attended six weeks of Instruction Classes on Sunday afternoons in preparation for the Christian life and water baptism. Following this I was water baptized by the pouring of water on my head and was given the right hand of fellowship.

When you became a member of the church, you were encouraged to wear a plain coat which had a collar similar to a priest's collar. I am sure it comes as no surprise that I never wore a plain coat. We were permitted to wear bowties but neckties were forbidden. Again, no surprise that I bought neckties to wear to church. This was pushing the limits and displeasing to my parents. One Sunday morning, I pushed the limits even further. I was wearing a pink necktie, which was too much for my dad. He said he wouldn't go to church unless I removed my necktie. As usual, I wasn't interested in compromising; my strong will won out. My dad backed down and went to church with his worldly looking son.

Many of the sermons included warnings against drinking, and the importance of outward appearance and how we dressed. This was supposed to keep us separate and different from the world and its sinful ways. If we dressed conservatively and looked different, this would hopefully keep us out of worldly places, like movies and bars. I am sorry to say that my heart had not changed and before long I was making bad choices and turned my back on living a Christian life. God gave me the freedom of choice and I chose to walk away from Him. I wasted many years of my life hurting others and myself. I continued a lifestyle of rebellion against the church, my parents, and God.

New Found Freedom

When I turned sixteen years old, my life took a turn, headed in the wrong direction, with the new freedom of having a driver's license. My friends consisted of eight guys who grew up in the Mennonite church. We experimented with our new found freedom and tested the boundaries. We were looking for fun and excitement, but our immaturity and lack of wisdom led us into activities that were less than best.

We realized having money was a plus and so we looked for a way to get some extra money in our pockets. We went to farmers ponds where there were lots of tame ducks. We caught them and took them to the local farmers' market to sell. I knew this was stealing but it seemed to be working at the moment. I got what I thought was a bright idea. Why not go directly into the farmers' chicken houses and steal chickens. We could place them in crates, then hide them in the cornfield until we could transport them to Green Dragon Market Friday night. We didn't think of this as a crime but soon found out otherwise, when we were caught and charged with burglary. I was eighteen, the oldest of my friends, and was the only one charged with a felony. The other boys, all under eighteen, were only charged with a misdemeanor. This wasn't good for my record or reputation as the word spread throughout the community. Throughout my life, I was teased and tagged as a duck and chicken thief.

Green Dragon was a place for youth to gather on Friday nights. The guys would size each other up and want to prove who was the toughest. We soon learned we were no match for the local town boys. They formed gangs and were good fighters with some members taking boxing lessons. They were armed with pipes, chains, and switchblades. We Mennonite boys didn't have a fighting chance and we were the ones kept on the run. One Friday night a gang set up a roadblock, knowing the way we traveled. They were stopping cars looking for us. I didn't own a pistol at the time but I did have a 30/30 Marlin rifle that I used for deer hunting. I kept that gun in the back seat of my car for a long time, thinking I could even up the odds if confronted.

I didn't have my own car, so I was at the mercy of my dad to allow me to use his car on weekends. Before I could use my father's car, I had to promise I would attend the Young People Meeting on Saturday night. This was a service held at our church as a positive alternative to secular options. One night, my group of friends and I sat on the front benches. The preacher was talking about how some of the boys were getting into a lot of trouble and we knew he was talking about us. At the conclusion of his comments, he asked the congregation to kneel for prayer. Upon kneeling, the ten of us boys promptly decided to leave. We crawled under the benches from the front of the church to the back door. We were a huge distraction to those who were trying to pray. The prayer ended with an "Amen" and upon arising the preacher saw the vacated bench where the troublemakers once sat.

Our parents required us to attend church every Sunday morning. Once at church, the troublemaker boys would sometimes skip Sunday School to participate in our own activities. We concealed our 22 rifles in the trunk of our cars. We knew most of the people were at church so we drove around the area looking for cats. It was a challenge for us to see how many cats we could scare off the porches. We would arrive back at church, just in time to gather in the auditorium for the main service. Much to my parents' dismay they realized forcing me to attend church wasn't working. I stopped attending church and lost the privilege of using my dad's car. I would have my friends drop me off at my girlfriend's house Saturday night and I would walk home Sunday morning. I recognized cars and people driving by me on their way to church. I felt embarrassed and ashamed, but not enough to change the direction I was going.

A group of us eight guys decided to build a cabin in Potter County, Pa. It was five hours away but was known for its abundance of deer. Most of the cabin members were also members of the Mennonite church and the guidelines agreed upon, prohibited alcohol in the camp. At the age of nineteen most of these friends had girlfriends and settled down. They married within several years and went on to follow the Christian upbringing we all learned as boys. I could have learned from my mistakes but instead, I went on to find a group of new friends. It wasn't long until I started bringing my own rowdy friends to the cabin and the alcohol rule was quickly broken.

It was time for me to have my own set of wheels and my father had set up a plan for his sons to succeed in reaching this milestone of new freedom. In our family we were all required to give 90% of any money we earned to our parents and could keep the remaining 10% for ourselves. Part of this deal included our dad buying us boys a car when we turned eighteen and my sisters were given a thousand dollars when they married to buy furniture. My dad helped me purchase my first car, a sharp looking red car. Shortly after I had the car, I refused to hand any more money over. I was a deal breaker and so my dad took the car back, painted it black and used it for his own car.

I was now on my own to find a way to acquire a car. I went to the new car dealership in town and they had the first 1955 Ford Fastback in the area. I said, "I will do whatever it takes to buy this car." In spite of having a very small amount to put down they agreed to work with me and gave me a loan. It was great for my ego while it lasted. The first night I had the car, I drove it into the city to show off my new set of wheels. Nobody had ever seen a car like this out on the road before. It was the first Ford Fastback in the area and I was proud to be the owner. I didn't have any trouble picking up girls with this car. Unfortunately, for me, my dream ride came to an end within a year. Once again, I didn't keep up my end of the deal so the dealership came and repossessed the car.

The next car I bought was a 1955 Chevy two-door hardtop. I customized the car and kept it for three years. I went on to buy a 1959 Chevy two-door hardtop. I was a motor head, and I "souped" up the engine and had a three 2-barrel carburetor on it. In the back seat there was a radio speaker which led to a convenient compartment leading to the trunk. I could pull out the speaker, reach back and get a beer whenever I desired. I was sure to keep several cases of beer in this secret compartment. My chances of getting caught drinking and driving were lessened with the cases of beer concealed from the eye of the officer. As drinking became a regular part of my life, I became more careless with the evidence. When I was stopped by the local police, they saw the open cans of beer on the floor of my car. In those days they didn't use breath tests but it was obvious I was under the influence. They would tell me to go home and followed me to make sure I arrived home safely. Shortly after the police left, I left and was back on the road again. They didn't enforce DUI fines and consequences as they do today. If they did I would have needed a second job to pay the fines and probably spent more time behind bars. I always planned well ahead to make sure I wouldn't run out of beer on Sundays. Bars were closed Sundays and were the only place to buy alcohol. The girls who wanted to party knew I always kept a supply of beer in my car and this served as good bait for picking up girls. It became well known to these girls when they hung around my drinking buddies and me they wouldn't be disappointed, if they were looking for a party Friday night, Saturday, and Sunday.

Most of my friends had new cars and we could recognize each other's cars while on the roads. When we saw one of our friends coming toward us, we would switch lanes. We passed each other on the opposite side of the road, they went in the left lane, while we switched to the right lane. This worked out well as long as someone else wasn't driving a car like ours. You have to remember, in those days you had about one fourth of the traffic you have today. If we made a mistake and switched lanes, but it wasn't our buddy, the driver would hit the ditch, to keep from having a head-on collision. We were old enough to have our driver's license but not old enough to have the wisdom to respect the gift of life.

We frequently spent the weekend at the hunting camp in Potter County, which was located forty miles from the New York State Line. The drinking age there was eighteen, so trips to New York were often an extension of our trips to Potter County. All we wanted to do was get drunk. I really don't remember much about what happened while in Potter County because we were mostly drunk or waking up with hangovers. We would go deer hunting during the archery season. When we came up short and failed to harvest a deer, we didn't want to come home empty-handed. We found another way to harvest deer, as night approached we would go out with a spotlight and find deer standing in open corn fields. We would chase them down with our car and try to kill a couple deer to take home with us.

We were always looking for excitement and found ways to make it happen. One of my friends yelled out to another one of my friends saying, "Get behind a tree because I am going to shoot." Fortunately this guy believed what he said, moved behind a tree and in a matter of seconds saw this guy put an arrow in the tree he was standing behind. We also played a form of "Chicken." We took turns seeing how close we could throw a knife at a guy's foot without hitting it.

One of the guys missed, and put the knife into a guy's brand new engineer boots. A fight soon broke out over his cool boots being ruined and the cut he was feeling in his toe.

When we were bored and couldn't think of any mischievous thing to do, we would go in to the local laundromat. Two or three of us would jump into the large dryers. The other guys would drop quarters into the machine and we would take a ride in the dryer. Sometimes there were women in the laundromat that would yell at us and then run out of the room. I guess they were thinking we would harm ourselves and didn't want to see what it looked like to see a human spun dry.

We would frequent our town's sportsman stores. One of the guys knew a lot about guns and kept the owner busy with questions, acting like he was seriously interested in buying a gun. Meanwhile the rest of us were walking around picking up items and putting them into our pockets. Shoplifting became a pretty big issue, as we found this as a source for meeting our need for hunting supplies.

We usually brought our motorcycles along to run the mountain trails. We also had target practice with our guns. One of these times when we went inside the cabin, my friend put a pistol to my head while another guy took a picture. Shortly after he went outside the cabin, he pulled the trigger and there was a live round in the chamber. He had no idea the pistol was loaded. Ten years later he told me the rest of the story. While the picture was being taken he was thinking about pulling the trigger, just for fun. This had him so worked up as he thought about what might have happened that he went home, sold all his guns and never fired a gun again. In a matter of seconds and with one little mistake my life could have tragically ended. This same weekend we were playing poker and only two of us had a lot of cash on us and everyone else was putting in IOU notes. At the end of the game the six guys using the IOU notes had taken most of our real cash. This just didn't seem fair to us and this created a huge argument and resulted in a big fight. There was no way we were going to drive home with these guys who had taken our cash. We had a buddy drive the two of us to Cherry Springs Park where there was a small airport. We used the remainder of our money to charter a plane to the New Holland Airport, which was another small airport, close to our home. My cash was all gone, but at least I came home alive.

Wild Living

A regular weekend activity was to attend dances, sponsored by a fire company. Our main purpose for going was to pick up girls or to pick a fight. During a fire company dance, I was involved in a fight when several cops approached me from the back to grab me. I didn't know who was grabbing me so I turned around to fight back and unknowingly slugged a cop. I was promptly taken to the police car and was enroute to the county prison. I was drunk and out of control. I pulled the badge off of the cop's uniform sitting next to me and went to hit him. They abruptly handcuffed me but that didn't stop me from trying to jump out of the car at every red light. It was my attempt to escape the consequences of my foolish actions but the consequences continued to follow me.

One particular night I was driving my three friends to a dance an hour away. We were traveling on a busy highway hitting 80 mph and passing cars on the right side. The main problem was, I was already drunk. I didn't really care that my friends were so scared they jumped into the back seat and were lying on the floor. I narrowly missed hitting a concrete bridge but was unsuccessful in navigating the next curve in the road. I ran off the road, drove through a farmer's fence and landed in a creek. I walked to the farmer's house and asked if I could use his house phone. He could tell I was drunk and wouldn't allow me in his house. I was giving him a hard time and he asked to see my driver's license. He took one look at my name and again at me and exclaimed, "Kenny Gingrich, you are my cousin." At that point I didn't know him from Adam but I did know that wasn't the best way to pay a visit to your cousin. The car was badly damaged but I wanted a new car anyway. Being drunk I envisioned my car insurance company's check in the mail. With this thought in mind, I jumped onto the hood and started dropping huge rocks on the hood and roof and finished up by kicking in the doors. The insurance adjuster came and questioned me on how the big dents got on the hood and roof. It didn't take him long to conclude I was lying and denied me any coverage. That night was one of the many nights I realized my life wasn't working out very well but that didn't stop me from drinking and driving.

When we became bored with the dances, we would find a way to make our own excitement. One night we were setting off fire-crackers. When the town policeman arrived and asked who was setting off the firecrackers, I said, "I was." He told me to get in the back of his car and as we were heading for the Justice of the Peace, I decided to change my story and said, "I didn't do it and you can't prove I did." Apparently the cop agreed with me and decided to take the law in his own hands. He took me for a drive in the country, far away from the dance. I appealed, saying, "My friends are back at the dance and they are my ride home." The cop replied, "I think I have a flat tire, could you get out and take a look?" When I got out to look at the tire, he took off and the joke was on me. I was stranded and my only option was to start walking. It was at least five miles away and by the time I got there, the dance was over with no one in sight. Again, I had no other choice but to start walking. The policeman achieved his goal of keeping me away from the dance, and in the early hours of the morning I achieved my goal of arriving back home.

Drive-in movies were a popular place for youth to gather. During the summer months and holidays they had all-night movies where you sat in your car to watch the big screen. We would crawl into the car trunk and fill it to capacity, to avoid paying the entrance fee. Once inside, we emerged from the trunk to enjoy the rest of the night. Some people were actually there to watch the movies but we went to drink, start fights and pick up girls. In the midst of a fight, a cop came and threw me into the back of his car. He was driving to the next trouble spot to pick up more guys. I think his goal was to round up a carload of guys to make his trip to prison worthwhile. At the next stop, I decided to dart out of his car and run. For some reason I grabbed his club and log book. I didn't have use for his log book but I probably did a favor for those whose names, addresses, and fines were recorded in the book.

I was pushing twenty-one years old and was with a fifteen-year old girl. On the other side of the drive-in property, we found a patch of grass to lay on to make out. The next day this girl needed to request her mother's help because she had poison ivy all over her body. She told her mother she went to the bathroom in the grass and that's where she came in contact with the poison. A couple months prior to this incident she was sitting on her front porch when I drove by. She waved at me and I waved back as the traffic light in front of her house turned red. The car in front of me stopped and I never had a chance to hit my brakes. My car slammed into the car in front of me and I figured that is what I get for being a girl watcher. I realized now I was looking to girls and alcohol to distract me from the pain and turmoil I felt inside.

There were several girls who hung out with my friends and me every weekend for a long time. On Sunday afternoon we would take turns making out with them. One night the six of us were parking in a cornfield and were mostly nude. We broke cornstalks, and started hitting each other with the cornstalks. The cornstalks stung but the sting of sin was worse in my life as one sin led to another. My friends and I would pick up girls and spend the night with them. In time this became boring so we agreed to switch partners. We would compete to see how many girls we could pick up and make out with in a night's time. A lot of these girls were 15-18 years old and had curfews. We would drop them off at their homes in time to meet their curfew, then come back later and park down the street. The girls would sneak out to meet us while their parents thought they were in their bed having sweet dreams.

Another girl I dated for a year was fifteen and I was twenty-one. I would be with her every weekend, picking her up Friday night and bringing her home Sunday night. Her parents didn't want me around for many reasons including being six years her senior. Her father was an alcoholic and her mother tried hard to keep us apart. We had a plan of escape for her to get out of the house and she knew the exact time I would arrive. We didn't have cell phones in those days so it took planning ahead. One night my girlfriend didn't come out of her house as planned. I walked down to her house and started throwing sticks at her bedroom window and calling her name. Out of the corner of my eye, I saw someone running toward me with an axe in hand—I was being chased by her mother. I jumped in my car and took off. It took a while for me to build up my nerve to go back again but I was willing to take my chances.

One night my girlfriend and I, along with another couple, plus one of his friends, went parking. My girlfriend and I were lying in the front seat, and the two guys and the girl were in the back. We were all pretty much drunk and soon there was a lot of yelling and commotion going on. Before we knew it she was yelling rape. We took the girl back to her house, she was intoxicated and could barely walk. No one wanted to help her into her house. She was drunk, underage and naked. My girlfriend who knew this girl insisted I help her. I carried her clothing to the door, rang the doorbell, shoved the clothing in her hand and ran. Her parents came to the door, called the police and pressed charges on all three of us for rape. We were told the cops were coming to pick us up. One guy's brother told us to pack a suitcase and run away to Florida. I didn't have much money and the other guys had nothing to contribute for our getaway. I sold a couple of guns and we took off. We were in Florida for a month but soon ran out of money, and couldn't find a job. We decided to head back home and face the consequences. The police picked us up and we had our day in court. My girlfriend testified on my behalf and I wasn't charged, but the other two guys were charged with rape.

This one lady I was seeing had a husband who drove tractor trailer and was gone for days at a time. When I knew her husband was out of town, I would go visit her. This lady rented out rooms in her house to other truckers to make a little bit of money on the side. Early one morning I entered her house and walked into her bedroom. I shook her and said wake up. I heard a rough voice asking, "What do you want?" I took off running down the stairs thinking it was her husband. She heard the noise, saw me and yelled, "Kenny stop." She explained she had moved to another bedroom, and moved this guy into her old bedroom. I stayed, even though I felt a bit uncomfortable, knowing I had awakened another man sleeping in her house.

One of the times while sitting in jail, I had a lot of time to think over my past. I decided to try to remember and count the number of girls I went out with. By the age of twenty-six I went out with over two hundred girls. I only dated two girls on a regular basis, including my first love and my wife. There is only one girl I went out with that I didn't drink before our dates. She was a Christian girl and I had a lot of respect for her. Otherwise I always had a beer or two before meeting up with a girl. This would relax me and I didn't have to worry about being embarrassed with my speech impediment of stuttering. I was known as a party guy who was always carrying on and seldom serious. I suppose this was the reason most girls went out with me, they were looking for a good time. I knew I was using many of the girls but some of the girls were using me too. I don't think many girls were interested in settling down with me or marrying me.

Partying, Police and Prison

I drank pretty much every night from the day I turned 21 until 29 years old. I would go straight to the bar after work and eat my supper there. My diet consisted of hamburgers, fries, or soup. I drank every night till 12 or 1 and then would get up the next morning for work. I repeated this day after day, year after year for eight years. Some evenings I would work as the bartender, paying myself throughout the night with drinks. I was using alcohol to numb the pain and emptiness I felt inside.

I lost my driver's license so many times for various violations of the law. After being notified I was losing my license for a year, I bought a horse. It seemed like a good idea but proved to be a bit too slow and constricting for my lifestyle. In my mind I questioned, how can anyone really stop me from driving when that is what I want to do? I went back to driving, got caught again and lost my license for an additional six months. Nothing stopped me from driving, until I was sentenced to jail for ninety days for driving with a suspended license. I was one of the younger guys in jail and some of the older guys who were homosexual were interested in me. They were chasing me and I found myself in a frightening situation with no place to hide. Amazingly enough, one of the inmates was a past neighbor of mine and took me under his care. He asked the warden if I could share a cell with him and his request was granted. In prison he had the reputation of being a tough guy you didn't mess with. He warned the guys not to mess with me, or they were going to have to answer to him.

My days were filled with listening and learning from the inmates as they talked about their lives of crime. They shared their plans on how they were going to rob this place or get even with this person. Many who were released were back in prison within a short time, showing they fulfilled their prison plan in the outside world. It was obvious prison did not bring the fulfillment of transformation. Prison did change me but for the worse. I was becoming meaner and rougher by the minute. One evening following a visit from my parents, I walked back to my cell block. The inmates were watching TV and an African American man was sitting in my chair. I asked him to get out of my chair and he said, "Make me." I walked away but my buddy said to him, "He might not make you get up but I will" and threw him a punch. A riot broke out with the sides predetermined by the color of your skin. The chairs started flying, the guards came running with billy clubs and tear gas in hand. The next day the warden called my friend and me into his office. He notified me that I had lost my "good time." This system encouraged good behavior. You were rewarded with points allowing for an early release. My heart sank, realizing any good points I had accumulated were gone, following the riot. My friend went on to convince the warden he was the one who started the fight and took all the blame. I kept all my good points through the kindness of a man who was known for his meanness.

While in prison, my grandfather died from an unexpected heart attack. My parents went to the warden and asked if there was any way I could attend my grandfather's funeral. Many of my relatives on my father's side are conservative Mennonites. They had black cars with black bumpers and the men wore black hats. I knew I wouldn't fit in very well wearing my prison clothing but I would be allowed to attend. Surprisingly the warden said he would arrange for a sheriff to escort me to the funeral. Arriving at the funeral in a sheriff's car would make enough of a scene so I appealed to the sheriff to remove the handcuffs. I didn't want to walk into the church with handcuffs on. The sheriff granted my request saying, "I know you only have a couple of weeks left to serve your sentence so I will remove the handcuffs." He figured I wasn't going to try to run at my grandfather's funeral. My parents brought my suit to jail for me to wear. I was thankful the sheriff wasn't wearing his uniform but instead wore a suit. He was considerate and discreet as he kept an eye on me from a distance. I felt awkward but it was good to be with my family.

My parents came to visit me while I was in prison. My mother wore her traditional Mennonite dress and prayer covering. She looked out of place but her love for me took her places way beyond her comfort zone. I hated being incarcerated and anxiously awaited the day I would be a free man once again. Finally, I received notice of my release date. I called my mother and told her the day and time I would be released so she could come and pick me up. She was looking forward to taking me home, hoping I would be a changed person. Unfortunately, I was already scheming and making plans for what I wanted to do with my freedom. I told my mother I would be released at 11 a.m., knowing full well I would be released at 10 a.m. When the door opened, I wasted no time in walking downtown to visit with some old girlfriends. When my mother arrived at the front desk, they informed her I was released an hour ago. They proceeded to tell her she needed to pay a fee for my release. She proceeded to tell them, if I was already released, she didn't see a need to pay any further fee. Apparently they agreed with her and she walked out of the prison with the money in her purse. Her next challenge was to find me but she wasn't successful and headed back home without her son. The next day I found a ride home. She was glad to have me out of prison but once again she would have to wonder what trouble her wayward son might get himself into. I regret dishonoring my mother and abusing the love she had shown to me in so many ways throughout my life.

A couple weeks following my release, I was back at a local bar, known for its frequent stabbings. I met five African Americans who wanted to go to a party in the city. None of these guys had a car or driver's license. They tried to talk me into driving them to the party. This time I had enough sense to refuse to get behind the driver's wheel, knowing I was in no shape to drive. A girl agreed to drive, who wasn't in much better shape than the rest of us. She was fighting a battle to stay on her side of the road and I was fighting a battle in the back seat. One of the guys placed his hand on my jeans. I asked him, "What do you think you are doing?" I kept pushing his hand away and fighting him off. It was the longest drive ever, into the city. As soon as they got out of the car, I got behind the wheel and decided to skip the party. I knew I wasn't about to get back in the car with this guy for the ride back home. This was one of the few times I opted out of going to a party. I don't know who gave them a ride home but I knew it wasn't going to be me.

By this time the cops had me marked. Being 21 years old, I was now buying beer for my underage friends. I confirmed the cops suspicion when they found minors in my car, along with eight cases of Budweiser and two cases of Rolling Rock. The cops followed me down to the police station and had me carry all the beer into their office. They asked, "Why are all these cases of beer in your possession?" I told them I liked to drink and wanted to make sure I didn't run out. They asked why I had two different brands of beer. I replied, "I get tired of drinking the same brand and like to switch sometimes." Upon further searching of my car, they found a pistol I hid under the dashboard. Of course I didn't have a permit, so they confiscated the pistol and charged me for carrying a weapon. They were trying to pressure the minors to admit I was buying beer for them, but they denied it. The officer placed the beer outside the station, on a porch. I asked him if he was planning to drink it and he replied he is not a drinking man. Later that night I went back and took the beer off the porch, once again having my beer, in my possession. With the next day being Sunday and the bars being closed, I stuck with my previous statement that I didn't want to run out of beer for the weekend.

We found a nearby wooded area which worked well for parties. Fifty or more kids would show up on weekends. Beer was the big attraction and I was the one who often supplied the alcohol. We had kegs on tap and twenty or more cases of beer, enough to last us the weekend. One morning most of the kids left to get breakfast, planning to return for more "fun." Two of us stayed at the party site and waited and waited but nobody was coming back. We came to find out the cops had set up a roadblock at the bottom of the hill. As the underage kids were leaving, they were being arrested one by one. I was drinking a beer when I saw eight policemen coming up the drive. They looked at the vast supply of beer; asked if we were having a private party, and who the beer belonged to. I claimed it as mine and they commented it sure was a lot of alcohol for two people. They proceeded to load up all the beer in spite of my appeal to leave a couple of six packs behind for me. At this point I didn't realize they were taking the beer to serve as evidence at a pending court trial.

All the kids received an order to show up in court and I was subpoenaed to be there as well. The court tried to pressure the kids to admit that I bought the alcohol for them. The judge pointed to the stacked beer cases in the corner and asked, "Is this your beer?" to which I replied, "no." I did buy most of it but not all of it. He responded by saying, "We happen to think it is." I responded back by saying, "In that case, if this is my beer, I think I will have one now because I am thirsty." I went over grabbed a beer and opened up the can. The judge wasted no time in telling me drinking was forbidden in the courtroom and an officer grabbed the beer out of my hand. All the minors were fined for underage drinking and I got off easy because there was no proof to convict me. The judge couldn't prove me guilty but I knew I was guilty on this and many other accounts. I was drinking whenever I could in an attempt to numb the conflict within.

Anytime we were looking for a bar fight, we knew where to go. Several bars had the reputation of being the roughest bars in the county. These bars had frequent stabbings, shootings, and had no problem with serving alcohol to underage patrons. I came to know three brothers from Virginia, who I called rednecks. They came to our area once a month with their own agenda, looking for a good bar fight. They asked me where we could go to get into a bar room fight. I suggested Mountain Top knowing they wouldn't be disappointed, since it was known as the roughest bar in the area. Six of us white boys walked into the bar where being white put us in the minority. We started pushing some guys around and the fight we wanted to pursue broke out into a real nasty brawl.

The owner called the State Police, who were already in the area, in anticipation of trouble. Realizing the police were called, we ran out of the bar and jumped into our Mustang and raced down the road. The police were right behind us with their flashers on. Some of the guys were yelling go, go, go and some were yelling stop. The driver did pull over long enough for the two officers to walk toward our car. We took this opportunity to take off and the speedometer reached 100 miles an hour. We were trying to lose the officers and they were trying to catch up with us. We rounded a corner, knocked off a mailbox and some bushes. We went over a bank and ended up trapped with nowhere to go. The police were right behind us, coming up to us with their weapons drawn. The police informed us they were getting ready to fire some rounds through the back window, to end the chase. I don't know if they were really going to do this but I do know I was sitting in the center of the back seat and would have been the most likely to take a shot. This was one of the many times I could have been killed but I believe the prayers of those who loved me preserved my life. My parents regularly prayed for my safe arrival back home. This one night was an exception and they were praying I would not come home. They saw eight guys outside the house waiting for me. God answered their prayer and I didn't get home that night. Only God knows what would had happened if I came home.

During the Vietnam War the draft was in effect. My friends and I decided to enlist in the Marines. We took the test and all passed. Being a baptized member in the Mennonite church, I had the choice to opt out of serving in the military. The government made an exception for young Mennonite men to go into an alternative service. These assignments entailed volunteer time served in hospitals, forestry conservation, or other services, to fulfill the pacifist stance of the church. I knew full well I wasn't living a pacifist lifestyle and the Marines looked like a better fit for me. Upon seeing my past record I needed a "letter of improvement" from five different branches. This included the local police, the State Police, the judge in my area, the probation officer, and from an official in Harrisburg, Pa. Four of them signed off, believing it would be a good move for me. They may have seen this as their way to get me out of their area, in hopes the discipline would turn me into a real man. The official from Harrisburg, who wasn't going to have to deal with me on the local level, refused to grant me his approval. When asked why he said, "After looking at his past records, I wouldn't recommend him for the Salvation Army."

In spite of my father's great disapproval and dismay, I brought a TV into the house, carried it upstairs and put it in my bedroom. My family thought I was the worst of sinners for bringing this evil into the house and begged me to get rid of it. At night I would turn the volume up as loud as it could go, disrupting my family's sleep, since all four bedrooms were merely separated by a small hallway. My mother would tiptoe into my bedroom, to turn the TV off, hoping I had fallen asleep. I would often snap back at her, commanding her to turn it back on. As time passed some of my family would sneak into my bedroom to watch TV while I was away but my father wasn't one of them.

While living this lifestyle on the weekends, I was miserable, mean, and mad during the weekdays. I would pick fights with my brothers. My older brother was stronger than me but refused to fight back. He chose to follow Christ's example of turning the other cheek. I was unpredictable and angry, and would do whatever it took to stay on top. He was making better choices as a young man than me.

My father had a gas pump at home, which he kept locked to prevent theft. The lock didn't stop me. I found a way to steal gas from my dad to go places which my dad was totally opposed to. I remember the day my anger was out of control and I hit my dad knocking the wind out of him. It was one of those times I felt really scared, seeing I had hurt my dad. This memory comes back to me bringing with it deep regret. I hurt my parents in so many ways but they continued to love and pray for me trusting God to bring a change into my life.

My parents spent a lot of money on my behalf, paying fines I couldn't pay and posting bail to keep me out of jail. I was bringing six packs of beer into the house and storing them in their refrigerator. This was so disrespectful, knowing my parents were totally against alcohol. They didn't throw the beer out, because they were afraid of me and what I had become. By this time my mother and father avoided having any confrontation with me because no matter what they said or did, I did it my way. My parents believed it was better to allow me to live in their home then to kick me out and bring more rejection in my life.

While still living at home and living this wild and crazy lifestyle, my youngest sister was hit by a car. She was walking home from a friend's house, after taking their dogs for a walk. My youngest sister was my favorite family member, she was the "little sister." The ambulance took her off to the hospital. I remember the day well when I was told they didn't know if she would live. I rushed into the hospital to see her. She was laying there in a bed with tubes and needles stuck everywhere. I knew I had to do something but I didn't know what I could do. Just like that God spoke to me and I went into the next room and prayed. Living the lifestyle I was living, I wasn't sure God would hear or answer my prayers. I promised God if He would let her live, I would turn my life around. This was one of many promises I made to God over the years. When I fell into troubled times, when I couldn't see a way out, I would offer Him a deal. "If You will only help me get out of this situation, I will change." Before long I was right back into my same old lifestyle. This time was no different, God did answer my prayer and my sister did live. So many broken promises but God remained faithful and was always there waiting for me.

SOFTBALL

During the years while all of this was going on, I still had time to be involved in softball. I went to many of the Men's Class A Fast Pitch Tournaments, traveling all over the country. Our team was called "S.H. Good," and we qualified to go to the National Tournament in Syracuse, NY. There were 70 teams in this tournament from the United States, including Hawaii, Alaska, and Canada. We won the tournament, ending a great season with this celebration of victory. In the beginning years of forming our team, we had several Christians on our team that wouldn't play in a Sunday morning tournament. We all made the sacrifice as we forfeited the game and took the loss.

On one trip, three of us drove to the tournament in my friend's car. The tournament ended on Sunday and we needed to be home by Monday morning. It was dark by the time we left for our trip home. Shortly after leaving, the alternator went out in the car. We drove to the next gas station but they couldn't fix our problem. We proceeded onto Interstate 81 and tried to run with the traffic.

"S.H. Good" two-time National Men's Fast Pitch Softball Team. Front row: Randy Sanger, Ronnie Sanger, Roger Hess, Bumpy Hess, John Oberholtzer, Terry Burkholder. Back row: Bob Martin, Billy Weaver, Mike Good, Dwayne Hostetter, Doug Hackman, Irvin Weaver, Eric Lichty.

The team I sponsor, major ISC Men's Fast Pitch Team.

We did have to be home in time to go to work so we did pass some slow moving cars. Fortunately we were blessed with a full moon, to guide us home. As we arrived in Lancaster County, it was just breaking light. A policeman blinked his lights at us, informing us our lights were still needed. Little did he know we were driving the last 260 miles without any lights.

The following year we won the National Tournament in New York and were invited to a tournament in San Francisco. We lost our first game but came back and won six games on Saturday. We thought we didn't have a chance on Sunday as we were facing five of the best teams in the tournament. Several of the ballplayers and myself decided to go out and party all night. These ballplayers were experiencing a batting slump, but the next day they came out of their slump and were hitting home runs and it seemed they could do no wrong. Every time a home run was hit the sponsor of the tournament would give the team a pitcher of beer. The opposing teams that were already out of the tournament and a friend of ours gladly drank all of the free beer. By the time the tournament was over he was completely wasted as he continued to celebrate our home run streak. I can't explain how it all happened, but we went on to win the tournament. During the ball games, it was our practice to intimidate the opposing team's players. We would sit right behind the backstop ridiculing the players. Several times the umpires called time out and made me leave the ball park. At the end of the game we hurriedly walked to our cars in fear of retaliation for our actions and words. Over the years I have had an attitude change and I continue to enjoy going to the games, but now with much improved sportsmanship. I was involved in softball from the age of 18 up to the present time. Today I sponsor a Men's Fast Pitch Ball team and enjoy going to the World's Major Fast Pitch Tournaments.

FAST AND FURIOUS RACING

At the age of nineteen my friends and I went to the local motorcycle dealer and bought ourselves new motorcycles. It wasn't long until we met other guys in the area who had motorcycles. They invited

Original members of Draggin Gypsies, Left to right: Leonard Newswanger, Jim Houck, Tom Martin, Dick Hurst, Bobby Reed, Ray Kurtz.

Left to right: George Dosch, Marty Dosch, Sonny Rhodes, Ken Gingrich, Hop Wenger, Dick Renninger, Harold.

us to their local motorcycle club which was part of AMA, sanctioned by American Motorcycle Association. They were holding poker runs and afterwards hosted beer parties at their clubhouse. This became a weekend habit, every weekend going to their club or to other motorcycle clubs to party. We were under the legal age for drinking but at these clubs there was no such law, much to our delight. We didn't go just to drink, we went to get drunk. Monday morning I was surprised to wake up in my own bed, not remembering leaving the clubhouse or how I arrived home safely.

In the 60's and 70's there were a lot of outlaw motorcycle clubs throughout the United States and Canada. Fourteen of my outlaw friends, decided to charter our own outlaw club. We named ourselves The Draggin Gypsy Motorcycle Club. Initially we held our monthly meetings in a motorcycle shop, owned by club members. Following the meeting we would party and conclude our evening with an adult movie. Back in those days these movies were in black and white and illegal. Unfortunately, people have the potential of watching X-rated movies in their own living rooms in today's culture.

One club member owned a plot of land in the Welsh Mountain and we thought this was a perfect place to build our clubhouse. We scheduled work parties which turned into beer parties, which resulted in very little work getting done. Since I had carpentry experience I ended up doing most of the work. We didn't have indoor plumbing so I built an outhouse. When I went to cut the hole for the outhouse I didn't know what size to make it. I needed a model and looked for the biggest lady there. I told her to sit on the board and proceeded to take a pencil and drew a circle around her bottom. I cut the hole much larger than a normal toilet seat should be. Most of the people using the outhouse had to prop themselves up on the sides of the board to keep from falling through the hole.

Racing appealed to me because it was fast and dangerous. My buddies had a super fast car and dared me to a race, knowing his car

Dirt track racing.

was faster than my motorcycle. I chose a country winding road for the start of the race. We took off and when I entered the first corner the road was covered with loose stones. I hit the brakes and started to slide and lost control of my bike, it felt just like I was sliding on ice. I was headed straight for a wooden fence but hit a two-foot ditch first. My bike came to a complete stop as I flew over the handlebars and over the fence. I escaped serious injuries but was seriously shaken. This was one of my first races and accidents, with many more ahead of me. If I had been smart and stopped racing at this point, I would have saved myself a lot of pain.

I was getting more involved in motorcycle racing including flat track, motocross, and hill climb events. I experienced firsthand the dangers of racing. Over the years I was involved in numerous accidents with broken limbs and lacerations. Every time the ambulance took me to the hospital, the nurses would ask, "Why do you do this?" I answered by saying, "This will be my last race." When my body healed, I went right back to racing.

My worst injury happened while riding during a dirt track race. I was leading the pack with twenty-five bikes behind me. I fell off my bike and felt the agonizing pain as several cycles ran over me. I survived but suffered a broken back. For the first time in a long time, I was forced to slow down for six months as my back healed. I was anxious to get back to work and one of my friends owned a motorcycle shop and offered me a job. I decided it was time to get out of the carpenters union and started working as a mechanic. George was not only the best boss I ever had but also one of my best friends. While working on Saturdays, my productivity was rather low. I was getting over a hangover from binge drinking Friday night. He gave me small jobs around the shop on Saturday mornings, realizing I wasn't capable of doing anything requiring a clear mind.

During the winter months we rode in the woods every Sunday morning to stay in shape for the upcoming racing season. It was more like racing through an obstacle course with everybody wanting to be out front. There were about twenty of us racing among the trees and a lot of guys ended up with broken bones. The bikes also suffered damages and kept a steady flow of work for me back at the shop. Monday morning when I came into work I was greeted with bent handle bars, damaged shocks, and other minor repairs. My challenge was to repair the bikes and have them ready to go for the following Sunday. Fortunately no one hit a tree hard enough to be killed during these crazy Sunday races. Throughout these years, I did lose several close friends, as a result of motorcycle accidents.

One weekend my bike was broken down and not having a bike to ride I took the weekend off. When I came to the shop Monday morning, my friend's car was parked out front of the shop. I asked my boss why his car was still there, I wasn't prepared to hear what he said. I saw he had trouble talking and I knew something terrible happened. He went on to say Dale fell off his bike coming out of the fourth corner. One of the bikes behind him ran over his head and killed him. His death was really hard on me and brought me face to face with the reality of the danger I was in each weekend. I used alcohol to ease my fears and grief and soon was back on the racing circuit.

All the motorcycle clubs had dirt drag strips. We would go to different clubs on weekends to party all night and to race during the day. Maple Grove Motorcycle Club had an eighth mile drag strip and sponsored dirt drags on Sunday afternoons. Years later they did away with dirt motorcycle drag racing, and sold the property to a new owner. They built a quarter mile macadam track for car drag races, where cars turned over 300 mph in a quarter mile. Today, national events are held here and it is well known as one of the largest drag racing locations in the nation.

I built myself a drag bike so I could run on this track. At one of these events I was going through the quarter mile marker, over 100 mph. I went to hit the brakes but my brake rod had fallen off and I had absolutely no brakes to slow down. I was able to gear it down and stopped before reaching the end of the strip. I went back to the pits to fix my brakes, to find out I didn't have the correct parts. My mechanic warned me it was absolutely unsafe to run another race. I ignored his advice and ran again, fortunately getting stopped in time. My mechanic tried to force me to face reality by asking what would have happened if my chain fell off? I never wanted to face reality but I knew the truth. Had my chain fallen off and without brakes, there was no way I could have stopped and my life quickly would have come to an end.

I became involved in scramble racing, now known as motor cross. I didn't want to miss out on any potential thrills so I built a cou-

Leader of the pack, beer can on helmet.

Hill climbs.

ple of bikes for flat track racing. The fans didn't have trouble picking me out of the pack. I had a beer can mounted on top of my helmet. They also had events called hill climbs and flat track racing. Flat track racing is a circular track on dirt and the bikes are not allowed brakes. I continued to build more race bikes to try to satisfy my insatiable desire for adventure and the opportunity to show I could be number one.

My life consisted of working every evening in the shop, repairing my bikes for the next weekend of racing. Friday and Saturday nights I went out to party and sometimes came home to catch a little sleep. It was hard for me to get up Sunday mornings, and load my motorcycles and head off to the races. All of the races were AMA sanctioned and had strict rules prohibiting drinking of alcohol during the race. I always drank going to the race and during the race. In the pits I carried around a large Pepsi cup, filled with beer. The officials knew me well enough to know I wasn't drinking Pepsi. They chose to ignore this violation in exchange for the good show I gave to the fans.

Later I built a bike for hill climbing. I had a 500cc Triumph running on alcohol gas and had one of the fastest bikes on the circuit. These hill climbs were so steep, a lot of the riders couldn't make it to the top, but would flip and come sliding down off the hill. At these events before the main event started we were given an opportunity to practice. Sometimes I would take courageous girls along for the ride. They sat on the seat of my bike while I stood on the foot pegs. I was the only rider that was crazy enough to do this. I took as many as five bikes to these hill climbs to run each bike in a different class, to gain more points, to win more trophies. The rider with the most points at the end of the year won the award for the best hill climber on the East Coast, our area was district six. I frequently took five bikes and won in all five classes. I also won the title "King of the Hill," which consisted of all of the winners competing, to earn this title. I remember proudly bringing home six trophies at a time, along with lots of points. For two years in a row I received the award for having the most points for the year. This earned me the title of East Coast Champion, the best hill climber for the year. I felt like I had finally proven that I was King of the Mountain. My bedroom was filled with trophies. Nevertheless, at night while lying in my bed, away from the noise and glamour, I knew I was missing the real purpose and meaning for my life.

Outlaw Living

I didn't always have a road bike to ride when the club members went bar hopping, so I took one of my racing bikes to ride with them. The problem was, the bike didn't have lights and had straight pipes that were extremely loud and thus illegal. It was impossible to go unnoticed and unheard by the police. I ended up with lots of fines for riding my illegal bike on public roads. We also traveled to surrounding states that held motorcycle events called Gypsy Tours. Our club bought a large army tent for us to sleep in. The meanest guy we had in the Draggin Gypsy Motorcycle Club was Bobby. He would fight anybody and very seldom would lose a fight. He usually took over the whole tent. Every time one of the members would try to go in he would throw us out of the tent. When the whole group went riding together to go bar hopping, it meant trouble. When we came to a stop sign or red light and Bobby was drinking, he would forget to take his foot off of the foot pegs. He would fall over with the bike usually falling on top of him. Someone had to get the bike off of him and put him back on the bike. At the next red light the same thing would happen again. During the Vietnam War there was a group of college kids protesting the war in one of our local cities. Bobby took his motorcycle right down the middle of the protestors knocking some of them down, causing injuries. When the police tried to arrest him, he beat up several of the cops. They finally got control of him and put him in jail. A couple days later he was out on bail. He was beat up very badly but we knew exactly what happened to him.

The Gypsy Tour was not an AMA event. It was featured by an outlaw club, which equated to-no rules. It was three days of drinking and racing, all night and all day. Their main events were drag racing, motor cross racing, and hill climbing. These Gypsy Tours drew the outlaw clubs from far and wide.

The following stories have been difficult for me to recall and even more difficult for my wife to hear for the first time, as I shared them, for her to type. I witnessed these events but didn't take part in most of them. I was wrong for associating with those who inflicted pain and terror on other human beings. God gave me a conscience, but I was doing a good job of ignoring it. The influence of my Christian home and the continued prayers of family and friends allowed me to keep some boundaries which I refused to cross.

The first several years these tours were basically fun events. More and more outlaw clubs started to attend these events including, The Sons of Satan and the Pagan Motorcycle Club. Drugs were becoming more prevalent and affected the bizarre behavior of the participants. It became an unsafe place, with the constant threat of being beat up or shot and with the possibility of anything happening at any moment.

Naturally food was a part of these gatherings but we had unnatural ways of picnicking. When we had pig roasts it was customary for us to chew on the pig's eyeball to see who could successfully break it. After eating red beet eggs all of the guys who had false teeth would take their teeth out and put them on a pile. The false teeth were covered with red beet eggs and other food particles. As gross as the pile of teeth were, we proceeded to find our own teeth by trial and error. We kept putting dentures in our mouth until we found the perfect fit. I thought this was very gross, and this time I was thinking right.

It was no place to bring a lady, nevertheless, I didn't have trouble finding a girl to go along with me to these events. They were anticipating three days straight of partying. I was surprised to learn that many of the girls who ran with these outlaw clubs came from respectable homes. The girls I invited along were sixteen and seventeen years old and I was in my early twenties. They lied to their parents, telling them they were going to their friend's house for the weekend, or some would sneak out of the house and just didn't return until Sunday night. We weren't staying at the Hilton but in a tent with no place to bathe and clean up. When I took them home they were dirty and dusty. I am sure they had a hard time explaining to their parents where they were.

These outlaw club members were in the age range of 25-50 years old but most of the girls were much younger. To be initiated as a club member, the girls needed to do whatever the members asked of them. One weekend we invited an outlaw club to our clubhouse for the weekend. They brought with them a girl they had drugged up and gave her as a token of appreciation for our invitation to our club. She laid on the sofa for the weekend for anybody to take advantage of her. I don't think she had any idea what was going on or what she had become involved with. I have thought about her throughout the years and wonder where she is today or if she is even living. My hope is she found good people to surround her with the respect she deserved and that she became aware of her value, as a person created by God.

I watched as an outlaw caught a child and placed a firecracker in his shoe. They lit the firecracker and blew off the whole back of his foot. Another time they threw a firecracker at a young girl, and it landed on her lap. She went to pick it up to throw it away but it went off in her hand, blowing off several of her fingers. A lady in the group who knew first aid had us search for her fingers in the high grass. She was hoping we could find them and have them reattached at the hospital.

There was one rule I saw enforced. You were not allowed to pass out from drugs and alcohol while wearing your club colors. Club members wore jackets with their club name inscribed, to identity the club they belonged to. It was considered a disgrace to the club's name if you passed out. The consequence was to be activated by a fellow club member. They poured gas on the fallen member and set him on fire. You would see the person trying to escape by running away while they were burning. In most cases somebody would catch them, throw them down and throw blankets or coats on them to quench the fire. Their life was spared but the consequence of severe burns and scars followed them forever. I have witnessed this several times and it is one of the most horrifying scenes you can imagine. It brought to my mind the many sermons I had heard about hell for those who refuse the gift of eternal life.

During the night when I was trying to sleep I heard shots being fired, followed by people screaming. It was a common occurrence for people to be shot at. Sometimes I would crawl under my truck at night to stay out of harm's way and to protect myself from being run over by a motorcycle while trying to get some sleep. One night I was sleeping under the truck when I was rudely awakened by a sharp jab to my ribs. It was a state policeman hitting me with the end of his rifle and yelling at me to get out from under the truck. I crawled out and became wide awake as I was surrounded by flashing lights, police cars, and state police everywhere. There were about thirty police cars that came to help with the raid that night and many of the guys were escorted straight to jail.

We were a problem for the police wherever we went. We traveled in gangs to and from our events. There would be hundreds of us riding through a town on our cycles. At the edge of these small towns we were greeted by the police escort waiting for our arrival. The police would try to escort us through their towns, all the side roads and red lights were blocked off. They weren't interested in our business and didn't want us stopping anywhere in their town. They knew that wherever we stopped there would be trouble and they were right about that. When we stopped at a bar, the first course of action was to throw out the bartender. By the time we left, the place was basically smashed and we had all helped ourselves to free drinks. When we traveled in large gangs the police usually wouldn't bother to arrest us for the minor laws we broke. On several occasions we ganged together to upset police cars. They were afraid of us and knew we were armed. When they got out of their cars, they often were carrying their rifles. One of our members did shoot and kill a police officer. He was given a life sentence and died while in jail.

There was a Pagan motorcycle member from my area who was raised in a more conservative family than me. One fateful night he approached a car parked on a back road, and found a couple making out. He killed both of them and concluded his act of violence by beheading them. His crime did not catch up to him for about six weeks. I was drinking with him at a bar, a couple nights after he killed this couple. He didn't show any emotions or signs that were out of the ordinary. I was stunned when the police arrested him for murder. I never imagined he was capable of being a killer, he was a very nice guy, when he wasn't on drugs or drinking. The night of the murder he was under the influence of drugs. He received a life sentence and died in prison this past year. Several years before he died he repented of his sins and asked for forgiveness. I believe I will see him some day in heaven. To have a murderer in heaven is difficult to understand and seems unfair to us as humans, because we rightfully desire justice. The reality is that Jesus paid the ultimate price for sin by taking the punishment for all sin on Himself. God sees this exchange as justice and freely forgives us when we ask. I lost several other friends who were shot and killed, which served as a reminder to me that I wasn't immortal.

A friend of mine was a bouncer at a private nightclub. His job was to card people as they entered the club. He always carried a stainless cigarette lighter in his shirt pocket. A guy he was carding got mad at him when he denied him entrance to the club. He pulled out his pistol and shot him at close range. Miraculously the bullet hit the cigarette lighter in his pocket and knocked him down. He had several broken ribs, but the bullet never penetrated through the lighter. I was putting myself in many dangerous situations and I thank God for granting me life through this precarious time of my life.

The outlaw gangs regularly traveled to Daytona Beach, Florida, for Bike Week. In the 60's and 70's it was completely different than it is today. On the streets of Daytona about every third car was a police car and every tenth car a paddy wagon to pick up the outlaws. The streets were filled with club members getting in fights and breaking the law in many different ways. I was younger than most of the members of the motorcycle gang, when I first went to Daytona. If I was partying with the college kids, I would dress like them, and when I was partying with the gang members, I would wear my colors. One night while partying with the college kids, I was drunk and jumped in the back of a stranger's car parked along the street. My plan was to sleep off my hangover. When the husband and wife got into their car, I was lying in the back seat and refused to get out. They called the police and the paddy wagon was not far behind. The police dragged me out of the car and threw me in the paddy wagon. When they opened the door of the paddy wagon, it was full of Hells Angels and Pagans, I was the only one in civilian clothes. We were all placed in the same jail cell. I recognized some of the Hell's Angels members from a previous party, but they didn't recognize me in my street clothes.

One night I went to party with the Hell's Angels at a bar. The cops followed us and surrounded the bar on the outside. They knew the potential for outlaws to cause havoc and they were right. Before long, pool tables were overturned, chairs were flying, the bartender was ousted. Things were getting out of control, I felt uncomfortable, and decided to leave. The cops grabbed me and gave me a choice to go back into the bar or get into their police car. They weren't allowing anyone to leave alone. I think this was their plan and hope for gaining control of an out of control situation.

The following year when I went to Daytona again to enjoy the events of Bike Week, I was caught while involved in an illegal activity. I went through a repeat routine of the previous year. I was thrown into the back of the paddy wagon and hauled off to jail. They usually locked up a couple hundred outlaw guys each night and a trial would follow on the next day. I would never carry my wallet, because I didn't want to have identification on me. I didn't want them to know who I was or enable them to do a background check on me.

That year I didn't have a driver's license and didn't want anyone to have that piece of information either. My friends went on my behalf to an attorney, to ask what kind of sentence I might be looking at. The attorney said if I was found guilty I would probably get a year on the chain gang. In Florida they were still using chain gangs as punishment. My friends packed my bags and came to the courthouse. I was sitting in the back of the courtroom waiting for my case to be called. My friends came in and informed me of my potential sentence if I was found guilty. They informed me my packed bags were sitting outside the door. They encouraged me to walk out the back doors and run. I had a couple of minutes to decide what I was going to do. Should I take my chances and run or face the judge and hope for mercy?

As I was contemplating my best course of action, I heard my named called. I went up front and stood before the judge, who proceeded to read the charges filed against me. He asked me how I pled, and I said, "Not guilty." He went on to question me about the crime and asked where I was from and why I didn't have my wallet or driver's license with me. I lied and said my wallet was stolen. He continued to ask me more questions and I continued telling him more lies. After the judge listened to my story, he concluded by saying, "It appears to me, you are trying to lie your way out of this." He instructed me to go over and sit down and said, "I will get back to you."

There was security all around me now and I was smart enough to recognize, I wasn't going anywhere. I sat there all day long, waiting to receive my sentence. When all of the other cases were heard and the court was closed for the day, he called me into his office. The judge said, "I am sorry you lost your wallet, you are free to go." As I look back on this day, I know, he knew I was lying to him, but he decided to extend mercy to me. For some unknown reason, I think he felt sorry for me and left me go.

Several years later one of my buddies who worked with me at the motorcycle shop, was getting married. He planned his wedding and honeymoon to coincide with Daytona Bike Week. We raced bikes together but he had no ties with the outlaw clubs. He asked his future wife if my girlfriend and I could go along with them on their honeymoon. His wife let us know we weren't to interfere with their honeymoon plans, but we could get together occasionally during the week. They stayed in a really nice motel which I couldn't afford, so we stayed in a nearby dumpy motel. I left my girlfriend alone in the motel a couple nights while I went out to party with other girls. I couldn't even stay faithful to one girl for one week. My girlfriend found out I was cheating on her and it was a very long trip back to Pa. She got back at me by embarrassing me when we arrived back at her house.

We arrived home on a Sunday afternoon and I went to drop her off at her home. The driveway was full of cars and she said all her brothers, sisters, and in-laws were there to visit her parents. She informed me I was not going to get away with just dropping her off. She had me carry her suitcase into the house and I was forced to face her large family. She introduced me to her parents and I didn't know if her parents knew where she was for the week. Her mother said, "Well, did you have a good time?" I felt really embarrassed and got out of there as fast as I could. I had just been faced with a respectable family and I knew I hadn't treated their family member with respect.

I was not a respectable man and I regret to say I went as low as to have a one-night stand with another man's wife. She told her husband what happened and he called and asked me to stop by his house. I wasn't aware of the conversation he and his wife had, but it became apparent as soon as I stepped inside the house. He cornered me and told me I had fifteen minutes to live. He informed me I was going to be dead by midnight. I knew what I did was totally wrong and I felt I deserved whatever was coming to me.

I was sitting on a chair in his kitchen when he told me to get up. I thought he was going to get a knife from the kitchen drawer or draw a gun. I thought at that moment I was going to die. You can't imagine the thoughts that flashed through my mind believing these were the last minutes of my life. The last thing I remember is getting out of the chair and then waking up and realizing I was lying by his screen door. I opened my eyes and could see him standing close by. I jumped up and somehow escaped through the screen door.

I ran down the road to a gas station where a man and his wife, with their kids in the back seat, was pumping gas. I tried to jump in to the back seat and was yelling that someone was trying to kill me. They were kicking and slapping me and trying to do everything they could to keep this wild man from getting into their car. I am sure I was pale and I had blood coming out of my mouth. At this point I wasn't aware of what all had just happened. I found out later, with one punch my upper and lower jaw were broken as I flew across the room. The car took off and I ran down the center of the road, trying to find a way of escape. I feared I was being followed.

I ran through the fields until I recognized a house where I knew the people who lived there. Their sleep was interrupted as I banged on their front door. Since they knew me they were kind enough to let me in. The state police were contacted and took a statement of what had happened. A day or so later the police came to my house, and wanted me to file charges. I refused, because I knew I was guilty and in the wrong for what I had done. After this incident I carried a loaded pistol with me and never went anywhere without it. I was building our first home, frequently working on the house at night. I carried the pistol with me into every room. This wasn't in the blueprint for how I wanted to build our first home. For years I lived in fear and was a living example of the truth, that the way of a transgressor is hard. The bartenders in the area knew I was carrying a loaded gun, but said they wouldn't report me or have charges filed against me. Perhaps they figured it was in their best interest to keep me around, being the loyal customer I had become.

At that time, I didn't realize the hurt and anger unfaithfulness and affairs bring to a man and his family. Only when it happened to me did I realize how deep this pain goes. Years later, my wife shared with me that she was involved in an affair. The table was turned and the shoe was on the other foot. I came to understand what people mean when they say, that unfaithfulness and divorce can be more difficult to work through than death. It certainly was a process for me to work through this betrayal and to eventually offer forgiveness.

During these years I thought I was "living high," but I actually was "living low." During the week when I was alone, I felt absolutely awful. I knew the things I was involved with were so very wrong. There are things I did and saw that are too disgusting to repeat and most of these years I lived in constant fear. The motorcycle club I belonged to required its members to carry a pistol. It was no way to live and I often thought about ending my own life.

I remembered what I had learned in Sunday School and it was clear who I was following. Satan had control of me and did a good job of tormenting me with feelings of hopelessness and despair. Satan haunted me with the lie that God would never forgive me for my past.

My life revolved around high-risk activities, running with a dangerous crowd, drinking and driving, and racing cycles. I was constantly living in fear, with the reality that I could be killed one way or another. I knew if I died, I would spend eternity in hell. When I thought about hell, the picture of the men running to get away from the torment of fire, came to my mind. Deep down, I knew God had a better plan for my life, than to live in torment and fear. God was lovingly waiting for me to choose a better life, for the remainder of my life on earth and for eternity, but I wasn't ready to accept His offer.

Meeting and Marrying Judy

I met my future wife, Judy, at a bar called Meck's, in New Holland, Pa. They featured a live band on weekends, providing a place to hang out to have a "good time." Judy was from Lancaster City, one of the larger cities in our area. She was a city girl and had one older sister, Sally. Her parents and sister were good people. Her parents made sure she went to church, even when they didn't attend. She was still attending church, at the age of 21, when I met her. Judy liked to get out on weekends and party, in spite of her parents being very strict. We both enjoyed partying and when we met at Meck's Bar we shared our first dance. We met again at another party, where some ex-Amish boys were throwing a party, with a live band, giving Judy and I another opportunity to dance.

The following week the Draggin Gypsies had a party at our clubhouse. Judy knew I would be there, so she came with her friends, looking for me. They were modest and well dressed, a contrast from most of the girls there. I sent her on her way as quickly as I could and told her I would pick her up, at her house, Saturday night. This was our first real date and I was proud of my beautiful date. In my opinion, she was part of the upper class, a class I never felt a part of. I set out to put on my best act in an attempt to impress her. I knew I was going to have to meet her parents before they would allow her to go out with me. I figured part of making a good impression was having an impressive mustache. For most of my adult life I grew a mustache and while my hair was dark brown, my mustache had a little red and white in it. I used my sister's mascara to fill in my mustache to match my hair color. After drinking Friday night and all day Saturday, I drove into Lancaster City to pick up my date. I knocked on the front door of her house. Her mother answered the door and asked, "Can I help you, who are you looking for?" In my nervousness, I couldn't remember her name. She said, "Just a minute," and shut the door on me, without offering me an invitation to come inside. She said, "Judy, the guy that is here to pick you up, doesn't even know your name." I failed in making a good first impression and had one strike against me.

Our first date included a movie along with some kissing. She excused herself to go to the ladies' room and looked in the mirror to check the status of her make-up. Much to her surprise her face was covered with black strokes of mascara smudged all over her face. She inquired about what I had on my face and I said to myself, "strike two." Talk about being embarrassed, I was certain this was my first and last date with her. To my surprise when I asked her for another date, she said yes.

We dated on and off while I continued to date other girls. About three months later she said something that surprised both of us—she was pregnant. I was 29 years old and that was the first time I ever heard that. I was in complete shock and didn't know how to respond. She informed me I was the one who was going to tell her parents about our baby and our plans to marry. I knew her parents didn't approve of her dating me. I felt I wasn't good enough for their daughter. I finally built up nerve and went to her father and said, "I would like to marry your daughter." He immediately asked, "Do you have her pregnant?" I said, "Yes." They only had two daughters and I am sure they long anticipated having a beautiful wedding for

Wedding day May 1970.

their daughter. They planned a nice wedding reception, for family and friends to share in celebrating our special day. It was going to be a big wedding and all around a big day. The more I thought about the changes that were coming my way, the more I was getting cold feet. I went to Judy and said, "I can't marry you, because I don't feel I am a responsible person and I just can't see myself married." I knew I was being a fool in more than one way, Judy was one of the nicest girls I ever dated. When my friends found out I wasn't going to marry her, they called me every name in the book. Some of them told me, if I didn't marry her they wanted nothing to do with me.

I remember riding my motorcycle to Judy's house when she was about three months pregnant. I asked her to hop on the motorcycle, to go for a ride. As we went to get on the bike Judy's mother ran out of the house and said, "Don't you take her on that motorcycle." I just took off and away we went. I left her mother standing there with her fear that her daughter and grandchild was going to be hurt. Her parents cancelled the church and all the plans made for the reception. Obviously they were very upset with me. Her father came to my parents' home, where I was still living, to appeal to me. He warned me that if I didn't marry his daughter it would be very costly for me and I would pay big time. Her mother suggested considering adoption, if I wasn't willing to marry and provide a home for her daughter and grandchild. This was about to be strike three but I came to my senses and chose to take Judy as my wife.

Looking back on this season of my life, I see the life changing decisions that were before me. My future would have been so different, if I hadn't made the decision to marry Judy and provide a home for our son. I would have lost the true blessings of having Judy as my wife and the joy of watching my son grow up to be a fine young man. I have so many good memories over the years and now have a wonderful daughter-in-law and grandson to complete our family. I believe God was working in my life and led me to make the final decision to marry Judy. We decided on a small outdoor wedding in my brother-in-law's backyard. He was a pastor and joined us together in holy matrimony in the presence of God and the wedding guests, on a lovely afternoon in May, and that was 43 years ago.

I brought into our marriage a mountain of debt, including car and motorcycle payments. We were married with a child on the way but didn't have any money for our future life together. We lived with my parents for a week until we could move into a small apartment in New Danville, Pa. Judy had bought a real nice car with her hard-earned money before we met. I told her she needed to sell the car so we could buy furniture and pay off my debts.

I was working night shift at an atomic power plant when I received the anticipated phone call from my wife. She was having labor pains and was on her way to the hospital. Several hours later we were blessed with a beautiful baby boy, we named Kenny. I loved my wife and son, but I was lacking the wisdom I needed to be a good husband and father. I was working long hours and a lot of weekends. When I did get a weekend off, I selfishly thought this was my time off to party with my motorcycle buddies. The first years of our marriage, I frequently left my wife home alone with our growing son.

One weekend I was leaving our apartment, to party with my motorcycle friends. She knew I wouldn't be home until it was time to go back to work, on Monday morning. She grabbed a couple of my most treasured trophies and stood on our front porch threatening to throw them at my car. I took off anyway, leaving her on the porch with her frustrations and with the trophies. During these first years of our marriage, Judy left me many times, hoping I would change my ways. Her mother discouraged her from coming back to me, knowing this was not the way marriage was meant to be; she was right about that.

Once again, Judy left and this time I was uncertain if she would ever return. We had a lot of Christian friends, parents and family praying for us during this tumultuous time in our marriage. My first cousin, Joyce and her husband Marty worked with us to help save our marriage. They played a large part in keeping our marriage together, for which we are thankful, to them and to God.

My mother arranged to have an evangelist named Martin to come and talk with us. My wife was now 24 years old and I was 31. We both agreed knowing something needed to change in our lives. He was a prison chaplain in Alabama and brought two ex-prisoners with him. They shared their testimony of how their lives have changed. I listened intently as the one man shared his life story which was very similar to mine. Due to his actions and lifestyle his wife left him, taking along their son, and he landed in jail, losing everything that was of value. God really used this man to touch my life and I could see how my life was headed for the same loss and destruction. The evangelist explained how asking God to forgive our past sins, was the key to a new beginning and a new life. He encouraged us with the fact we could also forgive each other and have a new start in our marriage. I chose to accept this gift of forgiveness and asked God and Judy to forgive me for my life of selfishness and wrongdoing. Judy attended church her entire life but never made a personal decision to be forgiven and to forgive. That night after hearing this message of hope, she invited Jesus into her life.

We experienced many positive changes in our lives as the inward change effected our outward lives. I stopped running with my old buddies and discontinued drinking and partying. I had a desire to be a better husband and father and to spend more time with my wife and son. We became involved in a local church and surrounded ourselves with other Christians who supported us in the new path we were taking. We continued to experience many opportunities to forgive each other for our failures, realizing this was our only way to move forward.

After 15 years of marriage I was tested with the greatest trial of my life. I am sorry to say I initially failed the test, but I am thankful to say I eventually passed the test. My wife shared with me, that she was involved with another man. During this time of crisis when I learned my wife had an affair all I wanted to do was get even with this man. My life completely changed, and all I could think of was how I could hurt or kill him without getting caught. When he got off work, I would wait for him beside the road. I thought when he came to a red light, I could push him out into the traffic so another car might kill him. One night I took my pick-up and ran through his garage door. I was carrying a pistol with me for a long period of time, trying to figure out a way to kill him, without getting caught. I went to a bar, where I knew some rough guys who would do anything for the right amount of money. I wanted to pay one of these guys to beat him up. I had so much hate in my heart, I knew Satan was completely taking over my life again. Some of my actions landed me in court. I sure wasn't thinking straight, I even carried a pistol into the courthouse. After the trial was over, I followed him along with his wife and son, to where they had parked their car. Someone knew I had a pistol and they notified the police. Before I knew what was happening, there were cops everywhere. I ran into a parking garage with cop cars running up and down the ramps, looking for me. Somehow I escaped without getting caught.

I forced my wife to go with me to this man's house. In the presence of his wife and son I had my wife sit at their kitchen table to tell everything they had done. His wife would not believe her. He told my wife she was jealous and because she couldn't have him she was making up this story. The affair included one time in his bedroom. To convince her that she was telling the truth she took it another step. She went on to describe the color of wallpaper and type of furniture that was in the bedroom. He died a few years later and I regret never going back to ask him for forgiveness for my thoughts and actions. I had trouble trusting my wife for years after this happened. I was always thinking if she did it once she may do it again. Every time we had an argument, I thought, how dare you talk back to me or yell at me, after what you did.

Anytime there is unfaithfulness, it is a challenge to get the marriage back on track and to a place of restoration. I found that Satan is always there to remind you of it and wants to use it to destroy the marriage. We personally experienced God's help and healing and learned we could have a restored marriage as we followed His ways. It was a process, but eventually we both forgave each other and received God's forgiveness.

Jobs, Right and Wrong

I learned a lot of life lessons from my various experiences in the work world. I have my father to thank for teaching me the reward and fulfillment of putting in a hard day's work. The only time I didn't have a job was when my body was broken and wouldn't allow it. The longest breaks I had from work was two six-months periods, while I recovered from a broken back. One wintry day I was involved in a truck accident with my friend, Mark. A school van hit us head on and the injuries included a broken back. Fortunately the school's insurance paid me for lost wages. The second time I was off work for six months was also due to a broken back. This was the time I was run over by several motorcycles during a race.

After my school days, I continued working on a farm until I decided the long hours of farming were not for me. My dad helped me get my first job as a carpenter at the construction company where he was employed. It was a fairly large company, constructing homes and churches, called Horst Construction. The first couple of years this company did not have a backhoe, and I was responsible for digging footers by hand. When they purchased a backhoe it sure made my job easier. They taught me how to pour and finish concrete and I moved on to working with concrete for several years. My good work ethic was showing and the company's 15 foremen frequently requested me for their job sites, knowing I was a hard worker. An older foreman appealed to the boss on my behalf, saying it wasn't fair I wasn't given a chance to learn the carpenter trade. The boss gave him the approval to work with me for half a year to teach me the basics of carpentry. I continued with carpentry for this company for five more years until another company asked me to work for them.

This new offer required me to join the Carpenters Local Union. I would start off making double what my father earned after his twenty years of carpentry experience. My father being the conservative person he was, believed working for the union was wrong. It sure looked right to me and so I agreed to start the new job the very next day. They informed me of the tools I needed, along with the restrictions of no power tools and no tools over 2 feet long. I had just bought a new 6'x 6' level, so I asked my dad if he would help hold my level while I cut a 2-foot section off of my brand new level. My dad graciously helped me, but I could tell it was difficult for him to watch the destruction of the 6-foot level as well as to process the change of his son being a member of the union.

I worked on many large jobs, including bridges and nuclear power plants, including Three Mile Island and Peach Bottom Power Plant. After the near meltdown at Three Mile Island, our union was called in to help rebuild the damaged reactor. I was considered a mill-wright as well as a carpenter, and that is why I was called to work there. The contractor was one of the largest ones in the world, called Bechtel from California. While working on this job, you had to go through security to get on the jobsite and the site was secured with a chain link fence around the whole perimeter. The first thing I learned on this job, was to put my work ethic aside. The foreman told me if I didn't learn how to slow down, I wouldn't have this job very long. The second thing I learned was to get rid of my regular size lunch bucket and purchase the biggest one available. The bigger the lunch bucket, the more tools you could carry off the jobsite. There were various ways to increase our take home pay. Working night shift, belt pay, using a torch, and working on a wall over 20-ft. high were all opportunities for increased pay. Our job was to set up concrete forms and we would be hanging on the back of these forms all night with a safety belt. When we felt we needed a break, we would knock out all of the lightbulbs so we couldn't see to work. We were not allowed to replace lightbulbs but had to wait for the electrician, who wouldn't come until the next shift.

The foreman knew I was a heavy drinker and he created a plan for me and others that came to the job drunk. The foreman would lock us in the gang box, where the tools were kept, and give us the entire shift to sleep it off. He didn't want to take the chance of having intoxicated men in high places. Everyone, including security, knew we were walking off with tools. Tools consisting of drills, torches, grinders, power saws, etc., went home with us in our lunch buckets. If the item was too big to fit into our lunch bucket we would disassemble them so we could carry it out piece by piece. The more we carried out, the more the company could back charge to the job. We used a lot of high-voltage copper wire, which we cut into two-foot sections and then stuck it through the fence. When we went out for our lunch break we loaded the copper into our pick-ups or car trunks. One night a pick-up load of new skill saws came on our job site so we dug a hole and buried them to run up the cost of the job.

When I was out of work the union would pay us to picket non-union jobs. During a huge snowstorm, our foreman asked us to go shovel the snow off of a building. I shoveled a couple of hours, knowing I was breaking the union rules because a carpenter was not allowed to use a shovel, which was considered a laborer's job. I was dreaming of warmer weather, so I came up with a plan. I threw my shovel down over the side of the building, went home, packed my clothes, and headed to Daytona Beach.

I also worked as a millwright, doing work for the RCA TV plant. The first person hired for a job working for the union, is the foreman and the second guy hired is the union steward. I was the first guy hired and they designated me as the foreman of this large job. I wasn't a welder and didn't know a lot about setting up machinery. My general foreman said not to worry about it, that he would help me work through it. I had twelve men working under me and we were installing a metal track to transport picture tubes to another area of the building. My men were welding this track for 4 days. The general foreman came to the jobsite and informed me the track was installed upside down. It took us another four days to grind the welds off and disassemble the track. I thought I was going to lose my job, but I also knew, being in the union, they couldn't fire me. The general foreman was gracious and told me everybody makes mistakes and that is how you learn.

When I was first married at the age of twenty-nine years, I had a lot of debt and a low paying job. We started our life together in a small apartment and later moved up to a mobile home. A friend asked me to go into the roofing and siding partnership with him. The construction business and the economy were very strong during this time. We became a fairly large company, needing to employ others for our growing business. I came to realize that running a business with integrity was the way to go and enjoyed some perks for a well run business. We purchased shingles and siding from local suppliers who gave us credit for the supplies we purchased. At the end of the year we were rewarded with credit points for free trips. We were blessed with trips to Hawaii, Bahamas, Mexico, Cancun, Rome and Italy. My wife and I enjoyed these opportunities to travel. When we had more credits than we needed we invited friends and were also able to invite some of my brothers and sisters to go along with us to enjoy the trips.

Business was booming and I thought all was going well. I was putting on roofs and siding for many large building contractors. The contractors told me to come and do the work without asking me to price out the jobs. I suppose they trusted me to give them a fair price. My partner and employees were aware I was turning over a good profit. I was taking multiple hunting trips and in one year I took six trips for big game in North America. I also booked a 28-day hunt in South Africa. Much to my dismay, when I came home, my business was basically wiped out. My partner and an employee went to the contractors and said they were going to take over the business. I decided not to make a big issue out of it and downscaled my business due to losing my contact base. It was a disappointment because I thought I had men working for me that I didn't have to watch over but I was wrong. Fortunately, I had purchased several rental properties prior to this happening and was earning income from them.

Knowing I was self employed and didn't have a pension plan I decided to continue buying rental properties. My accountant said I was paying too much in taxes and advised me to invest in more real estate for a tax write off. It was a good time to buy real estate properties and I was blessed with several good investments. My broker also encouraged me to buy stocks, which I did. Annually he asked me to come to his office to make decisions. I was busy with hunting, booking hunts, or maintaining the apartments, so I told him that was what he was getting paid for. I never read the monthly statements I received nor did I ever look in the paper to see what the stock market was doing. I only met with him one time in thirty years. At seventy years old I was required to start taking withdrawals and it looks like he did a decent job in making good decisions on my behalf.

My next and final job was working as a booking agent and guide. I booked hunts all over the world, mainly caribou and black bear hunts in Quebec, Canada. I guided most of my clients and had employees to assist me. I was also the camp manager, averaging 12-16 clients a week. My best year was when 300 hunters booked bear and caribou hunts. During the winter months of January, February, and

March, I was busy with Sportsman Outdoor Shows. I did as many as fifteen shows per year, with some shows running for nine days. The shows were the hardest part of this job. I was exhausted after three months of standing and talking about hunting and repeating the same things over and over. When the shows were over, I told my wife I didn't want to talk about hunting or answer any phone calls. I needed a couple weeks off to recuperate.

Entering my retirement years, I decided it was time to sell some property. I held a public auction to sell multiple townhouses. The day of the auction, a young man pulled up in a new corvette and looked at one of the units. He came over to me and asked if I was the owner. He went on to say he was interested in buying the properties and asked if I would accept cash for the down payment. He told me I wouldn't need to claim it as income. He carried a brown paper bag with him, filled with the cash. I told him I wanted to talk with my wife and attorney. I went back to him and told him we were not interested in making this deal and we will report the sale as income. As it turned out, he did buy all the townhouses.

With siding jobs and when selling hunting trips, I would frequently be asked how much less it would be if paid by cash. I was suspicious of these offers, wondering if they wanted to avoid a paper trail and possibly cheat the government out of their share. After all the years of cheating in various ways, it felt good to know those days were behind me.

I used the skills I had acquired over the years and built six different homes for my wife and son. We lived in them several years and then sold them for a profit. My wife put in a request for an in-ground pool with a bath house at the next house we built. It sounded like a good idea at the time of planning but turned out to be a huge mistake. I was frequently on hunting trips, my wife had a full-time job, and my son was too young to take care of the pool. Upon returning from my extended hunting trip, I was greeted with a green, algae-filled pool.

Baptism in our pool.

After several episodes of that, I told my wife I was not going to pay to have the pool pumped out one more time. I threatened to stock the pool with fish. We did use this pool for a baptism one Sunday and it was a blessing and served one good purpose. We settled the problem by selling the property, and building another house where we enjoyed the green grass in the backyard in place of the green pool.

I am grateful to my father for passing his good work ethic onto me. I learned valuable life lessons from my father and one of them, was the importance of work. He was a carpenter by trade and had worked on his chicken farm every night after work. We always ate supper together as a family but my dad didn't have a lot of free time to play with us children. I am grateful for the way he took his responsibility seriously to provide for his wife and seven children. The last couple years of his life, he often apologized to us, regretting he didn't take more time to have fun time with his children. I would try to reassure him, he was just doing what he needed to do in that season of his life. He was a survivor of the Great Depression, which gave him a perspective from that era. He saw firsthand, the time of rebuilding after a time of loss and saw the importance of maintaining a good work ethic. He was a man of integrity and was always concerned about being fair and honest in every way. Retiring from his career of carpentry at the age of 72, he questioned if it was right for him to collect social security. He needed to be convinced it was money he had already contributed for his retirement and it was fair and honest for him to receive it. He was very cautious and low risk, never putting a penny in the stock market. When the stock market was down, he would ask me with a knowingly grin, "So how is the stock market doing for you?"

His breakfast consisted of bacon or scrapple and eggs with a regular bedtime snack of cheese and pretzels. He lived a simple lifestyle, desiring to live by God's principles and with the intent to keep God first. After 97 years of a good life he left this earth and passed on to receive his reward in heaven. I miss having my parents to visit and talk with, but I am looking forward to spending eternity with them.

Judy's Life Story

I grew up in the city of Lancaster and came from a family that was very stable. My parents were always there for me. I went to schools in Lancaster City. I had one sister Sally who was seven years older than me, she is married to Galen Perry. When I graduated from high school, I got jobs working in some factories for a short time. The jobs after that were always working for large companies in the purchasing departments.

I got married at 21 years of age; we had a little boy the same year. My husband Ken was from Goodville. We didn't know each other very long before we were married. He came from a large conservative Mennonite family and I was raised Lutheran. He was

My sister and brother-in-law, Galen and Sally Perry.

73

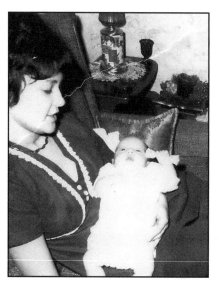

Judy with Ken Jr.

a country boy and I was a city girl. It didn't take long to know we were very different from each other. He was a very ambitious person with some real specific goals and I was content with the way things were, just working and taking care of my son.

The first year we were married he took me to Florida for a nice vacation just the two of us. He took me to Daytona Beach for Bike Week. When I got there I was scared to death being around those types of people. My husband was used to this but I certainly wasn't. I was glad when we got home.

Our married life started out real rocky and my husband did whatever he wanted even though he was married. I was home alone with a baby and had never been alone overnight in my life. This took some time to get used to this type of life. After about three years of marriage I thought it was really bad and I didn't know what to do. I would walk out with my son and would go live with my sister, or friends and then we would always get back together again. This was no way to live. Then my husband's cousin Joyce became friends with me and she and her husband Marty tried to help us from a biblical standard of living.

As our marriage kept getting worse and worse, we knew we had to do something. My mother-in-law asked an evangelist by the name of Martin to come and talk to us. I was at the point I just wanted to give up and move on with my life. The pastor came and brought two ex-prisoners to our house and they shared their testimonies with us. Then the pastor asked the big question, "Do you want to receive Jesus as your Saviour?" I said yes and we got down on our knees and prayed. This was the first time I ever did anything like this and I received the Holy Spirit. Right after these men left with the pastor my husband was so happy and then he told me he was unfaithful to me. Then I was really confused.

Life was pretty much the same as it had been; we fought a lot even though we both accepted the Lord. My husband continued to hunt and be away from home for many weeks at a time. We had a siding business and this gave him more money to hunt. It was a very successful business. We worked together as a team.

On my job I got closer and closer to my boss, I never could talk to my husband and here was someone willing to listen to me. Next thing you know we got into a relationship with both of us being married. I went to our church one night at the revival service and was convicted of what I was doing. That night I told my husband that I was unfaithful to him. My whole world literally fell apart. My son and I moved out of the house for safety reasons. A nice couple from our church took us in for three weeks. I had lost my good job and had no money. The people who took my son and me in were Lowell and Lucy a very committed Christian couple. They lived what they believed, and I thank God for them. After three weeks I went home and the relationship was still bad in our marriage. It takes years to repair a marriage when unfaithfulness is involved. My parents were worried about my safety. When someone isn't living close to the Lord the door is open for anything to happen and my husband was really out of control.

As time moved on I got another job and just existed and worked. My husband would take me on many vacations but our marriage still didn't have the love we should have had for each other. I do have to say God put the right people in our lives, through Karen and Howard who worked with us on many occasions with great biblical counseling and just being our dear friends and our Sunday school teacher.

I worked for a company in Leola for 21 years, and the 11th year I worked there I was diagnosed with CML, leukemia, which is a form of blood cancer. The type of cancer I have is chronic which means I can live a fairly long life taking chemotherapy medicine for the rest of my life. I have been in remission for the last 11 years. This gave me a whole new outlook on life. Each day is a precious gift from God, and I knew He was going to take care of me. Twenty years ago when someone was diagnosed with leukemia you would have a very short life span. Today with the latest technology and medicine we can live long productive lives.

When I was first diagnosed, I thought I was going to die in a few months. I went to my church and asked the pastor if I could be anointed. So I went on a Sunday night along with many of my family members and was anointed. I had seen this done many times in our church for emotional, physical, and mental healing for the person. I was very doubtful about this, but I went ahead. We are told you must have a clear mind believing that God will take care of you. Well that night I believed I was in no condition not to believe, He is the only one who can heal you.

The very next day on Monday, I had to go to the hospital and have a blood transfusion. When I was sitting there in the chair with my arm ready for the needle, my cancer doctor walked up to me and said, "What are you doing here?" I said, "Your nurse called me on Friday and said I needed a blood transfusion so here I am." He said, "You don't need one you can go home." What an answer to prayer, God had really healed me. Praise His name! Three weeks later I did have to have a blood transfusion.

I never missed a day's work in eleven years due to my illness, and the pills I take are $5000.00 a month but God has provided. I know I will have this 'til the day I go to heaven but God is in control. Sometimes people ask why certain things happen. If we let God take control of our lives He will walk us through the difficult times.

God has shown me in my job, and with relationships He is always there. We are the ones who move away from Him. He wants us to call on His name, and ask for wisdom and guidance. It's when we try to do things within our own power that things get out of control and messed up. God gives us all we need, so we can give to others in their need.

Our son and his wife wanted a child and could not conceive. After many attempts they tried invitro-fertilization, and they had a little boy. We call him our miracle grandchild. There are people out there who really want children and will provide a wonderful home and life for children through adoption and modern medicine and technology. He is our little blessing, and I thank God for Brady every day.

Now as I am retired, I look back on the years of working full-time and have some very fond memories of people who I worked with, and how many lives we touch. We get to know these people in a very personal way and get to share with them. I realize how many times I got to witness to people who called on me with my position, most were salesmen and salesladies. I shared with them about my illness and gave God all the glory. When you are told you have a terminal illness it sheds a light on you and you realize the brevity of your life. You have to depend on God more. The medicine I take is very expensive but I always have it available to me and it is always paid for.

My wish for my family and friends is that they see Jesus in me. There are people in my life that are very close to me and they don't know the Lord. All I can do is pray for them and share what God has done for me, and then let the rest up to the Holy Spirit to convict them. Sometimes the closest people to you are the hardest ones to reach, but nothing is impossible for God.

I remember leading my mother to the Lord years ago. We were in the car and I was taking her home and we sat outside of her house. I said, "Mother you need to ask Jesus into your life," and right there she did; we prayed together and she accepted the Lord. I remem-

My parents Richard and Mildred Black.

ber when Mom went to the nursing home, they had a bible study there and she didn't feel comfortable about answering the questions, so I would help her with her homework. She came to the Lord late in life and didn't know how to find the passages in the Bible, but she had a willing heart. We all grow at different paces in our walk with God, and we have to be patient with those who are still crawling. God knows the heart.

My father on the other hand didn't always agree with me on the spiritual level. One time we were driving up to some apartments my husband and I were building in Womelsdorf, and I said, "Dad look at the sign." It said, "You can have a home in heaven." His reply was, "Heaven is full." I really thought about what he said and was saddened he did not believe. It wasn't until he was diagnosed with lung cancer, that he had time to think. He was diagnosed and died within seven weeks. I prayed and prayed my dad would accept the Lord. He went to church, but did not have a personal relationship with Jesus. So when he was sick and in bed, I prayed I would get the opportunity to share with him. I remember going up to his bedroom, I had my Bible marked in so many places to share Bible verses with him. But in the end I just looked at him and said, "Dad you know what I went through and God took care of me and my life changed, and I said you need to accept the Lord before your life is over" and he did. My father was there for me in any and every situation and I could always count on him and my mother.

My mother never worked outside of the home, she was a stay at home mother. She was always there for me to share with. I think of the younger kids of today, and how they come home to an empty home. Many don't have any fathers or mentors. My parents always knew where I was or who I was with, they kept very close tabs on me. But even though they did that, I turned out very rebellious in my teen years.

When I met Ken we were both rebellious and wanted to do our own thing. When God is not the center of your life and you think you are in control, life can get out of hand. I thank God for the many people He has put in our paths—some who had wonderful marriages and did counseling with us, and the many pastors and just good Christian friends who stood by us and went the extra mile, for two people who were stubborn and headstrong. Their prayers and persistence kept me strong. Ken's family was very supportive in our marriage and I thank God for Christian brothers and sisters-in-laws. When Ken's parents were living we had many get togethers as a family—birthdays, anniversaries, reunions, vacations at the mountains. I got together with Ken's family more than my own family.

Over the years we built six houses and some of the time Ken got me involved. I am married to a very ambitious guy, when he sets his mind on getting a job done he gets it done. I am not of the same mind always. He is really a go getter. This can have its problems at times. We have done things I thought we could never get accomplished but when God is in the center of things it gets done.

My father was never a hunter or an avid sports person, he was a golfer. When I married Ken he was so involved in hunting. My father never left the family to take a vacation, we all went together and did things. Little did I know I would be selling caribou and bear trips for many years, and listening for hours to men telling me their experi-

Our cabin in Fulton County, Pa.

Our family. Front row: Our son Kenny, grandson Brady, daughter-in-law, Michelle. Back row: Judy and Ken.

ences while I was selling them a hunting trip. I met some very interesting people over the years and had many of them in our home.

We are also landlords in the Ephrata area and over the years have met some really neat people. We have a great couple living in one of our townhouses, they also have an outreach ministry. They have worked with many couples in their church and they recommend them to us to be tenants. Some people complain about being landlords but in most of our dealings, if you treat people fair and honest you can work with people in some of the most difficult circumstances.

We have had the privilege of owning a cabin in Fulton County, that my husband built. We have had numerous church groups and retreats held there, we also rent it out. God has been so good to us and we go there to enjoy nature and our family. You would be surprised how many people just want to get away from the rat race of work and the many activities that require their time and money. I hope we can share this cabin for many years to come with our family and friends.

Through the years I have been on many vacations and trips in America and to other countries. I have always looked forward to them with great anticipation and planning. But what we have to look forward to at the end of our life is more than we can expect or imagine. I am talking about heaven, may you join me on this promise and journey, only Jesus can give us.

When Ken's mother and dad died, there was so much peace knowing they were going to heaven. In many families they don't have the assurance where their family members are going. The family worked together getting the house sold and all that goes in settling the affairs. When God is in the picture everything goes fine.

May God bless you all and I hope you enjoy reading my husband's book. Remember this, Proverbs 3:5,6: "Trust in the Lord with all your heart and lean not on your own understanding; in all our ways acknowledge him, and he shall direct your paths."

The Challenge
of the Whitetail

I started hunting deer when I was fifteen years old. A group of us
built a cabin in Potter County, Pennsylvania; so, I've been hunting
deer for 55 years. During that time, I've seen a lot of changes. In deer
season, we'd usually have 14 hunters in camp; and, on an average day,
we'd see 30 to 40 deer per hunter. We didn't kill a lot of big bucks during those years, because most of what we saw were spike bucks—the
law required the spike be three inches or longer. When you shoot a
lot of spikes, you don't give the bucks a chance to grow bigger antlers.
A number of years ago, they changed the law. Now bucks in our area
need to have at least three points on one side and in parts of western
Pennsylvania the bucks need to have at least four points on one antler.
The current law protects a lot of two- and three-year-old bucks from
being shot. So, now we're harvesting more four- and five-year-old
bucks and the antler quality has improved.

Back in the old days, there were three times more hunters
in the woods than we have today. In those days, a young boy would
dream of the day he could be hunting with his father. Now that
there are a lot fewer deer in the woods, we're losing our young hunt-

Front row: Irvie Gingrich, Lloyd Weaver, Kevin Horning, Ken Gingrich. Back row: Calvin Weaver, Eugene Horning, John Martin, Barry Martin, Harold Horning, Carl Gingrich. Potter County Gang.

ers. When I was a kid, the majority of our activities took place outside of the home. Now the majority of kids spend their free time in the house playing video games or watching television, I think their attention span is much shorter. Most youngsters today don't like sitting out in the woods all day in the bitter cold, especially if they don't see any deer. There are a number of reasons we are losing our deer herd. It seems everybody has their own opinion. I believe the game commission contributed to the problem of fewer deer and bucks when they made open seasons on does. Hunters are their own worst enemy when they harvest does. A lot of hunters feel if they don't kill a deer when they are in the woods hunting, they had a bad hunt. Fewer does results in fewer fawns and fewer fawns results in fewer bucks. Many hunters say, "If it's brown, knock it down." They think if they don't shoot the does somebody else will. Some say they need the meat; however, if they can afford to buy all the latest gadgets in hunting gear and take days off work, I think they could afford to buy meat. Another factor that probably contributes to the decline in the number of deer harvested is the shrinking amount of forest land in Pennsylvania.

Here are some estimates on why killing does effects the deer herd:

> YEAR ONE – The doe you did not kill usually has, on average, two fawns each year—one doe and one buck. Now we have two more does and one buck the first year.
>
> YEAR TWO – Those two does will have two more does and two more bucks. Now you have a total of 4 does and 4 bucks.
>
> YEAR THREE – Those four does will have four more does and four more bucks. Now you'll have 8 more does and 8 more bucks.
>
> YEAR FOUR – Those eight does will have eight more does and eight more bucks, now you have a total of 16 does and 16 bucks.
>
> YEAR FIVE – Those 16 does will have 16 more does and 16 more bucks, now you have a total of 32 does and 32 bucks.
>
> YEAR SIX – Those 32 does will have 32 more does and 32 more bucks, now you have a total of 64 does and 64 bucks.
>
> YEAR SEVEN – Those 64 does will have 64 more does and 64 more bucks, now you have a total of 128 does and 128 bucks.
>
> YEAR EIGHT – Those 128 does will have 128 more does and 128 more bucks, now you have a total of 256 does and 256 bucks.

In a perfect environment, if all of the does survived from the one you didn't kill, in an eight-year period, we'd have 508 more deer. I hope hunters take this into consideration and understand why I say we can be our own worst enemy. Of course, this would be in a perfect environment. We have to take into consideration that a number of the does would be killed by hunters, cars, coyotes and bears. We also have more bobcats today than ever before and they'd kill some of the newborn fawns. In addition, some of the deer will starve from lack of food. I also hear some hunters saying, "We have to get the deer numbers down, because in the hard winters a lot of deer will starve." Since the climate is changing a lot and we don't have many hard winters like we did in the past, there are only a few areas in the state where deer might not make it during a hard winter. In most areas, there's feed for the deer, especially in agricultural areas. I must admit, in my lifetime, I've only shot two does but I probably shouldn't have.

There is another statistic that needs to be considered. When I started to hunt in Pennsylvania in the mid 50's there was only a two-week archery season and a two-week buck season, and a three-day doe season if you were lucky enough to draw a tag. Today the hunting season starts mid-September and runs to the end of January. There is a total of 120 days for hunting season. With this extra long hunting season there is an opportunity of harvesting a lot more deer than in the past. Also, back in the 1950's, if a hunter had a deer rifle it was usually a 30/30 with open sights, and a lot of the hunters were using shotgun shooting slugs. Your range when using these weapons are about 75 yards. Today the hunters are using high-powered rifles with scopes, that can range anywhere from 100 yards up to 1000 yards.

In the 1950's the archery hunters only had re-curve bows; their range was approximately 20-30 yards. Today with the compound bows and the cross bows their ranges are unlimited. This is another factor why our deer herd is decreasing.

I have been hunting the Eastern Shore of Maryland for years.

William Altman—Manager's son on Maryland Farm where I hunt.

The farm where two of us hunt covers 400 acres of woods surrounded by bean and corn fields. The landowner told us he wants us to kill 50 does off his land every year. This goes completely against my way of thinking, however, I do understand the landowner's need to have some of the deer harvested to protect against crop damage. If I didn't obey the landowner's rules, I feared I could lose my lease of this property and these woods are known as one of the best areas to hunt in Kent County. It borders the Remington Farm area and Remington Farms has a deer management program that was established years ago by Dr. Gary Alt, a deer biologist. He recommended that the doe-to-buck ratio in the area should be two does to one buck. That first year they killed lots of doe to achieve that ratio. From that point on, they kept detailed records over the next several years on the quality of buck harvested. The results showed no substantial quality increase in the size of bucks' antlers. My friend and I also manage our area to increase antler size. We only hunt archery on this farm and we don't kill bucks that score under 145 BC. As a result, we take three to four bucks that score 150 or better off this farm every year. Maryland allows each hunter to harvest 30 does and 6 bucks per season.

In Pennsylvania, I killed my first doe when I was eighteen years old. A couple of years after that they opened up a flintlock muzzleloader season in January. Up north, in Potter County, Pa., they always had a lot of snow in January. I decided I wanted to try hunting with a muzzleloader, so I bought a flintlock. When I was out hunting, it snowed and the humidity and the moisture in the air dampened my powder and caused misfires. On one day alone, I had over 15 misfires.

Later on that afternoon, I was on top of a mountain and saw a small herd of deer down close to the bottom. They were standing in a tight group, too far away to use my muzzleloader. At the time, I was only a teenager and did a lot of dumb things. This was one of those times. I thought I should shoot into the herd. I did and they all ran off, but I thought I saw one deer limping. It was a long way down there and I wasn't positive about what I saw. I went ahead and worked my way down to check for a blood trail in the snow. I did find a blood trail and started to track the deer. I didn't go very far before I saw a deer in front of me stumbling and falling. I saw it was a doe and she had her two front legs broken. She came to a river and jumped right in and had trouble keeping herself from drowning. The only thing sticking out of the water was her head. I had to figure out a way to get her back on the shore, but the water was too deep for wading. I had a drag rope in my knapsack, so I got it out and made a lasso. On my fourth attempt trying to lasso her, I finally got the rope around her neck and pulled her out on shore. This is when I had my hands full.

I had a wild and very active deer on the end of my rope. She had two broken legs, but other than that, she was in good health. I had a hard time holding on to her. She just kept going in circles and it was all I could do to hang on. I didn't know how to handle this situation. I couldn't reach my gun to finish her off, I pulled her over to a tree and tied her fast, then walked over and got my muzzleloader and loaded it. I tried to shoot her in the neck but she jerked and I missed. Then she really went wild. I had to load my muzzleloader again. On the second try I killed her. That was my second doe, I hunted the next forty years without shooting a doe. A couple of years after that second doe, I shot my first buck in Potter County, it turned out to be the nicest buck I ever killed in Pennsylvania. It was a nice eight point.

Non-resident, Trophy Hunting

When I got married, my wife told me I could hunt as much as I wanted but not to bring any meat home. She said she didn't like to cook wild game or the taste of it. I do like wild game but I thought I'd better listen to my wife. I asked myself why I am killing these bucks if we're not going to eat them? I made a decision from this point that I was not going to shoot any bucks unless I would mount them and put them on my wall.

I had a son and I couldn't wait until he turned twelve, so he could hunt with me. Twelve is the legal age to hunt in Pennsylvania, as long as you have a mentor with you. I tried to teach him the methods of deer hunting. I showed him deer trails and rubs, where bucks rub their antlers, and scrapes which the bucks use to attract does. I also pointed out the difference between doe and buck tracks in the snow. During Fall turkey season, about a month before deer season, I went up to our camp to build blinds in several different locations. I thought hunting out of a blind would be much easier for my son and give him a chance to kill a deer. That was long before pop-up blinds came on

Kenneth and Ken Jr.'s first buck.

Ken Jr. 177 Boone & Crockett harvested in 2013 in IL.

the market. When building blinds, I always look for a tree that had
fallen down and drag other logs to that tree and build a blind. Some of
the hunters in camp didn't think this was legal. At that time, the game
laws weren't real clear on this issue. That method worked and my son
killed a buck his first year hunting. Then, he killed a buck every year
after that for the next five years. I can truthfully say those early years
of hunting with my son were some of the best experiences I've had in
all my years of hunting. To this day, my son and I plan one or two
hunting trips together every year. The last seven years we've also been
archery hunting in Illinois. My son owns a car lot and is really busy
most of the year, so he doesn't get a lot of time off. When he does get
time off, we travel and hunt together. We have quality time to share
with each other, I always look forward to our hunts.

    We hunt in a lot of different places. For the last five years,
we've been hunting on a farm in Fulton County, Illinois. They only
take a couple of doe off this farm a year. The buck and doe ratio is
two does to one buck and it hasn't changed over the years. We'll often
see up to ten bucks per day. Some of these bucks are in the 140 class
range or more. Again, I can't see why we have to kill a lot of doe to
have quality deer management. There are more Boone & Crockett
and Pope & Young record book heads coming out of Fulton County,
Illinois, than any other state. Last year, my son was very fortunate to
kill a 178 Boone & Crockett buck. I average about sixty days of deer
hunting a year. In addition to Illinois, Maryland and Pennsylvania, I
also hunt deer in New York, Iowa, Kansas and Ohio as well as in Alberta and Saskatchewan, Canada. I spend about 50% of my hunting
time in Maryland.

    I bought a piece of land in New York state that was excellent for
turkey and deer hunting, so I hunted there for fifteen years. One year I
was hunting deer on my property when my Amish neighbors asked me
if I would be interested in going along with them to hunt and put on
drives for deer. There were about 14 Amish guys in the group and they

Ken's 161 Boone & Crockett harvested in Saskatchewan.

wanted me to drive them around to different areas helping them put on drives. On one of those drives, I was a stander and they told me to shoot anything I saw. They wanted the meat. Their policy was "If it's brown knock it down." While I was standing there, a couple of deer came out and there was a small buck in the group. I shot it. When the drivers came out, an older Amish man came up to me and asked if I had shot. I said, "Yes, I shot that small buck that's laying over there. If you want it, you can have it." He was all excited and he asked, "Do you mean to tell me you don't want that buck?" I told him I didn't. He walked over to the buck and all at once I heard a shot. I yelled at him, "What are you doing?" He said, "I had to shoot it. I don't want to go home and tell my wife a lie—that I shot it, when I didn't."

I've hunted deer many times in Saskatchewan on Indian reservations. On their reservations, Indians don't have to abide by game laws. It's their land and they make up their own laws. They will let you shoot whatever deer you see and as many as you want. They do charge

159 Boone & Crockett harvested in Alberta.

a trophy fee for each animal killed. I've had a lot of good hunts on reservations and killed several good buck. I asked one of the outfitters if he would be interested in having me book hunts for him. He said he'd like that. Then I explained his obligations he has to me. He had to promise he would bait one month before my customers arrived in camp and he had to build some more blinds. He assured me that all the requirements would be met. I should have known better, having dealt with Indians before. During the year, he kept calling me asking for money, and it got to the point where I told him I wouldn't send him anymore money. I said I would pay the balance for the hunters when I got into camp. The reason I did this is because the Indians only live for a day at a time. They don't plan for the future. I was concerned that when my customers arrived in camp in the Fall all of the money would be spent, and the Indians wouldn't be ready for the hunters. I went up a week earlier than my customers and found that the Indians didn't even have enough money left to buy groceries for my clients. I was glad I held some money back. We went out and bought groceries and extra corn and wheat for our baits. Everything was ready for the first group of hunters and we had a very successful season. That was my last year working with that outfitter.

Another time, I went on a seven-day hunt for elk and deer in Alberta, Canada. The first couple days we had bad weather conditions and we didn't see much at all. On the fourth day, we got up a little bit late and had a late start. As we were driving up a dirt road at daylight, the guide stopped and said, "There in that field is a real good buck." We drove down the road another quarter mile, got out of the pick-up and walked back up the road to where we saw the deer. Again, he said, "It's a monster buck." I said, "It doesn't look that big to me." He said, "It is a good buck, shoot it." I shot it and then we walked over to it. The guide looked at the deer and said, "Kenny I'm sorry. I thought it was much bigger than that." I asked him, "What are you going to do now?" He said, "I will use my tag and tag it for you." Then, on the last day of the hunt, I did kill a real good buck, but we didn't see any quality elk on that hunt.

The following year, despite the past problem, I booked another trip with the same outfitter. We really got along well. I was the only customer they had in camp that week. There were five of us in camp—me, my guide and three other guides without any customers. They asked me if I would mind if they went along on my hunt. I told them if they wanted to hunt that would be fine with me. There was no reason they'd have to sit around camp all week. All five of us had tags for elk, whitetail deer, bear, and wolves. We hunted for the entire week and none of us had an opportunity to harvest any quality animals. Still, it was one of my better hunts. All five of us were guides and we had a lot of fun, a lot in common and a lot of stories to share. They had a jet boat in camp and we spent a lot of time in the boat running up and down the river. The river had a lot of rapids and it was a very exciting trip.

My guides in Alberta. Dave in center of picture took his life.

My guide, Dave, was one of the friendliest guides I ever hunted with. During the week, he was sharing a lot about a girlfriend he had back in town and telling us how much he missed her. When I got back home a couple of days later, one of the other guides called me and said he had some bad news to tell me. He told me when Dave got back in town and went to his girlfriend's house, he caught her cheating on him. He lost his temper and beat her up pretty bad. Then he called "911" and reported what he did to her. After making the call, he walked outside of her house and, when the cops were coming down the street, he pulled out his pistol and shot himself in the head. I guess he couldn't face the reality of what had happened.

"Scent Free"

The past year, I hunted in Kansas and there were six other hunters in camp. They were all in my age category. Most of them were big game hunters and they hunted all over the world. They had hunted whitetails all of their lives. We had a lot of things in common and we had a lot of stories to share. This was also an archery hunt and these guys took the necessary steps to be scent free, as much as possible. They all hung their clothes outside at night, but I only saw the one hunter spray himself with scent-free spray. Over the years, when something new comes on the market, I'm usually the first to try it. I've tried almost every buck and doe lure, scent-lock suits and cover-up scent; and I've come to the conclusion that most of these things don't work. The only caution I take is to be scent free, I always hang my clothes outside. I can remember I was one of the first ones to ever use cover-up scent. I used to take raccoon lure and put it on my cap. The guys in camp thought I was crazy. That week in Kansas I saw 28 different bucks. I was in a ladder stand in a tree, about 12 feet high. I always keep a diary of what I see when I'm hunting. I know at least 12 of the bucks I saw walked within 15 yards of my stand. Two of them came in and put their noses on the ladder stand where I had left scent from my hands and boots a couple of hours earlier.

On an average year, I probably pass up shots at 60 to 70 buck. Most years, I only harvest one or two deer because I'm looking for bucks that score 140 or better. I guided for bear in Canada for forty years and I consider the bears' sense of smell to be equal to that of white-tail deer. Over the years, I did every test possible.

After my Kansas hunt, I went to Fulton County, Illinois, with my son on another archery hunt. In this camp, the outfitter usually had 12 hunters a week. I was the oldest one in camp. It was a completely different atmosphere than the Kansas hunt. Almost all of the hunters were between the ages of 30 and 40. This younger generation of hunters had been brought up watching outdoor channels and buying DVD's on deer hunting. They'd go on the internet for a lot of their information. Most of them believed everything they'd heard or read. They spent the entire week in camp telling each other what works and what doesn't. If you are one of those hunters who uses everything on the market and thinks it all works, then I recommend you keep on using those things. That way, you'll have peace of mind. One of the hunters had his bow lying on the back of my tailgate, and when I went to pick it up to move it out of the way, he yelled at me, "Get your hands off of my bow." I said, "I just want to move it out of the way." He said, "I don't want your scent on my bow." Most of the young hunters would take their duffle bags out in the woods, strip down naked in the cold and put their hunting clothes on. One of the hunters wouldn't even ride in the pick-up truck's cab. He would sit back in the bed and ride out to the stands in the cold. He wouldn't allow the guide to start his pick-up until he was in the bed of the truck, so the gas fumes wouldn't get on him.

When I'm archery hunting, I try to take a shower every day. When my son and I drove out to Illinois it took about 14 hours. When we got to the camp, we were tired and I didn't take a shower that first day. The next morning when I was up in my tree stand, I was on the side of a hill looking toward a cornfield. I saw a trophy buck working its way down toward me. It came within 40 yards of me and spotted me in the tree. As long as I didn't move he couldn't figure out what I was. He stood there for 15 minutes or more looking up at me, then all at once he ran off. I thought maybe he picked up my scent. He only ran about 60 yards, then stood in the briers for a half hour. Finally, he came out and started working his way over toward me again. As he went by, he kept looking up at me. He stopped a couple times and finally walked off. I should and could have taken him, but I was looking for a bigger buck. He was in the 140 to the 150 class.

That evening I was sitting next to the outfitter at the supper table and I was only wearing pants and a t-shirt. I might have had a little bit of body order. The outfitter and my son were real good friends; and the outfitter told my son if I didn't take a shower in the morning, I wouldn't be able to go out and hunt. After my son told me this, I told the outfitter I was sorry. I also told him about my experience the prior day when I was on my stand. I asked, "If my body odor was that bad, why did that buck stay around for so long?" After that buck walked away, I took out a small piece of toilet paper and dropped it out of the tree stand and found that the wind was blowing right toward him. I had on six layers of clothes and the outer layer was a rain suit. It is nearly impossible for a little bit of body odor to get out through six layers of clothes. The next morning, I told them I would do whatever they thought was necessary. They gave me scent-lock soap and shampoo and I took a shower. I always keep my clothes outside. That morning, I went outside and put my clothes on and they sprayed me down with scent-free spray. I thought I could smell the spray. If I can smell it I thought, I'm sure the deer can too. As I was walking to my stand, they gave me scent-free gum to chew. If all this stuff works like they say it does, I should have had a good day hunting. That day, more deer picked up my scent and snorted at me than ever before.

Many archery hunters think it is very important to take a container with them in the woods so they have something to urinate in. They think that way the deer won't get the smell of urine. Here's a test I've made hundreds of times over the years. I urinate near my stand and then watch as adult does or bucks come near my stand. I watch what they do. I've never seen them react to the smell of my urine. Maybe it's because the urine turns into ammonia in a couple of minutes. That's a proven fact. One time, I was sitting on the ground behind a tree and an adult doe came up right behind me and then walked on by. Then, she turned around and came back to me and licked my shoe. That was years before they came out with the scent-free products. When the first scent-lock suits came out, three of us bought them and wore them for one year. We had the worst luck with those suits and now none of us will ever wear them again. When they get wet they emit an odor.

In this day and age, with all of the information out there on how to keep yourself scent free, you try to do things right by using

Jim Smith in center harvested over 300 buck with bow hunting from the ground.

the latest products and methods recommended. At the same time, a lot of hunters take a thermos of coffee, hot chocolate, or soup out with them and drink it in the woods. I believe that smell carries much further than your body odor does. When you pull out a sandwich, most of your lunchmeat has a strong odor as does candy and lifesavers. Many hunters carry the latest high-tech gadgets with them when they're in the woods. They take cell phones out with them and when they're bored they text, play video games and search the internet. When they're playing with those things, they're not concentrating on hunting and they're letting their guard down. When I first started hunting, none of those items were available and I think we enjoyed hunting much more back then. It was peaceful, quiet and we enjoyed nature. One of my good friends, Jim from Maryland, spends more time in the woods than I do. In Maryland, you are allowed to harvest 36 deer per year. He told me he hunts from the ground and has killed over 100 deer with his bow. He also tells me he doesn't worry about being scent free. He keeps his clothes right in his kitchen and fries bacon almost every morning. After all my years of hunting, I'm not saying all the things I do are right, only that they worked for me.

The Mating Call
of the Gobbler

I have been asked a number of times, "What is your favorite hunt?" I tell them hunting male turkeys, called gobblers, in the spring, because it's a lot like dating. First you locate them, then you try to attract them. It's mating season and the gobblers are looking for the hens and the hens are sweet talking the gobblers. You go out

Eastern turkey from N.Y.

in the evenings and use an owl or crow call to get them to answer, and when you locate them you go back there early the next morning. Once they answer, you try to get within 100 yards of them without them seeing you. Then, you wait for them to fly down and gobble again to attract a hen friend. It's important to set up on the same level as the gobbler. I don't like to call a bird up hill or down hill. When I set up, I usually have three decoys with me, sometimes even more. My setup usually includes two hens and a jake. These days, there are more turkey hunters using decoys. Back when I first started hunting turkeys there wasn't a decoy on the market. In fact, I built my first turkey decoy by buying a goose decoy, painting it black, cutting off its head and getting my taxidermist to mount a real turkey head on it. That's what I used for several years, before they came out with turkey decoys. After getting set up, I'd start out calling using a box call and make a couple soft yelps. Then, using a Cody slate call, I'd follow up with a couple of soft clucks. Finally, I'd use a mouth call and make more soft clucks. I carry about five calls with me, depending on what the birds like to hear.

Turkeys make a number of calls including: yelps, clucks, putts, purrs, perts, kee-kee runs, fly-down cackles and gobbles. Both hens and gobblers yelp, but the gobbler's yelp is deeper, more bass like. Mother hens yelp to assemble their offspring. Young turkeys trying to get back with their mom or their flock use the kee-kee run. All turkeys yelp and cluck to communicate with other turkeys. Obviously, the fly-down cackle happens when a turkey is leaving its roost and flying to the ground.

Often the gobbler comes within fifty or sixty yards, hangs up and just stands there gobbling and strutting; saying to the hen, "If you're interested in mating, come over here." Your heart starts to pound. You either wait or make a few very soft clucks or purrs until the gobbler moves into shooting range. When he comes out of his strut and raises his head this is the best time to shoot. Then, he is out there flopping around on the ground and you run over, jump on him and finish the job. At this point, you're hooked for life on turkey hunting.

When I originally began hunting deer in Potter County, Pennsylvania, there were no turkeys in the area. Several years later, they opened turkey hunting for the first time. During those days, if you were lucky enough to locate a turkey in the Spring, you had no trouble at all calling it in. They would answer and respond to any call or caller. They were really curious at that time, because they had never heard hunters calling them before. In those early years, I wasn't very smart about turkey calling either. I thought I was pretty good with my calling, so I entered my first turkey calling contest. I finished in second place, not bad for my first competition. Only trouble was there were only two of us calling in that contest. I usually don't tell anyone I finished in last place, just that I finished second.

It was during my second season when I killed my first Spring gobbler. The following year, I killed a Fall turkey with my rifle. During the Spring season, gobblers are the only legal harvest. In the Fall, you can shoot gobblers or hens. Usually, the best way to hunt in the Fall is to locate a flock and break it up. Then you sit down and call like a turkey trying to get back together with its flock.

Back in those days, there were only two well-known manufacturers making box calls. One made Lynch calls and the other made the Ben Roger Lee box calls. Ben Roger Lee was from Alabama. He would come to Galeton in Potter County, Pennsylvania, to an area called Potato City. Then, he'd put on a seminar on turkey calling. After the seminar, he would have a table set up with all of his box calls. At that time, the calls sold for $10.00 each. I paid for one of the calls and Ben told me to help myself to any call I wanted. His personal call, the one he used to put on his seminars, was sitting back away from the rest of the calls. I thought that was probably his best call if he was using it to demonstrate calling. Since he told me to help myself to any call on the table, I selected his personal call. When I got back to the cabin the next morning, I picked up the call to practice with it and examined it a little closer. It didn't take long for me to see he had used this call quite a bit. Most of the lettering on the side of the box was worn off.

Over the years, I got to know Ben Roger Lee pretty well. One time I was flying to Texas to hunt the Rio Grande turkey in Corpus Christi and Ben was on the same plane. He was headed to Oklahoma to hunt. Since we knew each other, we booked seats together. There were three seats per row and Ben had the window seat and I had the aisle. Ben weighed over 300 pounds, so he almost took up two seats. The center seat was open; and when the airline stewardess walked by, she recognized Ben. She asked Ben if she could sit next to him, because her husband was an avid turkey hunter and she would like to talk to him. Before Ben and I got on the plane, he had told me he just had his stomach stapled and was having trouble holding his gas. When the young stewardess sat between us, Ben silently started to pass gas. The smell was so bad it made my eyes water. People sitting around us kept looking at me, thinking I was the one passing gas, I was very embarrassed. Ben kept talking to the stewardess and acting like there was nothing wrong.

I met up with him a couple years later and he told me he had lost over 100 pounds. I thought it was great that he had lost so much weight. A few years later, he was in a car accident and he burned to death.

For years I got my turkey every Spring. Then, one year the season was winding down and I didn't have my turkey yet. I was planning on hunting the last eight days of the season mainly in Tioga County, Pennsylvania, near Cedar Run. One of my hunting friends, Glenn, had a camp on Pine Creek, and the only way to get to his cabin was by taking a boat across the creek. I really wanted to hunt in that area, because I knew there wasn't much hunting pressure there; because most hunters wouldn't have the means to cross the creek. On the 10th day of the hunt, the last day of the season, I got up early and climbed the hill behind the camp. I reached the top of the mountain at first light and sat down and made a couple of soft tree calls with my Cody slate. A gobbler on an opposite ridge answered my call. This was the first bird I had heard in eight days. The last thing I wanted to do was leave my current spot, climb down off that ridge and climb to the top of the other one. However, since I hadn't heard any other bird for eight days, I knew I didn't have a choice. So, I climbed down off the one mountain and up to the top of the other mountain. When I reached the top, the gobbler was still gobbling. I slowly worked my way over within fifty yards of the bird and set up. Then I made a couple of soft yelps and heard a few yelps in return. I looked to my right and there was another hunter sitting there calling. I wondered, how did he get in here? Turned out, he was working that bird before me, so I stopped calling. A couple of minutes later, I saw him put the gun on his shoulder and shoot. I saw the turkey flopping on the ground. I walked over to the bird, got there the same time as the other hunter, shook his hand, congratulated him and headed down off the mountain. Did you ever see a grown man cry? You would have if you would have been there that day.

Several years later I bought a cabin in up-state New York just across the Pennsylvania line. My next door neighbor, Sam, was an avid hunter. He had lots of coon dogs and was a real woodsman. He was born and raised in that area and knew the woods really well. He knew where a lot of the turkey roosting areas were and where the birds fed. When he was out at night hunting coons, he'd often run into turkey roosting areas. Many evenings I'd go with him to locate birds and pinpoint their roosting areas. Then, at dark, we would get the dogs out and go coon hunting.

At that time, there were a lot of people from out of the area moving in, buying land and posting it with "No Trespassing" signs. Sam wouldn't pay any attention to the "No Trespassing" signs. He would hunt coons, turkeys, pheasants and deer anywhere he wanted to. He told me that most of the locals didn't care if you trespassed on their land during turkey season, but you should stay off their land during deer season. He said, "If anybody gives you a hard time, just tell them you know Sam." I decided this would probably not be the best thing to say if I got caught trespassing. Often at night when we went raccoon hunting, a landowner's lights at the house would come on and the owner would come out and yell, "This land is posted, who are you?" Sam would yell back, "I am Sam. Who are you? If you want to make something of this, come out here." As soon as the owner heard Sam's name, he'd go back in the house and turn off the lights. However, Sam did warn me about one area. He said, "Don't ever get caught trespassing on this guy's property because he has a lot of young sons and if they catch you, they will beat the tar out of you."

A couple of years later, while hunting in that area, I saw four gobblers out in a field. The farmhouse was down in the valley about a mile away. This was a temptation I couldn't pass up. I wanted to go after those gobblers and I didn't think that land belonged to the farmer Sam had warned me about. I thought if I park up the road about a mile, circle around and come in from the back side, nobody would see me. When I got to the open field where the turkeys were, I crept down through the woods and came out right at the edge of the field. The turkeys were only 30 yards off. I shot and missed, and all of the birds flew down the valley right toward the farmer's house. The farmer's boys must have seen those turkeys up in that field. As soon as I shot, I heard the motorcycle, an ATV and a pick-up start up. I looked down the valley and saw all three of the boys coming up across the field. I didn't have time to run, but there was a brush pile and a bunch of briers right in front of me, so I dove into them. The boys came up across the field and stopped right next to the brush where I was hiding. They yelled, "We know you're here somewhere and when we find you, we're going to beat the living tar out of you." Actually, they used a word much worse than tar. All three of them searched the woods looking for me. They knew I couldn't have gone very far in that short period of time. I was laying face down shaking. When I lifted my head up enough to see where they were, I could have touched them. A couple hours later, they gave up looking for me and went back to their house. I continued to lay there a while, before I had the nerve to get up and work my way out of the woods.

I had another neighbor only a couple of miles away. His name was Bill, the inventer of the Cody turkey calls. When I first started hunting with him, he made his first slate call. Later, he came out with a glass call and then with mouth calls. Cody calls are well

Rio Grande turkey from Texas.

Merriam turkey from Wyoming.

Osceola turkey from Florida.

known, very popular and some of the best calls on the market today. I hunted with Bill for a good many years and he taught me a lot about turkey hunting and calling. Fortunately, over the years, I've had the opportunity to turkey hunt with a lot of well-known call makers. They included a number of people from Pennswoods and Quaker Boy calls. I learned a lot from those professional callers.

One of my major goals in turkey hunting has been to achieve a grand slam. That means I'd have to harvest each of the four species of turkeys. That includes the Eastern turkey found in states along the eastern seaboard; the Rio Grande bird living in Texas and surrounding states; the Merriams roaming the midwestern states; and the Osceola turkeys located in the southern part of Florida below Route 4 which runs from Daytona down to Tampa.

Obviously, I had harvested an Eastern turkey in Pennsylvania, so the second turkey I went after for my grand slam was the Rio Grande bird. To accomplish this I hunted with a Quaker Boy representative. When you're hunting in Texas, you have to be very careful where you sit to call. They always tell you to kick the leaves around the area where you are planning to sit to chase off the snakes (they have a lot of poisonous snakes in Texas) and also to make sure you don't sit on a cactus. The first morning out, we heard a bird about a mile off. My guide got out his call and started calling. I told him he was never going to call in that bird, because it was too far off. I said, "Why don't we get up and move toward him." He told me to get out my box call and to call as raspy and as loud as I could and he'd do the same thing. We called and called loud and raspy; and, after a while, we could tell the bird was working its way toward us. It took the turkey a couple of hours before it came in close enough for me to kill it. That was the farthest I ever called in a bird.

My next turkey harvested in the slam was a Merriam. I hooked up with an outfitter from Wyoming named Ralph. He took me out the second day of the hunt and we drove down a mountain road. He parked his pick-up behind a big brush pile and we climbed out of the truck. I asked him how far we would have to walk, so I could decide what to wear. He said, "Not very far." Right on the other side of that brush pile, he had a blind set up. That was the first time I had ever hunted out of a blind. As the sun came up and it began to get light, I could see a number of toms coming in to our decoys. I never saw so many turkeys in one area in my life. I shot my bird and it was one of the easiest turkey hunts I have ever been on.

The last turkey in the slam was the Osceola. My wife went down to Sarasota, Florida, and I went with her so I could hunt turkeys southeast of Sarasota. The Osceola is one of the hardest birds of the four to call in. They usually only gobble once in the morning and that's pretty much it for the day. Hunters usually set up along dirt roads and ambush the turkeys as they walk by. I completed my slam in Florida. Over the years, I've killed several of the Osceola turkeys. I still head south to hunt them when my wife is on vacation in Sarasota. The hunting season opens in mid March in Florida.

Now that I've completed my grand slam, I'd like to go after a Goulds turkey in Mexico to complete a Super Slam. The best way to hunt this bird is to walk through the woods and shoot them out of trees. It is nearly impossible to call in the Goulds. Right now, I wouldn't feel real comfortable going to Mexico to hunt Goulds, because the drug cartels may decide to hunt me. It's just not safe to hunt in Mexico.

During the last several years, most of my turkey hunting has been in Pennsylvania, Maryland and New Jersey. New Jersey has more turkeys than anywhere I have ever hunted. I usually have the best results in New Jersey when I use six or more decoys. I have used as many as fourteen decoys set up at one time. (See, gobbler hunting is like dating. The more females you display, the more males you attract.) Right now, I am having the best results using a Mike Lapp box call. Mike Lapp lives several miles from my house in Pennsylvania. Over the last six years, he has finished in the top five at the National Turkey Federation outdoor show in Nashville, Tennessee. He custom builds all of his box calls and you usually have to wait a year or more when you order a call from him. His calls are some of the highest priced on the market. I feel they are well worth it, because the Lapp call is one of the best sounding box calls I have ever heard. The last several years I have been hunting with a personal friend from my area. He is one of the best turkey hunters I have ever hunted with. He never leaves his guard down for a second; he hunts hard; thinks like a turkey; and goes at it from dawn until noon. (Our legal hunting hours in Pennsylvania in the Spring).

Many turkey hunters hunt hard in the first hours of the morning then give up later in the morning. I know my weakness in turkey hunting comes when I don't hear a bird for a long period of time. I get depressed and overcall which isn't good. When I hunt with my friend, our biggest problem is our hearing. We don't hear a lot of the birds that an average hunter hears. When we do hear a bird, we look at each other and wonder where the bird is located. He'll point one way and I'll point another. One of my partner's best moves comes when he imitates a turkey flying down out of a tree. He carries a turkey wing with him and slaps it against a tree. It sounds exactly like a turkey flapping its wings as it flies out of the tree. He'll follow up with a fly-down cackle. Then he takes the wing and slaps it in the leaves on the ground to imitate the bird landing. It's an effective technique.

So far, the biggest turkey I've ever killed had a 16" beard, 1-5/8" spurs, and weighed about 25 pounds.

Turkey hunting is a wonderful activity, but it also can be very dangerous—especially in the Spring—as more and more new hunters begin hunting. Hunters tend to get very excited when they hear turkeys gobbling or yelping, and sometimes that leads to beginner's errors. Years ago I was hunting with a friend in Alaska. He was one of the most safety conscious men I've ever been around. He was always checking our guns to make sure they weren't loaded and that we had the safetys on especially when we were handing them to each other, as we climbed in and out of the boats. He reprimanded us if he saw us doing something unsafe. A year after I was hunting with him in Alaska, he was hunting turkeys in Pennsylvania and he accidentally shot another hunter. He mistook the hunter for a turkey. He walked over to where he thought the turkey would be and saw the wounded hunter lying there. He tells us now, as far as he can remember, he went into shock and walked away leaving the wounded hunter there to die. Fortunately, one of the other hunters in his group heard the shot, found the wounded hunter, fortunately the man survived. The shooter walked back to camp and, according to others in the camp, didn't show any emotion at all. A couple weeks later, when he was sitting in church, what had happened all came back to him and he shouted out loud what had taken place. It's hard to believe someone could shoot another hunter during Spring turkey season when you're only allowed to identify and shoot gobblers. Hunters are supposed to look closely at the turkey before shooting to make sure it's a male bird. How can you mistake a human for a turkey?

You can't be too careful, I consider myself a very safety conscious hunter but I almost made this fatal mistake. One time I thought I saw a turkey moving and it was another hunter. This was in an area where I had taken a rowboat across the river to get to the hunting area. I didn't expect to see other hunters in that area; I thought I was alone. It was during the Fall season and I heard a turkey calling and heading in my direction. There were a lot of thick pine trees and I was looking under the trees trying to spot the turkey. It was dark looking into the pine trees, but I saw some movement.

I kept watching and was certain it was a turkey coming my way. I layed down, propped my rifle on a tree stump and was getting ready to shoot when I realized I was looking at a pair of black boots. You can't imagine the feeling that came over me. I thought to myself, it doesn't matter how safety conscious you are, accidents can still happen.

My friend Ken, who was wearing an orange vest was Fall turkey hunting when he was shot with a rifle. Ken was sitting on a log next to a tree, calling for turkeys. Another hunter heard the calling, saw some movement and shot him through the back with a hollow point bullet. The hollow point fragmented upon impact thus breaking two ribs, cracking two ribs, damaging the left lung, stomach, and intestines and ruining the spleen. Due to blood loss to the brain, sight was lost in his right eye.

My first hen turkey.

The hunter came to Ken's aid and called 911. Ken was in the woods a mile back from a traveled road. An ambulance crew carried him to a four-wheeler which transferred him to the ambulance where they treated him and then airlifted him to Geisinger Hospital in Danville, Pa. This took about 4 hours. Ken was very fortunate as the surgeon said a matter of a few minutes more and he might not have made it. After 12 days in the hospital and 2 months of recovery at home, Ken was back to work and still enjoyed turkey hunting with his son, grandchildren and friends.

I accomplished my final goal in turkey hunting, one week before my book was to be printed. I always wanted to harvest a gobbler with a bow and this morning I harvested a gobbler. There were five toms that flew down off of their roost and landed in an open field in front of my blind. There were two nice gobblers in the group, the one I wanted was out of reach for my bow, it had a 10-inch beard. I chose to take the other gobbler that was 25 yards away. It was also a nice tom, his beard was a little over 9" long. I felt fortunate to harvest this bird. I shot it with an expandable broad head and it dropped right on the spot.

Now that I achieved this goal in turkey hunting, if there was anything else I would like to accomplish, it was to harvest a hen turkey with a beard. I only ever have seen a couple hens with a beard in my lifetime. If you are fortunate to see one, they will only have a 2 to 3-inch beard. The very next morning after harvesting my gobbler with a bow, I went out hunting again, since I had two tags for turkey. At the break of dawn I couldn't believe what I was seeing. A turkey was coming into my decoys and I saw it had a nice beard. I kept looking at its head and I saw it wasn't a gobbler, it was a hen. I shot it and it had a 5-inch beard.

This just goes to show if you spend enough time in the woods, luck will come your way. If there is anything else that I could possibly ask for, it is to harvest a turkey with a triple beard. I have harvested a turkey already with a double beard. The ultimate goal would be to harvest one with five beards with a total length of 27 inches which is the world's record.

Ken, Judy and Kenny Jr., 1991.

Gingrich Family. Front row: Lois Ann, Mother, Dad, Susie. Second Row: Millie, Irvie, Carl, Ken, Lorraine

Judy, Ken, Kenny, Michelle, grandson Brady.

My parents, Irvin and Edna Gingrich, on their 65th wedding anniversary.

My Family—Left to Right: Charlie & Millie Wert, Carl & Ruth Ann, Ken & Judy, Lois Ann, Amos & Lorraine Hess, Irvie & Marlene, Nelson & Susie Martin.

Two-year-old Kenny Jr. at Easter, at the Log Cabin Trailer Court, Blue Ball, PA.

Two-year-old Kenny Jr. looking forward to see his Daddy race.

My family on a fishing trip with Ed Page Outfitter in Ottowa, Canada.

Grandson in trophy room riding a bear.

Pappy and Brady hiking the STS trail in Potter County, PA.

Brady and Pappy fishing for bass in Maryland.

Sledding at four years old at the homestead in Goodville.

My transportation was a horse when I lost my driver's license.

Our wedding in my brother-in-law's backyard, at Peter's Road, New Holland.

Best man Irvie and Maid of honor Marlene Gingrich.

This 1965 Mustang was the first one on the road in my area, hauling my 500cc Triumph Hill Climber.

My 1970 Dodge Challenger hauling my race boat.

1959 Chevy two-door hardtop, which I customized with a three-2 barrel carburetor.

Judy and our grandson at Blue Ball "Town Hall Restaurant," where I ate breakfast for the last 30 years with my friends, discussing politics, religion, sports, and hunting.

Raft trip on Snake River in Jackson Hole, Wyoming, with my wife and son.

Our mountain home in Woodhull, New York.

Judy and I on a salmon fishing trip in Plattsburg, New York.

One of the first dirt track scramble races I won.

Bob, George and myself preparing to go to a race in Flint, MI.

My friend Pooch and his wife's wedding at the Dragging Gypsie Motorcycle Clubhouse, in the Welsh Mountains.

Our Dragging Gypsie Club camping out at one of the many Gypsie tours.

I am on the right side on the starting line at a hill climb.

Viewing the steepness of the hill, from the top.

My guide and I in Zimbabwe.

The three trackers that were with me on my 21-day safari. They did an excellent job helping me track my wounded animals.

My sable that was harvested in Zimbabwe, Africa.

My guide and I with the Kudu.

Some of my mountain lions and the Alaskan brown bear.

Black bear and the Grand Slam of the four turkey species.

North American Game I harvested.

African Game I harvested.

*Our trip to Alaska in 2012, where Judy and I met Lance Mackey, four-time win-
ner of the Iditarod, through the Yukon and the Alaskan Wilderness.*

North American Big Game

I have had plenty of experience hunting bear and deer in Potter County, Pennsylvania, but now I was going to go on my first out-of-state hunt.

Lee Sample from New Holland, Pennsylvania, was the owner of the bar where I hung out. He asked me if I was interested in going on a black bear hunt with him and Jesse. He said they were going to Timmons, Ontario, in Canada to hunt bear. Of course I said, "Yes!"

We arrived in Timmons a day earlier than scheduled. That night we went downtown to a bar where we met a guy who worked for a Canadian railroad. He told us he was seeing a lot of bear along the train tracks. At that time of the year, early May, the bear are out feeding on roots and grass. They're the first things they feed on after coming out of hibernation.

Bears hibernate for six months. When they come out of hibernation, feeding on grass opens up their digestive systems. After their systems open, they start to feed on meats and fish. The man told us if we bought him a fifth of hard liquor he would take us out and show us where he was seeing the bears. Considering the condition he was in now, he sure didn't need another fifth of liquor today. When we dropped him off at his house, he was in bad shape.

We picked up this guy the following morning. His wife wouldn't permit him to take his rifle with him. I guess she knew what shape he was in. We walked down the railroad tracks about four miles and it was hot; it was lunchtime, so we stopped. Lee, Jesse and I laid down on a big flat rock near the tracks to take a nap. We had a hard night, with little sleep.

We awoke to a couple of shots. Our non-professional guide had taken one of our rifles and was shooting at a cow moose, which was not in season. We asked him if he had killed it, how was he planning to get it back to town? He said it would have been easy, because his buddies worked for the railroad and he would have flagged the train down and put the moose in one of the boxcars. Then they would have dropped off the moose when they got to his town.

The following year, the three of us booked a trip to Tennessee to hunt wild boars. I didn't know anything about wild boar hunting. I bought a couple of hunting magazines and read up on hunting wild boars. The articles really made it sound dangerous.

When we got down to Tennessee, the outfitter opened some gates and we drove into a high fence area. They called this a high-fence-hunt on a reserve. I thought we were going on a fair-chase hunt. If I had known what type of hunt this was, I would never have participated. However, it was interesting to watch the dogs chase the wild hogs and corner them. Then they'd pull the dogs off and shoot the wild pigs.

This reserve only covers a small area; whereas, larger reserves usually encompass a couple hundred acres. In the small reserves, the game can't get away and I don't consider the hunt a fair chase. They also have other game on this reserve including turkeys, white-tail deer, sheep and goats. My two friends shot three or four of the species. The outfitter talked the hunters into leaving their game with

Lee Sample and I on a high fence hunting in TN.

him, so he could mount the trophies. A year later, Jesse got one animal out of the four he had shot. We didn't receive ours. Jesse called
the outfitter and was told that as soon as we sent all of the money
down and paid him in full, he would send the trophies to us. We all
paid him in full. A couple months went by, but our trophies never
came. Jesse called and found the phone was disconnected. Jesse and
Lee drove down to Tennessee to find out what was going on. His place
was locked up and he was gone. They asked some of the neighbors
what happened to him. They said as far as they knew he moved to
Alabama. We never got our trophies back.

I had another disappointing experience with a game reserve.
About twenty years after the hog hunt, I was hunting turkeys in northern Pennsylvania. Spring gobbler season in the state is only open until
noon time. I knew there was a game reserve near where I was hunting,
so I thought I would take a drive over and check it out.

When I got there I asked the owner how much it would cost to hunt on the reserve, and if I didn't see something I wanted to shoot, what would the charge be? He quoted me a very low price and I decided to go on the reserve. Then he had me sign his guest book. I signed it and looked down over the names of other people who had hunted with him, and to my surprise, I saw a guy's name in there who I knew very well. Every year this guy got his turkey and a nice buck. I had considered this guy a real hard hunter and sportsman. I don't consider hunting inside a fence a fair chase. (More and more hunters are hunting this way.) The owner took me inside the fence and told me to sit down next to a tree. He said I should see game within a short period of time.

The whole area was completely bare. There wasn't a blade of grass anywhere, because animals had eaten it down to the ground. I was watching to see if I could see any animals coming. It probably wasn't more than 15 minutes when I saw lots of animals coming toward me. Right behind the animals I saw a guy walking and waving his arms. I heard him saying, "Shew, shew." The animals went by me and he came up to me and asked, "Why didn't you shoot?" I told him there was nothing there I wanted to shoot. He told me to stay right where I was and he would be back in 15 minutes. He was again herding animals toward me. I didn't shoot. He walked up to me and asked why I didn't shoot? I had seen enough, so I paid him his fee and left. If this is what the sportsmen of today call hunting, I don't want any part of it.

My next hunting trip took me to Lynchburg, Virginia, for white-tail deer. I went by myself. My plan was to hunt the week before New Years and party there on New Year's Eve. I figured I could party hard and nobody in the area would know me. New Year's Eve was on Monday night. Hunting was forbidden in Virginia on Sunday; so, I thought, since I was in Lynchburg, I would go to the Lynchburg Baptist Church to worship. The pastor was Jerry Falwell and I often watched him on television, so I went to his church to worship. After listening to his sermon, when he gave an invitation to come forward, I went up and recommitted my life. After that, I had an opportunity to talk to Jerry in person. That Sunday changed my plans for New Year's Eve. Now, I had no interest in partying, so I returned home that same day.

When I killed my first bear in Potter County in 1976, there were only seven bears killed that year in Pennsylvania. Thirty years later, they are now killing nearly 300 bears alone in Potter County. Bears kill as many deer, if not more, than coyotes. Interestingly, we have more coyotes than we have bear. In Pennsylvania, the growing bobcat population is another danger as bobcats kill a lot of newborn fawns. It's no wonder the deer herd is decreasing in size.

When two of my friends and I went up to Potter County for bear, it was my first year hunting bear in Pennsylvania. I set up on the top of a ridge behind our camp. On the ridge across from me, I saw five black spots moving around. Back in those days, I didn't carry binoculars, so it was difficult to identify animals at a distance. I thought those black spots might be raccoons. One hour later, I looked to my right and saw five black bears coming toward me. The bear in the front was the biggest, so I shot it. I soon realized the leading bear was a sow and she had four cubs with her. I knew I had made a mistake. The two older cubs ran off and the two smaller ones climbed up a tree. The cubs in the tree looked down at their mother and bawled. I really felt bad about what I did. It was very unusual to have four cubs together. Looking back on that, after talking to game wardens, I believe another sow bear probably adopted the two younger bear cubs.

My First Alaskan Adventures

My two friends, Lemar and Alvin, and I hunted in Alaska on two occasions. Both of our hunts were unguided, so we did everything

Alvin Sweigart, Lemar Mast, and I hunt in Alaska for the first time.

on our own. We flew into Anchorage, Alaska, and from there we flew to several different villages. From the villages, we chartered floatplanes and flew back into the bush. It was our first time flying on a floatplane and we had all our luggage, tents, and food sitting on the dock. The pilot looked at our groceries and asked how many days we were planning to hunt. Then he told us before he flew us out we should buy twice as many groceries as we had, because the weather conditions up there change a lot, and he might not be able to get back in to pick us up until several days later than scheduled.

We loaded everything on the plane and the pilot said he knew he was overloaded. We were taking off on a river. As we were picking up speed, all at once, the plane just stalled. We were stuck on a sandbar, so we all had to get out and push the plane off the sandbar. We finally took off and the pilot flew us about fifty miles out into the bush and landed on another river. We unloaded the plane on the shore and the pilot told us he had written in his schedule to pick us up in eight days. He gave us a time when we had to have our luggage down on the shore. We had no radio contact with him so we couldn't be in touch. That meant it could be many more days than scheduled, depending on the weather, when he could fly in to pick us up. We carried all our gear up to an old trapper's cabin. It had a dirt floor and there were creatures running all over the place.

When bush pilots fly you into an area, you are not allowed to hunt the day they drop you off. This keeps you from spotting game from the air, landing on a lake, stalking the game and shooting them the same day. We set up our camp, and still had several hours before it got dark, so we went for a walk. Alvin and I were walking about a quarter of a mile apart when I saw a bear going past Alvin. It was a big bear. He didn't shoot and it headed right toward me. When it got within shooting range, I had to make a decision if I was going to shoot it or not. The plane was gone a couple of hours already and I knew there was nobody within miles of us. Alvin is a hunter who

My first moose in Alaska.

goes strictly by the books and I give him credit for that. He is one of the best hunting partners I ever hunted with. He is also a woodsman and very knowledgeable about nature. I learned a lot over the years hunting with him. Since he didn't shoot the bear, I didn't feel I should shoot it either.

A couple of days later, I shot a moose on a Sunday. Alvin would not hunt on Sundays, but he would not leave any meat lay out and go bad. So, Alvin, Lemar and I worked all that day to get the meat and horns packed back to camp. A couple days later, Alvin shot a bear and wounded it. We got on the bear's blood trail and tracked him to his den. He crawled down a hole and we could hear him groaning. We thought it was his death groan. It was getting dark and we had to make a decision on how we were going to get this bear out of his den.

Alvin told me he was going to crawl down the hole and it was my job to hold onto his legs. If anything happened and the bear was still alive, he'd yell and I was to pull him out fast. When he was crawling in you could still hear the bear groaning. It was so dark down in the hole Alvin couldn't see the bear, but he felt around and felt some hair. He finally figured out it was the bear's leg. Alvin pulled the bear out even though it still wasn't dead. We were not thinking. If Alvin would have gotten hurt bad, we had no radio contact to call for help. The pilot did fly in and pick us up on schedule. We flew back to the village and from there we flew to King Salmon, which is down on the Alaskan peninsula.

Our next hunt was for caribou. Again the pilot flew us out into the bush and we set up our own tents. We were going to be in this area another eight days. The first four days we didn't see any caribou. The fifth day, when I was out on the tundra by myself, I saw something moving in the distance. I got out my spotting scope and found out I was looking at another human being. I knew there were no other camps within miles of us, so I couldn't figure out why a man would be out there walking around. I started to walk toward him and he spotted me and started walking toward me.

When I got close to him, I saw his pants and coat were all ripped up. I asked him what he was doing. He said he'd been out here wandering around for the last four days. I told him, "Over the last couple days, there were planes flying around and they were flying low. I guess they are out looking for you." He said, "I don't think so." I told him if he was lost for four days I was sure they were looking for him.

I took him back to our camp and that evening got some salt water and soaked his feet. He had blisters all over them. We gave him some of our clothes to wear. The next day when I went out hunting I told him to stay in camp, in case a plane would fly into our camp looking for him. I went out, not too far from camp, and shot two caribou. I was getting ready to butcher them and quarter them when I saw the lost fellow coming toward me. He asked if he could have one of the caribou I shot. I said, "Sure." He said he would cape out the caribou and butcher it for me. He pulled out a switchblade knife and started

Lost hunter and crazy man.

to cut on the caribou like a wild man. He said, "Oops, I cut myself." He cut his finger pretty deeply and wrapped a hanky around the cut and kept on butchering with his other hand. After a little while, he said "Oops, I cut myself again." He was bleeding very badly. I looked over at him and he had the switchblade knife stuck through the palm of his hand. The tip of the knife was sticking through his hand. He pulled his knife out of his hand and took his hanky and tried to bandage it. At this point, I didn't want to hang around and see anymore. I took two of the quarters and packed them back to camp.

I wanted to get away from him. I thought this guy was crazy. When I got back to camp, there was a plane circling our camp flying very low. I ran inside the camp, got into our duffle bags and took out as many pieces of white clothing and underwear as I could find. I took the clothes and made a SOS on the tundra. The plane flew over again and dropped something out of the window. I went over and picked it up. It was a quart of oil with a note wrapped around it. The note said, "If you have Larry (The note listed his last name, also.) make a circle with the clothes and we'll know you have him." I knew his first name was Larry but I didn't know his last name, however, I was sure they were searching for him.

So I made a circle, the plane flew over again and tilted its wings back and forth. That's the way the bush pilot lets you know they got your message. The plane flew off because it couldn't land on the adjoining lake with wheels. I ran out to where Larry was butchering my caribou and I told him what had happened. I told him to get back to camp as fast as possible. "I think they'll be sending in a floatplane to pick you up," I told him. I had a hard time trying to convince him that a plane would be coming in for him. By the time we got back to camp, there was a plane on the lake and a game warden waiting for him. They put him on the plane, took off and that was the last we heard of him. Anytime there is a plane out searching for you up there, you are partly responsible to pay for the rescue.

I guess we weren't experienced hunters and campers when we established our camp. We had set up our tents right on the beach near the water. When we went out hunting the following day, it poured rain all day. By the time we got back to camp, the lake had risen about two feet and the whole bottom of our tent was full of water. Our sleeping bags were soaked, our food was wet and our bread soggy. That night we had to sleep in wet sleeping bags and it was cold. The sun didn't come out for a couple of days, so we couldn't dry out our sleeping bags or our wet clothes.

Three years later, our same group of three went on another unguided hunt to Alaska. (Back in those days, you could hunt for bear, moose, caribou and goats without a licensed guide.) We flew into Anchorage first, then into a small village and from there flew into the bush. Our plan was to stay at this location for six days. We were hunting mainly for moose, but there were a lot of grizzly bears in the area. One afternoon on the hillside right behind camp, we counted 12 different bear sightings. Three of us were sleeping in small tents and at nighttime we had a lot of high winds. We had trouble sleeping at night because the pots and pans were blowing around and rattling. We thought maybe there was a bear outside getting into our cookware. We did all of our cooking outside over a campfire.

Alvin shot a nice bull moose about the fifth day of the hunt. When he shot the moose it ran into some alders. The alders were about six feet high and the area was very thick. He cut a space out around his moose, so he could field dress it. He worked at this all day. That evening he came back to camp with the liver and a small portion of the meat. He asked us if we would go along with him to pack out the meat. The next morning, we all put on our backpacks and headed out to pick up the moose meat.

When Alvin walked into the brush where he shot the moose, the first thing he said was, "This isn't the way I left the moose last night." It was covered up with dirt and grass. Just about that time a

Alvin with the bear that charged him.

grizzly bear came running out of the brush right toward Alvin. Fortunately, he still had his gun in his hand, but he didn't even have time to put it up to his shoulder and aim. He shot at the bear right from his hip and the bear dropped dead a couple feet away. None of us had a grizzly bear license; and they are illegal to kill without a guide, plus the season wasn't even open at that time.

We knew if we couldn't prove Alvin shot the bear in self defense, there was going to be a large fine. The only way a game warden might accept your story about self defense is if you can show where the bear clawed you, or you had a limb missing. We got all of the meat back to our camp and left the rest of the bear where he shot it. The area where the bear was shot was several miles from our camp and no one would have been able to find it in the thick alders. The only person who knew we were hunting on the lake was the pilot who had dropped us off.

The pilot was supposed to come in and pick us up the next day, so we tore our tent down and packed up all of our luggage, meat, and gear. We had everything ready and we waited for the pilot. He didn't show up and we had to set up the tent again. We were stuck out in the bush for five extra days. The pilot finally flew in on the sixth day. During those five days, we had a little butter and salt and liver from the moose. That's what we ate every day. We also caught some fish but ran out of butter. We cooked the fish in water and ate it like soup. The broth from the fish is high in protein.

When the pilot flew in and saw all the horns and luggage setting on the shore, he said he didn't think he could fly it all out in one trip, but he would try. We loaded up, went out on the lake and tried to take off. We were overloaded and couldn't get off the water. The pilot told us to take our carry-on bags and put them on Lemar's lap. He was the biggest guy in our group and you always want to get the most weight in the front seat of the plane.

We piled all of our heavy items on Lemar's lap. Then the pilot told the two of us who were sitting in the back to get out of our seats, lean as far forward as we possibly could and rock the plane. You rock the plane so the floats will lose contact with the water. When a lake is really smooth, it's hard to take off. The pilots like the water to be a little rough, so the floats won't drag as hard. After the third attempt, we finally made it into the air and flew back to the village.

Alvin wanted to call the game warden and tell him what he had done illegally by killing the grizzly bear. I tried to tell him just let it alone about the bear, that no one knows that he shot it. Alvin said what he did was wrong and he wanted to report it. He called the game wardens down in Anchorage, and they told him that they would fly up the next day. When the game wardens arrived, Alvin told them the whole story. The game wardens asked, "Are you sure you killed the bear?" Alvin told them he definitely killed the bear. The game wardens said, "This is our hunting season and we are very busy and it will take a day for us to fly in to look at this bear you shot." The wardens asked him again, "Are you sure you can find the bear?" He told them he was sure he could lead them directly to the bear.

Finally, one of the game wardens went outside and I went with him. He asked me, "Can't your friend Alvin take a hint as to what I am doing? We don't have time to pick up the bear. Can't you convince your buddy that he didn't shoot the bear?" I said I would try but I didn't think I could convince him to say he didn't kill the bear. They wanted Alvin to tell them he didn't shoot the bear. Again, Alvin said it was wrong to shoot the bear. He was going to take the fine and the consequences of shooting the bear. At that point, the game wardens told Alvin, "If we go after that bear and you did shoot him, it will be a fine of over $1,000.00 or a year in jail." Alvin said, "I will take the consequences for shooting the bear." Finally the game warden said, "Ok, we are not flying in to see the bear, but tomorrow morning I want you down in Anchorage and within a couple days you'll have a hearing." Alvin flew down to Anchorage by himself and Lemar and I flew out on another five-day moose hunt.

When Alvin appeared in court and told the judge the whole story, the judge told him he had never had a case like this since he was on the bench. The judge said, "I have no proof that you killed this bear, only your word. I don't know how to write this up." When the hearing was all over, they gave him a $350.00 fine and the judge told Alvin, "When you get home, do me a favor and send me a picture of the bear; so I have something on record to show that you did indeed kill the bear." When Alvin got home, he sent the judge a picture of the bear, and that was the end of the bear ordeal.

After his day in court, we met up with Alvin and we all flew into an area to go on a mountain goat hunt. On goat hunts, you spend a lot of time glassing hillsides looking for mountain goats. You usually find goats on the highest peaks. They like to stay up high on rocky ledges to stay away from danger. I spotted a goat from camp early one morning knowing it would take me about half of the day to get up to it. I started climbing after the goat by myself while the other guys stayed in camp, so I didn't have a chance to tell them where I was going. Hunting a goat by yourself can be very dangerous. I kept pulling myself up the rocky ledges. I finally made it up to where I had last seen the goat. I crawled around the rocks looking for the goat and spotted him on the other side of a rock slide. I shot him and he tumbled a couple thousand feet the whole way down the rock slide. Since I didn't have any ropes with me or friends to help, there was no way I could get down to the goat.

The guys told me later they were spotting the hillside where I was hunting. When they saw me in their scope, I just looked like a little dot. I had to leave the goat there and climb down off the rocky ledges. I found it's a lot easier climbing up than getting back down. I got to a point I could not put my legs down far enough to feel the next ledge. I kept trying to let myself down far enough so I could get my foot on a rock. I had my rifle over my shoulder and I got so frustrated that I was going to take it off my shoulder and throw it down off the mountain. Then, I thought I would try it one more time. I just stretched my leg a little bit further and felt a rock sticking out far enough, so I could let myself down. When I got the whole way down off of the rocky peak, I sat in a corner and the wind was blowing real hard. I just sat there and shook all over.

Hunting mountain goats, even with a guide, is the hardest hunt you will ever go on. We flew out of that area and into another area to hunt moose again, since two of us hadn't harvested one yet. We flew into an area where there were a lot of Alaskan brown bears. Brown bears are much larger than grizzly bears. A good-sized grizzly will get as big as 8-1/2 ft. tall, while a big Alaskan brown bear will measure 10-1/2 ft. and weigh up to 1000 lbs.

We set up our tent for an eight-day hunt. There was a trapper's cabin only a hundred yards from where we set up our tent. I said

Trapper's cabin after a 10-day hunt.

to the guys, "Why don't we just stay in that cabin?" Alvin said, "We don't know who the cabin belongs to, so we better not use it." The next day a game warden flew into our camp in his Piper Cub plane. He said to us, "Are you guys crazy staying in a tent? There are a lot of brown bears in this area. Let me tell you what happened to me last night. "I was stuck in the bush because of fog and couldn't fly out, so I slept in my plane, (Look at my side window)" On his window, there were two mud prints from big bear claws. They went down over the whole window. He told us to go over and stay in the trapper's cabin. Alvin and Lemar were out hunting that day and I was around camp doing some chores. When I looked out across the valley, I saw a big brown bear coming right toward camp. Again, it was a time of year when you were not allowed to shoot brown bears. He got pretty close to our camp, and since I was alone, I decided I better get up on the cabin roof. I crawled up on the roof and the bear kept walking around the cabin looking up at me. He was at least a good 10-feet tall. After about an hour, he walked off. That evening, when the guys came back to camp, I told them about my experience.

Earlier that day Lemar shot a fox and he skinned it out inside the cabin. After he was finished skinning the fox he took the carcass outside and threw it off the front porch. It was already dark at this point and he came in running hollering, "Bear, bear!" He was so shook up he could barely talk. We looked out and the bear was coming up on the front porch. It was the same bear I had seen earlier that day. We slammed the door closed and took a couple of old boards and wedged the door shut as best we could. The old cabin's exterior walls had boards nailed on the outside. There was one window over the front porch and one window on the back of the cabin. For a couple hours, the bear kept walking around the cabin looking in the windows and doors.

Our lanterns ran out of fuel and the extra fuel was out on the porch. None of us were going outside to get it. The lanterns went out and it was pitch dark in the cabin. We decided to tape our flashlights to our rifles. After a while, the batteries in our flashlights started to go dim; so, we took turns using our flashlights to save on battery power. We knew if our batteries would go dead and the bear pushed the door down, which he could have done with very little effort, we'd be in big trouble. If he came inside the cabin and we didn't kill him with the first shot, we would be in great danger. Early in the morning, we didn't hear him anymore. Alvin said, "Let's try to get some sleep." I knew none of us would be able to sleep. A couple of hours before daylight, the bear came back. Finally, at daylight, he left again. We breathed a sigh of relief.

Facing The Elements

One year, three of us went on an elk hunt in Salmon, Idaho. The most interesting event during the hunt took place while we were heading into camp. The outfitter only had about 8 horses for the guide and the hunters. All of his supplies were brought in on a Willy army Jeep. They had this Jeep rigged to go through deep water because we had to cross the river numerous times. Some of the places where we crossed were over 4 feet deep. They had the gas cap wrapped in plastic and they had it sealed tight, so no water could get into the gas tank. They also had a hose attached to the carburetor coming up through the hood, so water wouldn't get in the carburetor. They had a wire hooked to the carburetor for the gas throttle. They put chains on all four tires. A couple of the hunters, including me, rode into camp in the Jeep. When we had to climb up a real deep bank, the driver would tell a couple of the biggest guys to get out and sit on the hood, so the Jeep wouldn't flip over backward.

When we finally got into camp, they parked it up on a steep hill facing down; so, in the morning, when they wanted to use it, they could coast downhill to get it started. That hunt was one of the coldest I have ever been on. The mountain streams would freeze from the bottom up and the water would run over top of the ice. When we went out in the morning, we could hear the limbs snapping on the trees. When the temperature gets down to 20 to 30 below zero, limbs freeze and you can hear them snap.

The first morning when they went out to start the Jeep, the transmission was frozen solid. They couldn't move the gearshift lever. There was a hole in the floor board; you could look through and see the transmission. They took Coleman gas and dumped it all over the transmission, then put a match to it. The flames were burning higher than the dash on the Jeep. They left it burn until it burned out. That heated the transmission enough that they could shift gears. The next problem we had was when the brakes froze up. When we took it out of gear, it still wouldn't move. They took Coleman gas again and poured it over all four of the brake drums. They left it burn until a couple of the tires caught fire. All at once the brakes left loose, they shifted into neutral and started to coast, then ran off of a real steep hill and into a tree. If that tree wasn't there, the Jeep would have run into our cabin.

A couple of days later I saw the biggest mule deer I have ever seen. I didn't have a place to prop my gun to shoot and it was about 150 yards off. My guide told me to lean my gun on his shoulder, so I did. When I shot, it just about busted his eardrums. He had forgotten to hold his ears. One of our guides had heart problems, and he should not have been in camp. One night his heart stopped for a short time, fortunately, one guy knew CPR and got the guide's heart going again.

When we left camp, we were packing out all the supplies because we were the last hunters for the season. The Jeep was loaded about 6 feet high with supplies. One guide had to sit on top of the supplies, because there wasn't an extra horse for him to ride. On our last crossing of the river, the Jeep got halfway across and it flooded out. It just sat there. They couldn't get it started again. The ice was starting to freeze all around the tires, so one of the guides rode out and went to town and got some dynamite. When he came back he blasted the ice open enough, so they could pull the Jeep out of the river.

One time, I was going into British Columbia on a ten-day, mixed-bag hunt for a lot of different species, including moose, goats, bear and elk. We were going in on horseback. It was a one-on-one guided hunt. There were only two of us. We had a pack train of 10 horses—the guide would always take the lead and I would be riding in the rear. My guide was an Indian, a man with very few words. He hardly talked at all during the entire trip. We'd ride all day, going back into the area where we wanted to hunt. That night we would set up a spike camp and the next morning tear it down. Then we'd

Indian guide with few words and me.

ride all day again, stop and set up camp. We would do this every day for ten days.

My guide would ride right past game and wouldn't point it out to me, unless it was something he thought I wanted to shoot. We would turn the horses loose at nighttime, so they could graze and eat grass. He had a device he would put on the horses' two front feet to keep them from walking or wandering too far from camp at night. They would have to jump to get around. This way, the horses couldn't graze further than a couple of miles during the night. The next morning the guide would go out and round up the horses.

I always liked to help around camp wherever I could, but this guide wouldn't let me help him at all. He would set up camp by himself and tear it down. He'd put the saddles on the riding horses and the pack saddles on the other eight horses every morning. Then, he'd take all of them off at nighttime. I had to just stand around and watch him work. One morning, while he was out rounding up the horses, I thought I would start a fire and make coffee before he got back. I thought a cup of coffee would be nice for him when he got back. I was pouring the coffee into the coffeepot when he came walking into camp. I heard him yelling at me, but I couldn't understand what he was saying. I wondered what I did so wrong. He told me, "You never pour coffee into the coffee pot. You dump the coffee into your hand first and then dump it in the coffeepot." I asked, "What are you talking about?" He claimed the coffee tastes better if you pour it into your hand first. After that, I knew I couldn't do anything right to please this Indian.

When you are on a pack-trip hunt with horses, you don't carry your gun over your shoulder when you're on the horse. Your rifle will catch on low-hanging tree branches. Actually, you have to duck down to avoid the branches. They have a system where they fasten a scabbard onto your saddle and your rifle goes in it. This way it is always out of the way and it's much easier to ride. We were riding all day one time and that evening when I got off my horse, I went to get my rifle out of the scabbard and it was gone. Right away, I could only imagine my rifle lying along the trail. Maybe my horse stepped on it, or it might have come out and slid down a rock-slide.

My guide wasn't carrying a rifle, so the next morning we had to retrace our steps looking for my rifle. I was sure we would never find it. If we did find it, it would probably be damaged, along with the scope, and I wouldn't be able to hit anything. Our only choice was to ride back to the base camp and get another rifle. That would be about a three-day ride, and then we'd have another three-day ride back in. I thought my hunt was over. We spent the best part of that day looking for my rifle. Then, when I was riding by a tree, I saw my rifle hanging there undamaged. A branch sticking out from the tree had caught on the sling on my rifle and pulled it out of the scabbard. It was just hanging there. What are the chances of that happening?

One time, Gail and Junior and I went to Montana on an elk hunt. On this hunt, you hunted mostly on foot. They had pick-up trucks that would take you to a base camp. The camp had all the tents, a couple bunk beds and a cook tent. Our cook was a young girl from a local town. She began messing around with one of the hunters and Ty, the outfitter, told her she was fired and had to leave camp. She called one of her friends from town to come out and pick her up. In the meantime, she and Ty got into a real big argument. When her friend got there and picked her up, they only drove down the road about a hundred yards when she got out of the pick-up, took a rifle and started to shoot through the camp. We all got behind trees. Ty called the police and they came out and got her.

We didn't have a very good hunt. Ty told me if I was interested in coming out the following year, I should enter a lottery drawing for an elk tag. The hunt area is right next to Yellowstone National Park. It takes place in December and January and it's only a two-day hunt. They open up the season on a Friday and Saturday for the two days, then again on Sunday and Monday for two days. The hunt then shuts down for the rest of the week and opens up again the same way the following weekend. This takes place over a five-week period. It is very cold out there at that time of the year, but your opportunity for killing a 6x6 bull elk are very good; however, it's very difficult to draw a tag for this hunt. The hunts take place outside the north gate of Yellowstone National Park in a town called Gardner.

I was lucky and drew a tag for the hunt. I was scheduled to hunt Monday and Tuesday. Another one of Ty's customers was a young kid from Texas who drew a tag for Friday and Saturday. I asked Ty if I could come out a couple days early and go in with him and the kid from Texas. He said that would be fine. Ty's ranch was about 200 miles from Gardner. He told me to fly into his town and we'd drive down to Gardner from there. (Ty was also a pilot and he had his own

Horse trailer I rolled over.

plane.) In the morning we loaded a couple of horses in a horse trailer. Ty pulled the horse trailer with a Land Rover.

Our first stop, a couple miles out of town, was a small private airport where Ty kept his plane. He told me he was going to fly his plane down to Gardner and fly around the area to see if he could spot the elk herd. He told me to take the Land Rover and the trailer down to Gardner. The trip to Gardner would be an all-day drive pulling a horse trailer on icy roads and I would have to cross a mountain about 12,000 feet in elevation. I was not looking forward to making this trip.

Ty was warming up his plane and he taxied down to the end of the runway where I was with the Land Rover and the horse trailer. I had just pulled out of the airport and was making a sharp left turn. The road was covered with ice and the horse trailer slid off the road, upset and slid into a ditch. The horses were lying in the horse trailer upside down, kicking and trying to get up. Ty saw what happened and he jumped out of his plane and came running over. We finally got the gate opened on the horse trailer and got the horses out. We called a tow truck and had it pull the horse trailer back onto the road. We loaded up the horses and Ty said, "I think I will leave my plane here; we can drive down to Gardner together."

We arrived in Gardner that night and checked into a motel. The next morning we heard a knock on our door, opened it and a game warden was there. He told us he was telling people not to go out that morning because it wasn't safe. It was 30 degrees below zero and the wind was blowing hard. Ty thought we would be okay, so we went out and waded through deep snow. We saw a couple nice 6x6 bulls and there were other bulls on the hillside. I had my mind set on a 7x7 bull elk. I had never killed a bull elk, and seeing all those nice bulls made me greedy. I thought for sure I would be able to kill a 7x7 bull.

I didn't shoot anything that day, so we went back out the next day—my last day to hunt. (I was limited to a two-day hunt.) Early that morning, I had passed up shots on a couple of 5x5's and one 6x6 elk. I thought I could do better. What we didn't know at the time was many of the elk had moved out of that area during the night. That evening, as it kept getter darker, there were a lot of cows coming out of the pines. I promised Ty he could have my meat. He kept saying, "Shoot something!" It was so dark I could hardly see through my scope. I kept waiting thinking with all those cows coming out of the pines there had to be a bull in the herd. Finally, I realized I didn't have a choice. I had to take a cow. That taught me a lesson—don't be greedy. We tied a rope around the cow elk and two of us drug her out. It was mostly downhill, but we were in deep snow, so it was hard work and we didn't get out until late that night.

One of my friends, named Mel, was working on a cattle ranch in Jackson Hole, Wyoming. His wife, Sara, did the cooking for the ranch hands. Mel invited me to come out and hunt elk with him. I planned my trip so I would be there for four extra days. That way, I could do work around the ranch. We bailed hay and, since I was a carpenter, I did some repair work around the ranch. I got to know the owner of the ranch pretty well. He was a wealthy man.

The ranch owner told me I could ride up to his cabin a couple of days earlier than my scheduled hunt. Mel said he would ride up and join me to hunt for a couple of days. The owner told me the cabin was stocked with food, so I wouldn't have to pack any groceries. The next morning they saddled up a horse for me and gave me two packhorses. They put me on a horse trail and told me to follow the trail right to the camp. I should be there by noon.

I was riding a horse and leading two others. I held two lead ropes in one hand and my horse's reins in the other hand. I was only about a mile from the ranch when one of the lead ropes got caught under my horse's tail. He took off bucking down across a meadow and I flew off the horse. I had an awful time catching those horses, because I didn't know any of their names. I finally caught them and walked for the next mile or two leading them. Eventually, I built up enough nerve to get back on my horse and we rode another mile or two going up over a steep mountain trail. The trail was just wide enough for the horses to fit between the trees. Again, the rope from one of the horses I was leading caught under my horse's tail and he took off bucking like wild, going straight down off the mountain between all the trees. I got bucked off and had to catch all three horses again. When I finally caught them, I decided to go the rest of the way to camp on foot. I wasn't about to get back in the saddle again.

I was in camp a couple of days when a snowstorm hit and we ended up with a foot of snow. The next morning the snow made for perfect hunting conditions. I was out in the woods sneaking along and caught a bull elk bedded down. I was only about fifty yards from him when he got out of his bed and I shot him. I gutted him out, but I knew if I tried to lug him out right then it would be pretty dark by the time I got back to camp. The next morning, with a couple pack-

Al Sheaffer and Walt.

horses, I went back to where I shot the elk. When I got there, the two hindquarters were just about eaten off. A bear had come in during the night and fed on the carcass. I cut off the two front shoulders and the back straps, caped out his head, cut off the horns and packed him out. Mel came in the next day and we hunted a couple of days trying to get him an elk.

To expand my hunting territory, I bought a cabin with 70 acres of woodland in New York State. The area had a lot of turkey and deer. My neighbors were Walt, Jenny and Chris. They were the best neighbors. When I was up there by myself, they had me down for dinner many times. They mowed my grass for me and never charged me a cent. Walt was a coon hunter and also hunted turkey and deer—a real woodsman. When I first met him he said to me, "If we ever get into an argument, please just back off. I don't want to argue with anybody, but I have trouble with my temper. I don't want to have to hit you and I know I will. So, I'm just warning you up front to just back off." All of Walt's neighbors knew this about him, too. One year, I asked him if he would be interested in going with Al and me on an elk hunt in Idaho. He said he would like to go along.

The outfitter lived right on the western border of Montana. We were going to ride into the Bitterroots in Idaho. We had a pack train of 15 horses. We packed all of our horses and started out early in the morning. The outfitter told us it would be an all-day ride and we should get into camp that evening, right before dark. We were just about to camp when we saw a guy walking toward us. As he got closer, we knew something strange was going on. His pants were all ripped and he wasn't wearing the right clothing for that time of year. At night, the temperature would drop down to zero. It was cold and we offered to take him along into our camp.

This guy wouldn't go with us, but one of our guides put him on a horse and took him back out to the base camp. They rode all that night and part of the next morning before they reached the base camp. The guide turned him over to the authorities and we found out later that he had a mental problem. He had walked into the woods trying to commit suicide by either starving or freezing to death. This wasn't the first time he had walked off into the woods.

That evening in camp each of us was introduced to our personal guide. It was a one-on-one guided hunt. Walt's guide was a guy about 6'5" and he weighed 270 lbs. Walt was only 5'9" and weighed about 170 lbs. That evening, we were setting around camp telling a lot of stories. The big guide was sharing stories about his barroom fights. He sounded like a rough guy.

The next morning my guide and I were hunting on foot. We hadn't gone very far when he told me this was his first time guiding. I already had that figured out before he told me. He was a real nice kid so in the nicest way I could, I asked if he would mind if I hunted by myself. I just felt I had a much better opportunity hunting by myself, because the kid was talking all the time.

That morning Walt and his guide had started to climb up over a real steep hill behind camp. Walt was a heavy smoker. This guide started walking up over the hill with his long legs. He covered a lot of ground in a short time. Walt could not keep up with him and he was running short of breath. The guide yelled at him, "Hey you, let's keep moving." Walt yelled back at the guide, "My name isn't 'hey you.' I'm Walt and you come back down here." The guide told me later he hadn't heard what Walt said. Walt was down there making motions for him to come back down. The guide went down to Walt and asked, "What's the matter?" By this time, Walt was taking off his coat and leaning his rifle against a tree. He raised his fists at the guide and said, "You and I are going to go around and around." The guide tried to calm Walt down. Walt wanted to fight him right there on the mountain the first day of his hunt.

After this incident, they became real good friends. I told Walt later that the guy would have beaten the tar out of him. Walt said, "Yes, he probably would have, but he would have known I was there." Later in the hunt Al and Walt got into an argument. I knew Al well and I had warned him, before we even went on the hunt, not to argue with Walt—because he punches first. The next day Al wanted to leave the camp and go back to base camp, but there wasn't a spare horse to take him back to the base camp. Al said, "I'll walk out." The guides told him it would take him all day because he had to cross over one high mountain, and the last couple of days there was a cloud hanging over that mountain. They thought the mountain was getting a lot of snow, maybe two or three feet. A couple of days later, when we were crossing over that mountain, we found about four feet of snow. The horses even had trouble getting through it. I said to Al, "Do you think you would have made it out on foot?" He responded, "No, I wasn't thinking."

Dall Sheep Hunts

I had a friend named Bill who had never been on a big game hunt and he asked me to go on a Dall Sheep hunt with him. The hunt was going to be in Yukon, Canada. A Dall Sheep hunt is one of the higher priced hunts, so Bill had to go to the bank and borrow money to pay for the hunt. We flew into the city of White Horse. From there, we boarded a floatplane and flew into the base camp. The outfitter picked out one of the guides at the base camp and told him he'd fly him into the area where we'd be setting up a spike camp to hunt sheep. The main guide had never guided before for sheep, so the outfitter wanted to fly him around and show him where we'd be hunting.

When we first met these guys, I knew we were in trouble. You could tell by their appearance. One guide looked like he had just climbed off a motorcycle. He was wearing motorcycle boots and a leather jacket. Chains were hanging out of his pockets and all kind of pins were hanging from his motorcycle hat. Since this was Billy's first big-game hunt, I told him I'd take the motorcycle guide and he could have the other guide. We were planning on getting up early the next morning and packing back in with our horses. We had a good day's ride or more to get into where we were going to set up spike camp and hunt. The next morning, when we got up and were ready to go, we looked outside and found we were socked-in with fog. You couldn't see more than a couple hundred feet. The guides weren't about to pack in that day. When you go into a new area you're not familiar with, you have to have topographic maps and be able to look at the mountains and the surrounding landscape for directions.

The next morning we still had fog and it lasted for five days. It was so thick we couldn't even get out of camp. There was a bunch of old western books there and Bill kept himself occupied by reading them. I'm not a big reader, so I spent my time walking in circles

Little Bill on the big horse.

around our camp for five days. As I was thinking about what this trip was costing me per day, it made it even worse. If Bill had to borrow all of this money for the trip, I couldn't understand why he was relaxed. On the fifth day, I told my guide I had to get out of camp. "I am going crazy, just take me for a ride," I said. The guide said, "You won't be able to see anything." I told him I didn't even care. He could put a blindfold on me. Just get me out of this camp.

Finally, on the sixth day, the fog lifted and we packed our horses and headed out. My friend Billy was only about 5'4" and had short legs and was a little bit on the heavy side. Bill's horse looked like a work horse compared to the other horses. When they put a saddle on the horse and gave the horse to Bill, it took two of us to lift him up into the saddle. The horse was so fat that Bill's legs stuck straight out when he was in the saddle. He couldn't let them hang down like a rider would on a normal horse. Bill stayed in the saddle all day. He didn't want to get out of the saddle, because he always had trouble getting back in. When I'm riding a long time, I always get off the horse as much as I can and walk it, so I don't get stiff. That evening when Bill climbed out of the saddle, he couldn't even stand up. He was that stiff.

On the first day, we rode all day. Billy and I were on the last two horses and it was getting dark. We could see that the guides were talking among themselves and looking at their maps. I told Bill I thought we were lost. I rode up to the guides and asked them what was going on. They said, "We have to tell you we are lost." We rode for another couple hours, until it was dark. The head guide said, "Let's tie the horses here. Get out your sleeping bags and we'll sleep here for the night." It was cold, snowing and wet.

The next morning we started off and rode until about noon. I heard the two guides talking loud, cursing and yelling at each other. I rode up to them and asked what was going on. Turns out, we were riding into another outfitter's camp. Outfitters usually place their camps forty to fifty miles apart, so we were riding into trouble. We made a couple of adjustments and rode for another fifteen minutes. Then I could hear the guides arguing again. I asked again, "What's going on?" We had made a complete circle and were riding into our own camp. We had ridden for a day and a half and ended up right where we started. The guides went into camp, got on the radio and called the outfitter and told him what they did.

The owner told them to stay there and he would fly in. He came into camp with two other guides; one was a young kid and the other one was an Indian. He told our guys to get in the plane that he was going to fly them back into town. The outfitter came over to us. This was the seventh day into our hunt. He told us these new guys would be our guides for the remainder of our hunt. The Indian he just picked up at a bar in town. He told us the Indian was drunk now, but he would sleep it off and by tomorrow, he would be fine.

The next morning we started off again, and the Indian guide

was on the lead horse the whole day. I never saw him pick his head up and look around. He had his head hanging down the whole time. I guess he was getting over his hangover. The younger guide was busy chasing the horses around trying to keep them on the trail. That night, we reached the area where we were going to hunt and set up camp. The Indian turned out to be one of the best sheep guides I ever had. Everything's good that ends well and this trip did. Bill and I each got a nice sheep.

The Brady Bill

When President Reagan and Jim Brady were shot in 1981, they passed a bill that banned assault weapons and required a background check for anyone wanting to purchase a gun. It was called "The Brady Bill." About a year after that, I went into the local sportsman shop to purchase a rifle. I had purchased many guns there in the past. I filled out all of the necessary paperwork. They called it in and when the salesman got off of the phone, he said, "Kenny, I can't sell you this gun." I said, "Dick don't talk so dumb, call it back in again." He called them back again and they denied me again. Then I asked him, "What's the next step?" He gave me a form to fill out and send to a courthouse in Harrisburg, Pennsylvania. A couple of weeks later, I got a reply back. It said that I had a federal offense on my record and I would never be allowed to buy guns again or have guns in my house.

Back when I was 18 years old and I stole some chickens, it was considered burglary—and that was a federal offense. I took all of my guns out of my house, because I was told that federal agents would come and take them from me. After a couple of years went by and I hadn't heard anymore about this, I also did some research. Pennsylvania Game Officials told me I was not allowed to have guns, but the only way it would ever become an issue would be if I shot someone while hunting. To this day, at 71 years of age, I still can't buy a gun.

My Alaskan brown bear, with Ken and Gale Sensenig.

On another trip my friend Gale and I went up to Alaska to hunt brown bear on the Alaskan coast. I shot a brown bear four years earlier, and you are only allowed to kill a brown bear every four years. Still, I didn't feel comfortable taking a gun to the airport and I didn't know what was going to happen when I needed to buy a hunting license in Alaska.

The outfitter was in camp and he would make fun of everything Gale and I said. When we told a story, he always said, "That can't be true." I had never been treated so badly in any other camp, by an outfitter. We spent a lot of time with our guide out on the hillside glassing for bear and asked him why the outfitter was being so nasty to us. He said, "I'll tell you why, but don't let it get back to him. He thinks you and Gale are undercover game wardens. He knows he is being watched, because of some of the unlawful things he has done in the past."

On this hunt Gale paid the full price and I only paid half price. I wasn't allowed to shoot a bear until Gale shot his. We were guided one on two. I went on this hunt mainly for the experience of the hunt. One time, I was glassing a hillside and saw a bear up on top of the mountain. Gale and the guide went up after it, hoping they could stalk it and kill it. I watched them through my spotting scope and they were only about 50 yards away from the bear and didn't see it, due to the brush. I watched them and the bear. The bear either heard them or smelled them and took off running across the hillside. All at once, he turned and came down off the hill toward me at a fast run. I was thinking, if he just turns a little bit more, he might come within range, and I might be able to get a shot off. Right about then, he turned and ran within one hundred yards of me. I shot him. I paid half price and got a bear. Gale paid full price and didn't get anything. Sometimes life isn't fair.

The Lost Feeling

On another trip I took four of my friends out to Idaho to elk hunt. It was scheduled to be an unguided hunt. The outfitter packed us in on horseback, set up camp and supplied us with food. After that, we were on our own and we were about thirty miles from any town. For a couple of the guys in our group, this was their first elk hunt; and they were concerned about getting lost. I told them, when we booked the hunt, I would be their guide and their camp manager. I told them, "As long as you don't leave this valley, you won't get lost. When you leave the camp in the morning on foot, you can walk down the valley from camp or walk up. You can hunt on either side of the valley. That gives you a five-mile area to hunt. When you are ready to come back to camp at night, leave your area about a half hour before dark. Just follow the horse trail in the valley and it will lead you right back to camp and you can't get lost."

The first morning I walked up the valley about one mile and

saw there was a husband and his wife who had set up a camp there. They had horses with them. I stopped and talked to them and asked whether they had been seeing any game. He told me he and his wife rode up to the top of this mountain a couple of days earlier and there were a lot of meadows up there. He said, "The elk come out early in the morning and the evening to graze in these meadows. There's a lot of elk and mule deer signs." After they told me that, I knew where I was headed for that day. I knew it was going to be a hard climb up to the top of this mountain, but by the time I got there, I would still have a couple of hours to hunt before I had to start down again. When I reached the top of the mountain, I could see that everything he told me was true. There were elk signs everywhere. The top of the mountain was flat, and I started to wander around not paying any attention to the direction I was heading. When it was time to come back down, I didn't know if I had walked in a complete circle or where I was supposed to head to get back to camp.

I walked out on a point hoping that I would be able to see smoke from our camp, but I couldn't. Then I tried climbing down from that point, not knowing if I was in the right valley or another one. When I tried to climb down, I kept running into rocky cliffs. I didn't feel comfortable crawling down over those rocks, especially since it was starting to get dark. I knew then I was going to be stuck out there overnight. I ran around trying to gather enough wood to last me through the night. I stayed awake all night keeping the fire going. It was windy, cold and starting to snow hard. The sparks from the fire were going up in the air and the wind was carrying them pretty far away. The grass was dry, so when sparks would land on the grass, I was kept busy most of the night running around putting the sparks out. I surely didn't want to start a forest fire. All night there was a pack of wolves howling not very far away from me. I didn't know whether I tasted good or not, but that made me feel very uncomfortable.

I spent the entire next day walking. There are usually a lot of horse trails in those mountains, but I couldn't find any of them. If you follow a horse trail far enough it will always bring you out to civilization. I did find some orange ribbons tied on branches where somebody had marked their hunting spot. I followed them for a while and they disappeared. I kept walking and I saw metal tags on the trees saying Montana National Forest. That's how the National Forests in many states mark their property lines. I wasn't hunting in Montana—I was supposed to be hunting in Idaho. When we set up our camp, we were about 15 to 20 miles from the Montana border. I knew I had a journey ahead of me.

The next day I was walking and I found a horse trail that was being used. I knew that because there were fresh horse droppings. At that point, I knew I was going to come out somewhere; but I didn't know if I should go to my right or left. I took a guess and started down the trail to my left. I walked about two to four miles, then I recognized the valley where we had our camp set up. I started up the valley and there was our camp not very far away. The guys were really worried about me. They didn't know if I had had a heart attack or broken a leg. If something like that happens to you, they may never be able to find you, even with a search party. I didn't have a compass and that was before they had GPS's. I wasn't carrying a compass because I wasn't planning on going out of the valley to hunt. The guys gave me a hard time. I was supposed to be guiding them and keep them from getting lost, instead I got lost.

The first time I hunted brown bear in Alaska, I was hunting on Kodiak Island and the outfitter's name was Dick Rohrer. He had called me a couple months earlier and told me that one of his hunters had canceled on a brown bear hunt. He wanted to know if I wanted to come in his place. He said he would give the hunt to me at half price. I was pretty young at the time and really didn't have the money to go on this hunt. A brown bear hunt is one of the more expensive hunts involving North American game. I went to the bank and took out a loan. The only catch was that I had to be there on Kodiak Island in less than a week.

I flew into Anchorage and down to Kodiak Island. There were three of my friends, Tim, Bob and Dave, from my local area, living on Kodiak Island. I spent a couple of days with them. They were all working in the fishing cannery factories. When I got back home from this trip, a couple weeks later I got a call from Tim's brother. He told me Tim was out in the bay fishing when his boat capsized, and they never did find his body.

On this trip I went over to Dick and Sue's house. I stayed there that night waiting on my luggage and guns to get there. They got lost somewhere between Harrisburg and Anchorage. We waited an extra day before we flew into Dick's camp. Since my luggage never came, I needed clothing and hunting gear. Dick and I were about the same size and weight, so he fitted me out with his hunting gear and gave me a pair of his waders. The next morning, at base camp, Dick asked if one of us wanted to go on a backpack hunt. There were four other hunters in camp and I was the youngest. Dick took me aside and told me my best chance for getting a big bear was much better on a backpack hunt. So, my guide and I put all of our dry food, sleeping bags and tents in our backpacks and took off on foot. I was carrying about 60 pounds and my guide was packing about 70.

Later in the day, we came across a real big bear print in the sand on the beach. I stepped into the track and my boot didn't even cover the whole print. If you take a bear's foot print and measure the width of the print and add one inch on each side of the print, that will give you a rough estimate of the total length, in feet, of the bear that made the track. That's how you know if you are on a real good bear or not. We walked a little bit further and we saw where a bear had rubbed his back on a tree. I tried to reach up to the top of the rub on the tree. I couldn't reach the top of the rub. I started thinking, if these bears are that big and we have to sleep out for the next ten nights in a

My Alaskan Kodiak bear.

Sleeping under the stars.

little pup tent, that made me nervous. Of course, that's what we had to do.

All day we would sit on a hillside and glass until we saw a bear that was big enough to go after. We would go after it and try to stalk it. By the time we got over to where we saw the bears, they would often be gone. Every night, when it was a nice clear night, we would lay our sleeping bags on top of the grass, instead of sleeping inside the tent. It's much safer to sleep outside than inside a tent. If a bear jumps on top of your tent at night when it's dark, you would be rolling around inside the tent, in your sleeping bag, and have a tough time getting to your gun.

At the time of the year we were hunting, the nights were very short. You only had about four hours of darkness. We were going into the last day of our hunt and I still didn't have a bear. On the morning of the final day, we stalked a bear and got within about 75 yards of him. My guide whispered to me, "That's a really good bear. Take him!" I knew that you had to try to break their shoulders, so they wouldn't be able to charge you. I shot and the bear came running straight towards us. Fortunately, your guide always carries a gun to back you up.

I fired the first shot; then the guide shot; then I shot again and we kept shooting. The bear finally dropped within a couple yards of us. I had fired four shots and the guide fired three. My guide only had one more round left. After looking over the bear, I found we had hit him six out of the seven shots we'd taken. We worked about three hours to skin the bear out. The guide took the hide and the head and put it in his backpack. I put all of the rest of the camping gear in my backpack. The hide and head weighed about 110 lbs. and my backpack weighed about 90 lbs. The bears live weight was over 1000 lbs. and it measured 9'6" in height. We walked all of that night and got back to base camp late the next morning.

Increase of
the Bear Population

M y friend Glen and I were planning a bear hunt in Timmons, Ontario, Canada. About a month before we were scheduled to leave, I went to a local fish store market and bought two garbage cans of their leftover waste, including fish heads and guts, to use as bear bait. Then, we set those two garbage cans out in the hot sun for a month. By the time we were ready to head north, all of the waste had turned to liquid. When we reached the border with Canada, we had to go through customs. We were confronted by a young female customs agent who said she wanted to look in the back of our pick-up. As soon as she opened the pick-up gate and smelled the waste, she told us to leave, "Get out of here!" So, this time we got through customs in a hurry.

When we arrived in Timmons and met with our outfitter, he told us we were in luck. One of his baits was set up right on the edge of a local hayfield and there was a real big bear feeding on that bait. He said the only problem might be that I would have to set up among a pile of hay bales out in the field. I told him I wouldn't have any trouble doing that if there was a real big bear feeding on that bait. I set up in the field the next morning before dawn. By 10:00 a.m. the temperature had risen into the 80's and I found that mosquitoes were nesting in among the bales. It was the largest swarm of mosquitoes I had ever seen. I hadn't taken lunch or water with me that morning so around noontime I left the haymow, walked out to my pick-up and drove a mile to a local grocery store. I was only gone about a half hour, but when I got back to the field my bait was almost all gone. Turns out the bear had been watching me sitting in the haymow and he just waited until I left before he had lunch. So, no bear but lots of mosquitoes. I wasn't happy.

The next year, a couple of my friends told me about another outfitter, Ed Page, located in Quebec, Canada. They didn't have his phone number, but told me he lived in a small town north of Ottawa called Masham. In May, I drove up to Masham, by myself, went into

Front row: George Martin and Ken. Back row: Glen Houck, John Sweigart, Leonard Martin, Tim Shirk.

town and asked a few people if they knew where Ed the bear outfitter lived. It didn't take long for me to locate Ed. I went to his house, introduced myself and told him I was there to hunt bear. That was the beginning of a long friendship. I hunted with Ed for the next ten years. During that period, he educated me in the sport of bear baiting and hunting, which enabled us to kill a lot of bear. Actually, that's where I got my start as a bear guide. One of the early years, while hunting with Ed, he told me to go to a local store and buy a couple of pounds of bacon. Then he gave me a frying pan and a little propane gas stove to take out to the baiting area. He said, "Cooking bacon is one of the best ways to bring a bear into your bait."

Well, that's what I did. After frying the bacon, I put the pan in my knapsack and left it at the bottom of the tree, then climbed up into my stand. I stayed in that stand until after dark and didn't see a bear. I couldn't understand why. Then, all at once, I heard the pan and stove rattling. I looked down at the bottom of my stand and saw something walking off into the woods. I climbed down out of the stand and turned on my flashlight. I could still hear the pan rattling so I followed the noise, because it was very dark. Finally, I saw it was a bear carrying off the pan. As I shined my flashlight on him, I could see his eyes. I yelled three times to get him to stop, but he kept going, and it was too dark to pick him up in my scope. Finally, the bear dropped the knapsack and disappeared in the woods. Well, at least I got my knapsack back.

During the summer months, I took my wife and son up to Ed's for bass fishing. Bass fishing is great in that area and my wife enjoyed walking through local swamps catching frogs for us to use as bait for the bass. Over a 10-year period, Ed gave me my first experience booking hunters and I brought him quite a few. This got me started in booking bear and caribou hunts, and doing outdoor sports shows. When I first hunted with Ed, there weren't many white-tailed deer in that area. The snow and the cold kept the population low. In fact, I was with Ed when he saw one of his first white-tail deer in the area. Now 50 years later there are lots of deer along with moose.

I met a bear outfitter at one of the outdoor shows. He was from Val Dore, Quebec, about 300 miles north of Ottawa. He asked if I would be interested in bringing some customers up to his camp and guiding for him. I worked for him about five years and then left. The main reason I stopped working with him was because he never furnished enough bait. I had learned that if you have enough bait at each site, bears will stay there and feed and won't move out of the area. If you keep bait at your sites, the bears stay in the area and only go back about 50 to 100 yards into the bush or woods to bed down. One week, I had a whole camp filled with fathers and sons. Some of the kids were only 12 years old. One young boy shot a bear right at dark. When he came back to camp and told me he'd shot a bear, I told him we didn't have enough time to go out that night looking for the bear. We'd get up early the next morning, have breakfast, then go find his bear. That night he described to me where he hit the bear and I was pretty sure we'd find it a couple of yards behind the bait in the bush.

The next morning, the boy and his father, I and one of our guides, who had guided there for years, went out looking for the bear. We didn't take our guns and we all had short-sleeve shirts on. We started tracking him at the bait, saw a little bit of blood and began following it. We tracked the bear for several hours. About noon time, with the mosquitoes getting really bad, I asked our guide if he knew where we were. I was worried we might be lost. He said we couldn't be more than three-quarters of a mile from the dirt road. I agreed with him. We had walked all morning and only covered about three-quarters of a mile. The bush up there was so thick you had to push your way through it. We kept walking, and walked in a circle and came right back to the same spot. At that point, I thought we might as well admit we were lost. The guide said the road wasn't too far off. Then he said he wasn't sure whether we should walk north, south, east or west, but he knew there was another road about 15 miles away. At that point, I knew we were in big trouble. It was around noon time and nearly impossible to walk a straight line following the sun, because it was directly overhead. The best time to follow the sun is when it's coming up or going down. We walked until late afternoon while the mosquitoes and black flies dined on us. The boy was crying and the father was getting nervous. I didn't tell them I was real concerned, but I knew I didn't want to spend the night with all the bugs biting us.

Back at camp, they were so concerned they'd called the game warden and the fire company to form a search party. You don't want to spend a couple of days in this type of environment. Later that afternoon, we came upon a 30-year-old logging road. It was tough to see the road in some places, but we followed it as best we could. Finally, we came to an area where thick brush covered the entire road and we could hardly get through it. The guide suggested we turn left. The group began walking off, but for some reason, I just pushed my way through the brush. After about ten feet, I could see a dirt road in front of me that looked like it was being used on a regular basis. I called out to the rest of the guys and they followed me out to the road. We followed that road for about five miles and arrived at our camp.

One day, the guide and I caught a little bear cub. We brought him back to camp, put a dog collar on him and tied him to a tree. We thought we might be able to tame him and have a nice pet. We tried holding and feeding him, but when an animal is born in the wild that doesn't work. About a week after we caught him, he got loose and was gone.

One of my hunters shot a bear on our first day in camp. When I went to pick the bear up, I turned it over and saw it was a female and she had milk. I looked around knowing the cub would be close. Cubs don't leave their mothers. I looked up in a tree and there at the very top was the cub. I went out every day after that and placed milk at the bottom of the tree. By the following morning, the milk was al-

Our bear we couldn't tame.

ways gone, and the cub had climbed to the top of the tree. A bear cub, without his mother, will not make it alone in the bush unless another female bear adopts him. Otherwise, a male bear will always kill them. I continued feeding that cub for two weeks. When he wasn't picked up by another female, I realized I'd have to shoot him. I didn't want to do that, but I knew that would be a better way for him to die than to have a male bear kill and eat him. When I went out the next morning with my rifle and looked up in the tree, the cub was gone. Fortunately, I didn't have to shoot him.

One year, I had a customer in camp who bragged about what a good shot he was. He was a big guy with a big ego and told everybody in camp he would kill the biggest bear. He told me he had brought a bear call with him. I had never heard of a bear call. I really didn't like this guy, but I always tried to treat all of my customers fair. I put the braggart on the worst bait I had. It had only been hit one time in a

Biggest bear shot for the season.

couple of weeks. His stand was about 20 yards from a dirt road, and every time a truck went by on that road, the hunter would be covered with dust. (I usually don't treat my customers that way. This was the first and last time I did something like that.) The first night, when I was going out to pick up my hunters, I had to drive by his bait first. When I got there, he was standing out along the road. I wondered what type of a hunter leaves his stand a half hour before dark. Is he scared? I pulled up, stopped and asked, "What are you doing standing out on the road?" He said, "I shot a really nice bear." I could hardly believe him, so I walked in and there on the ground was one of the biggest bears any of my hunters had ever shot. Then he said, "Let me show you what I have on my movie camera." The video showed the bear he shot lying on the ground and another bear, just as big, standing right next to it. So, I guess I gave him a much better stand than I thought I did.

Challenges of Working with Outfitters and Guides

There was a game warden, named Danielle, covering this area, and he heard about me operating out of this camp and bringing hunters up. The following year he called me and told me he was a bear outfitter and asked if I could bring him some customers the next year. He was French and I could hardly understand, what he was saying on the phone, but I could understand, "Bring me some hunters next year, I have lots of bear." I thought being a game warden, he should know the area well, and maybe there are lots of bear in his area. Things weren't going very well with the outfitter I was currently using. We would argue every year about him not having enough bait for me like he promised. This became a big issue. So the following year, I asked two of my good friends if they would be interested in going up to this new camp. I told my friends, it sounds like there are a lot of bears in this area. I also told them I didn't know much about the new outfitter, but they could go at my cost. That would be about half of what my current outfitter was charging.

I told my friends before they left for the hunt, while I was working with my regular outfitter, I would drive over to the new area and look at the game warden's baits. That way I'd be able to tell if there was a lot of activity on the baits. I drove over there one day and found that he had only five bait sites, but there were numerous hits on those sites. I called my friends and told them to come up. It really looked good. They came up a couple of weeks later and both of them killed bear their first night on their stands. The outfitter told me if I would bring up 30 to 40 hunters the following year, he would set up sixty bait sites. I told him I would, but I knew I was taking a big gamble bringing up that many customers. There was no way I could be sure he would do what he promised. The main thing I was asking of him was that he have all the bait sites set up and all the bait I needed for those sites. I didn't want to have to complain to him everyday about running short of bait. The next year, I got up there a couple of weeks early to make sure he had everything he promised me. He had the bait sites, but when he showed me the amount of bait he had for the season, I told Danielle, "That's not nearly enough. We'll need to have at least three times more than what you have." He did double the amount of bait he had, but I still felt we needed a lot more. Over the many years I worked with him, having enough bait was a continuing issue.

He would have cakes, cookies and pie from the bakery in Val Dore, but the cookies would be in wrappers and it would take three hours to unwrap the cookies before we could go out baiting. During those three hours, I should have been building stands and checking baits. Up to this point, every outfitter I'd worked with complained I used too much bait. (They should have told the bears that.) I told Danielle, "Just give me eight of your bait sites. I don't care which areas they are in. Then give me all the bait I need for those sites and let me bait the way I want to. I will prove you are wrong. Having enough bait at each site to hold the bear on that site is really important. Eight of my good friends will be coming into camp in two weeks. I'll bet you, seven out of the eight guys will kill bears the first night." He took me up on the bet.

When my friends came into camp, I told them about the bet. I said, "You guys will all see a bear the first night. You have to promise me you'll follow the instructions I give you. This is real important to me." I told them: "No eating in the stands; don't use bug spray; don't smoke; and don't move around in the stand." I took them out to their stands that evening. Once they were in their stands, I walked to the bait sites and made noise banging buckets. The bears know the banging signaled that someone was putting food out for them.

Shortly after I got my eighth hunter in his stand, the sky turned black and we knew a real bad storm was coming. It started to blow and poured so hard I couldn't see to drive my ATV. I got off the ATV next to a big brush pile, dug a hole under the brush and crawled in. The rain poured until after dark. When I went back to pick up the hunters, it was still pouring. Originally, my hunters were using 5-gallon buckets for seats. When I picked them up, they had their buckets over their heads. Needless to say, we didn't kill any bears that night. I told Danielle that was not a fair test for my baiting and asked if we could hold the bet over for the following night. He agreed. The following night, seven out of my eight hunters shot bears. I think that proved my point.

Outfitter Danielle with wife and daughter.

Danielle, the outfitter, had a very pretty wife and his 17-year-old daughter was the prettiest French girl I had ever seen. When I went out baiting on my ATV, she always wanted to ride along with me. She liked to ride on the back of the four-wheeler. Her mother always asked me where I was going and how long it would be before we got back to camp. I don't know if she didn't trust me or her daughter. I told the mother she had nothing to worry about, because I was fifty years old and the daughter was only 17 and she could get any man she wanted.

The next year I brought Danielle 50 hunters and was again faced with the problem of not enough bait. He was always coming up short on bait. So, I was doing all of the baiting; taking customers out to the bait sites; and going out to retrieve the wounded bears. Danielle was a people person. He enjoyed sitting around camp with the customers talking. I knew I had to make a decision, because I thought I might have 70 to 80 hunters the following year, and I knew Danielle couldn't take care of that many hunters. There was another outfitter about 30 miles down the road. So, one day I drove down there and asked him if he would be interested in taking some of my bear customers the following year. He was interested and we worked out a deal.

Somebody saw my pick-up truck down there when I was working out a deal with the other outfitter and told Danielle. Danielle got very upset with me. He said, "How dare you go down there talking to him when you are working for me?" I tried to explain to him that he didn't provide enough bait for the sites and certainly not enough to take care of 80 hunters. I explained my plan for the following year was to give him 40 hunters and to take the 40 additional hunters down to the other outfitter. He was very, very mad and I knew my plan wouldn't work. So, I made plans to take all my customers to the new outfitter. Being a game warden, Danielle knew I was working in Canada guiding without a green card. (The Canadian government requires a green card for any non-Canadian working in Canada who gets paid.) Since my customers weren't paying me in Canada, I didn't think I needed a green card. If I were getting paid in Canada and the United States, I would have had to file tax information in both countries. My income was coming from the hunters I booked and charged in the United States.

The following year, I went to Canada a couple of weeks ahead of my customers to make sure the baits were ready. The outfitter gave me two French Canadian guides. One of the Frenchmen drove me around the first week to look at the roads and the bait sites. Since GPS's weren't out yet, I had to draw maps outlining the bait sites on paper. I marked roads and turn-offs the best I could with ribbons. The guide kept a case of beer in the back of his pick-up and he'd drink a case of beer every day. I knew that was going to cause trouble when my customers arrived.

Every time the guide was baiting, he'd pour a bucket of bait into a 50-gallon drum, beat on the bucket, then yell as loud as he could, "Hubba, Hubba." I asked, "What are you doing?" I knew the bucket banging would attract the bears, but I didn't know about the yelling. He told me the yelling called the bears into the bait and it worked. I thought this was interesting, so I decided to have some fun. After I placed customers up in their tree stands, I'd bang the buckets and barrels and yell, "Humba, Humba." Customers would ask me what I was doing. I'd tell them, "I'm calling in the bear." Shortly after I'd leave the site, the bear would come into the bait. The hunters thought it was great that I could call bears. I never told them why those bears were coming into the bait—it wasn't me yelling, it was the sound of the baits being poured into the drums.

The first group that came into the new camp was a party of 14. They were all husbands and their wives. The cook I was supposed to have in camp for the season called and said she wouldn't be there the first day of the season. That meant I was stuck with the cooking

Party of 14 in my bear camp.

for that day; I don't consider myself much of a cook. While I was in the kitchen preparing the meal, there was a knock on the kitchen door. When I opened it, I was confronted by two Canadian customs officers. They asked me, "Do you have a guy in camp by the name of Ken Gingrich?" I told them that was me. They asked what I was doing. I said, "Right now I am cooking." They asked if I was getting paid to cook. I told them I wasn't.

The officers told me to come outside because they wanted to talk to me. We got in their car and they questioned me for a couple of hours. Then they took each one of my customers and questioned them. They asked them what I did for them. My customers told them I did the baiting, guiding, and skinning of their bears. The customs officers told me I was in big trouble. They said I wasn't allowed to be working in camp. I tried to explain to them that I wasn't getting paid in Canada, and they told me that didn't matter. They said I was taking the job of a Canadian. I told them, between bear and caribou hunts, I bring over a half million dollars of business into Canada each year. They told me that didn't make any difference. "You are up here taking a Canadian's job."

They served me with a warrant scheduling me to be in court the following Saturday. Another boss I worked for in Canada guiding caribou hunts was an attorney, so I called him and asked what I should do. He said, "I'll drive over there on Saturday and I'll represent you in court." It took him six hours to get to Ottawa.

I knew who had reported me. It was Danielle, the game warden I had worked with the previous years. He was the only one in the area who knew where I was working and he was mad at me for using another outfitter. When we went to court, everything was spoken in French, so I couldn't understand what was being said. The attorney from Montreal interpreted for me. The judge told him I could be in camp, but I wasn't permitted to do any work. I was only allowed to sit around and talk to customers. I couldn't carry any bait, use a chain saw or take anyone out to the baits. Nicolus, owner of Safari Nordik and my acting attorney, told the judge he couldn't ask me to just sit around camp not doing anything. After some discussion, they dropped the charges, but every year after that I had a lot of trouble getting through Canadian customs.

The town of Val Dore is known as one of the wildest towns in Quebec. The main street is a mile long and runs through the center of town. The saying is, "Nobody can make it from one end of the town to the other if they have one drink at each bar and night club." You can't drink all that alcohol and still walk. There are more night clubs and bars on the main street than businesses, and that's where a lot of my bear hunters and guides would party on weekends. It was a great temptation to go with them, especially when you're away from home for eight weeks during the hunting season.

Encounters with Bears

Two men who hunted with me flew over from Africa. One of them had three large farms with 100 black African men working for

Three hunters from South Africa.

him. The other guy was a pilot who flew 747-airplanes from Johannesburg to New York once a week. These guys lived in an area where they had leopards and lions, but they were afraid of the black bear. I'd say about 70 percent of my hunters feared bears. The remaining 30 percent only got scared when it got dark. Chris, the pilot, would get up every morning and go for a jog. He would run 10 miles a day. The very first day I saw him running along a dirt road where he thought it was safe for him to run. I said to him, "I think you are the only person I know who can out-run a bear."

I put the other African hunter in a blind on the ground because he was hunting with a rifle. I always try to put rifle hunters in ground blinds—the kind that are hand-built out of logs. It's a lot easier for them to kill a bear with a rifle if they're sitting on the ground leveling their rifles and shooting straight at a bear, instead of shooting down at them from a tree stand. The best shot is a head shot because that'll kill the bear on the spot, making my job easier. I don't have to track them and the bullet usually won't penetrate through the bear's skull causing an exit wound that would damage the hide for mounting. I put all my archery hunters in tree stands. The archery hunters usually feel much safer hunting out of a tree stand.

When I'm out baiting for bear, I carry a container of vanilla spray. I spray the vanilla around the bushes at the bait site. If the hunter is with me and turns his back while I'm spraying, I'll spray some of this spray on him. It's a real good coverup scent. If a bear circles the bait and comes up behind the hunter, he'll catch the scent of the hunter and not go to the bait. I sprayed some of the vanilla on one of the African hunters and a bear came in right behind him on the first night. The hunter told me he felt there was something behind him and turned his head a little bit and found the bear's nose was about a foot away from him. One night he was asking me questions about the American culture and where I think the culture is headed. We talked about the kids in America who don't respect their parents, teachers and the law. I pointed out a lot of the kids who get in trouble only have one parent and are on drugs. I asked him if they had the same problems in South Africa. He said, "Not in the white community." In Africa, this hunter lived about 70 miles out in the country. He said there were no churches within 70 miles of his home that white people could attend. As a result, his family held church regularly in their own home. He said, "The Bible answers any questions we have and we try to follow the Bible's teachings in raising our family."

The 40-year-old pilot, did cause a problem for me. He was trying to befriend the outfitter's daughter who was a 17-year-old French girl. He said to her, "If you come back with me to Africa, I have a new home I just built and I'll give you a new Mercedes and a vacation home." She told her parents what he offered her. Her father threw him right out of camp, bags and all. He was gone in a hurry and that was before he was scheduled to leave.

Being a bear guide is one of the most interesting jobs you could ask for. I had more funny experiences with my hunters than you can imagine. I'll share some of them with you. I usually pick up

my hunters around nine and ten o'clock in the evening when it's dark
and they're finished hunting for the day. One time I was going out to
pick up a hunter named Mark. He was first on my list. When I was
about a half mile away from Mark's site, I rolled my window down
to see if I heard any shots. Just before dark is a prime time for hunting, but during that last 15 minutes, it's very difficult to see through
your scope. Just then, I heard a shot and I drove down to where I had
dropped Mark off that evening. By the time I got back to his stand, it
was pitch black and he was still up in the stand. When hunters don't
come out of their stands after dark, it tells me they are scared; they
won't come out until I arrive. When I reached his stand, I asked him,
"What did you shoot?" He told me he shot a bear. He said, "I could
barely see him through my scope. All I saw was black." I told him to
stay in the stand and I'd check out the bait and see if he hit the bear.
I walked down to the bait to check for blood and found a couple of
small drops. I didn't have to walk far before I saw it lying there dead.
Then, I hollered up at him, "Yes, you got him." When he climbed
down out of his stand, I held it up with one hand and said, "It's a very
nice raccoon."

He came back hunting with me the next year and I put him in
a ground blind. He was sitting next to some big rocks and a bear came
in behind him. He couldn't hear the bear walking on the rocks, but he
did feel warm air blowing in his ear. He turned his head and the bear's
nose was right in his ear. (I don't remember whether I had sprayed him
with the vanilla or not.) The bear took off running and the hunter got
off a shot but missed the bear, but some things do end well. I put him
in the same stand the next night and he got his bear.

Another time, I had a young kid hunting with me. There was a
logging road running right past his bait and his tree stand was just up
the road about 60 yards. A bear came out and approached his bait. He
shot at it, but didn't know if he hit it or not. This happened early in
the afternoon. He was afraid to walk past his bait, so he went directly

to the main road from his stand. He came running into the camp where I was working yelling that he had shot a bear. His stand was about five miles from camp and he had run the whole way looking over his shoulder to see if the bear was following him. He told me he never stopped running from the time he left his stand. When he reached camp, he was still shaking.

I had a young French Canadian boy working for me and it was his first year guiding. One evening before anybody came into camp, I asked him if he would be interested in going to one of my baits and sitting there until

Young hunter ran 6 miles to camp.

dark to see what's coming into the bait. I showed him how to use my portable tree stand and how to climb the tree. He started to go up the tree but didn't get any higher than six feet. He told me he was afraid of heights. I told him, "If you're afraid to go up any higher than that it's fine." The guide didn't have a hunting license so he didn't bring a rifle with him. When he came back, he told me that a bear came over to his tree and started climbing up. He said he had to keep kicking it in the head to stop it from climbing up the tree. That was his first experience with a bear and he was afraid of them the rest of the season. He told me he had a problem with drugs. He said he smoked drugs in his own house, but didn't do it out in public. I said, "That's a problem with me." He tried to assure me I wouldn't have any problems with him in camp, I knew, even if I told him he couldn't use drugs, he'd do it behind my back. I also told him, "If we have any trouble at all, you'll be gone. I don't want you smoking around any of my customers during the hunting season." I had a lot of problems with him. The younger generation of French people have a problem with Americans, and to be truthful, Americans feel the same way about some of the French Canadians guides. Almost all of the French guides who worked for me didn't appreciate me telling them how to guide and they definitely didn't like me managing the camp.

Most of the French young people didn't want to work long hours and they wanted to party practically every evening. As a bear guide, I averaged around 17 hours of work a day. I worked from 6:00 in the morning until 11:00 at night. I'd usually take five ATV's up to camp and I'd always ride a 600cc Yamaha, which is a fast machine. I ride it because I have to cover a lot of ground in a day's time. If I have 90 baits, I bait 45 every other day. Most days I would put 80 to 90 miles on the ATV. That's on rough logging roads and very rocky terrain. Over the winter, they have lots of snow and in the spring it melts off and washes the logging roads out. There are a lot of holes in the road and a lot of rocks.

I always loved speed, since I was a motorcycle racer a number of years ago. In my later years, I still like to ride fast. Every year I take one or two real hard falls, either rolling my bike or flipping it. One time I hit a washout and I flew through the air and the 400-pound ATV landed right on top of me. I had a lot of trouble getting it off of me, but I was lucky I wasn't seriously hurt.

The most dangerous situations I confronted was when I was out baiting all day and looking for new areas to put up bait sites.

I'd be back in the bush 30 to 40 miles. If I had been hurt bad, back there, nobody would have known how to find me. Our cell phones didn't have any reception and our walkie-talkies didn't carry that far. People in camp always told me to let them know where I was going in case I didn't come back and needed help. That way they could come looking for me. I told them I didn't know where I'd be by the end of the day and it would be impossible for me to pinpoint my location.

I had a lot of occasions when my ATV broke down and I had a long walk to get out to a main road where somebody could pick me up. I like to ride fast, especially when I'm taking a young customer out to a bait site. It scares them, because sitting in the back makes it seem like you're going twice as fast as you really are; there were lots of sandy roads and loose gravel where I could get the ATV to slide through the corners. One time, I had a middle-aged man in camp. I guess some of the customers were talking about me taking them on a thrill ride. So, that night when I was taking that middle-aged guy out to his bait site, he told me he was afraid of four-wheelers. I promised I would definitely drive safe, because I could see he was really scared. I was going back a logging road in low gear, as slow as the ATV would go. He told me to go slower and he had his arms wrapped so tightly around my belly I could hardly breathe. I said, "If we go any slower we will stop." We could have walked as fast as we were going on the ATV.

Over the winter, we'd have a lot of bridges washed out and have to rebuild them quickly before our hunters arrived. We'd do that by cutting down four trees up to 30 feet in length. Then, we'd lay two of them side by side and wire them together. After we had the second set wired together, we would place the sets next to each other across the creek. You could drive across the logs, but you had to be real careful you didn't run off them. Some of the bridges we built had 16-foot drop-offs.

Outfitter's daughter and I on ATV. Mike Hackman, Ross Houck, Jim Harsh, Dennis Scritchfield on back of swamp buggy.

One year, I had an older gentleman from my local area in Pennsylvania who asked me if he could work in my camp. He said he would like to stay the entire season. I asked him if he ever rode a four-wheeler and he said he was afraid of them. So, I told him he could work around camp skinning and butchering the bears we brought in. He was wondering what his pay would be. I told him the job didn't pay much, but he could make out pretty good on tips from the hunters. He told me he had a hobby collecting bones. I asked him what type of bones he collected. He said any type of bones that come from wild animals. I told him he could have all the bear bones he wanted.

The first thing we do before the season starts is to dig a pit. It's usually 8' x 16' x 16' in size and we throw at least 60 bear carcasses into that pit each season. In a couple week's time, that pit gets very stinky. The older gentleman would go out to that bear pit, wade around in those stinky carcasses and cut off the heads.

The following week, I told him I had 16 guys coming into camp, and we needed him to take two of the hunters out to their bait sites on the first day. He usually only had to do that one night, because four or more of the hunters would have shot their bears on their first night. He told me he could do that. I said I'd let him take the two hunters down the road about five miles from camp. I told him he couldn't get lost. The next day I took him down and showed him both of the baits. I put a white five-gallon bucket at the first bait site, another white five-gallon bucket at the second bait site, finally to help him, I placed a third white five-gallon bucket where he had to turn off the main road. All he had to do was drive down the main road, cross over a wooden bridge and on the other side of the bridge was the first white bucket. Then he'd turn right onto a logging road and drive down that road a quarter mile until he saw the first white bucket for a bait site. Then he'd go another half mile to the second white bucket at a bait site. I told him, "Just turn around and come out the way you came in." The next morning I told him, to drive down again to make sure he knew where the baits were, so he'd feel comfortable about finding them. He drove down again and when he got back he told me he had no trouble finding the baits. He said, "I am ok now." My customers came in the next day and I had two hunters for him to take to the baits. All of a sudden, he told me he didn't think he could find the baits. I couldn't believe what I was hearing! Instead of having five customers that night, I had seven hunters to take to their bait sites.

One evening as I was taking four hunters to their bait sites, a big bear crossed the road about a quarter mile ahead of us. I stopped my truck, told all four guys to get out of the truck, take their rifles out of their cases and put a round in the chamber. (Two of the hunters, Lemar Mast and his son Daniel, were from Morgantown, a town near my home.) I told the hunters we'd go another eighth of a mile and walk along the edge of the road looking down over the side. I didn't think the bear would go far and thought we'd probably find him down over the bank feeding on leaves of white birch trees. At this time of the year, they love to pull over white birches and eat the buds off the tree; that is exactly what that bear was doing.

One of my hunters shot the bear and it dropped right on the spot. Four of us went down over the bank, tied ropes to the bear, dragged him back up to the road and threw him in the back of the pick-up. After I dropped the other three guys off at their bait sites, I took the bear back to camp where I had a young French Canadian girl cooking for me. She was from Montreal and had never seen a live or dead bear. I went into the kitchen and told her I had a dead bear in the back of my pick-up and asked if she wanted to see it. I had a tough time trying to coax her outside to take a look at the bear. She finally built up her nerve, walked out to the pick-up and looked over the tail-gate. Turns out the bear had been shot in the spine and wasn't dead. Just as she looked over the tailgate, the bear raised both of his front legs up in the air and she took off running. I wasn't about to shoot the bear again while it was lying in the back of my pick-up.

There were a couple of guys in camp who had already bagged their bears. They helped me carry the bear and placed it on the table in the meat house. When we laid the bear on the table, he was still moving his front and back legs. I waited a while thinking he might die on the table. I got four hunters to hold his legs down; he was paralyzed, but his legs were twitching from nerve impulses. I cut off his head, assuring his death.

Another time, I was dropping off three Amish hunters on the last night of their hunt—none of them had shot a bear yet. The group included a father and his two sons. I asked the father if he or his boys would care if I shot a bear for myself. He said that would be okay. I told him not to tell the boys if he hears me shoot. I drove up the road a couple of miles and set on one of my baits. Right before dark, an average size bear came out and walked up to the bait. I shot it but I didn't kill it. I could have shot it again, but I didn't want the boys to hear the shots and know I'd killed a bear. When only one shot is fired, it's tough to tell where the shot came from. When you fire the second or third shot, it's easier to pinpoint the location.

I decided to cape that bear out right on the spot. There was a five-gallon bucket sitting on the bait, so I decided to put the hide in the bucket and cover it up and put it in the back of the pick-up. No one would know I shot it. The reason I didn't want the hunters to know I shot a bear, is because I usually don't harvest my bear when I have paying customers in camp hunting. This was the last day of the hunt, so I chose to harvest a bear. I started to skin the bear out, and while I was skinning him, he tried to crawl away, into the brush. I drug him back and tried to hold him down the best I could.

On another hunt, four of us were in my truck returning from our bait sites at dark. All of a sudden, a bear stood up on the road right in front of us. I told one of the hunters to get out with his gun and shoot the bear. He did, then the bear made one leap into the brush. Our headlights were right on the bear when the hunter shot. I thought he had made a good shot, so I walked into the brush look-ing for the bear. I found a good blood trail and started to track him. One of the hunters yelled at me and said, "Should I bring a gun?" I said, "No, I think we are going to find him dead." We kept tracking that bear for another half hour. Usually, when I track a bear and have hunters with me, I do carry a gun, especially if I think the shot was not a good one. I don't let any of my hunters carry a gun when it is dark, because they're often scared. If they see movement in the dark, there's a chance they'll shoot another hunter.

When we finally found the bear, he was on his back, usually dead bears are on their stomachs. I didn't give it much thought at the time. I just leaned over to roll the bear onto his belly, and his two front legs reached out and tried to grab me. I jumped back and he just missed my head. Turned out, like that other bear, this one had been shot high in his back. It broke his back, but didn't kill him. I told one of the hunters to hurry back to the truck and get a gun.

Retrieving a big bear.

On a different hunt, I went out to pick up a hunter at dark and found him standing along the road. He had had a long walk from his bait site to the road. I asked him if he'd shot a bear. He said, "Yes, it's dead and it's lying right alongside the bait. Here are pictures of the bear." I said, "Good!" Then I told him we'd first pick up the rest of the hunters and then come back to pick up the bear with the ATV. After we got the rest of the hunters, we rode back to the bait and there was no bear there. The hunter said, "It was lying right here. I showed you pictures of it. Where did it go?" I started looking around on the ground and saw blood drops and drag marks. We followed the drag marks for a couple hundred yards and found the bear lying there. We loaded the bear on the ATV, rode out to the truck then drove back to our camp. The next morning I thought I knew what had happened with that bear. There must have been a bigger bear in the area which found the dead bear and drug it away. That had happened a couple of times to me before.

I love it when a hunter tells me the bear he shot is lying right next to the bait. That saves me a lot of work. I don't have to go out the next morning and spend half a day looking for the bear. I always tell the hunters that when they shoot a bear and it runs off to always listen carefully for the sound of a death groan. Try to pinpoint where the sound came from. That way, when I have to go looking for the bear, it is much easier for me to know where to start searching.

One night I dropped a father and son off at the same bait. The son was about 12 years old and the father didn't want him sitting by himself near the bait. I said it was alright even though I don't like to have two people sitting in the same blind for six or more hours. It is nearly impossible to keep them quiet that long and sound carries a long way. (This is usually a problem too, when you have a hunter and a photographer in the same blind.) That evening when I went back to pick up the father and his son, I found them standing along the road an hour before dark. I thought I had two more guys scared to be in their blind after dark. I pulled up to them and asked them what they were doing out on the road. To my surprise, they said, "We both shot bears." The father said the first bear came in and stuck its head into the 50-gallon drum that was lying on its side and his boy shot that bear. Then about fifteen minutes after the boy shot his bear, before they went over to it, another bear came in and stuck his head into the drum right next to the dead bear's head. Then, the father shot the second bear with his son's gun. I figured when I got back to that bait, I would have to track two wounded bears. When I arrived at the bait, I saw something I had never seen before. Both bears had their heads inside the same drum. That made my day!

In the area where we have our bear camp, there are a number of Indian villages and a lot of the Indians are heavy drinkers. If they come into camp and ask for cigarettes and beer and you give it to them, you can be assured they'll be back for more. A couple times when there was no one in camp, they walked through all of our sleeping quarters then opened our coolers and helped themselves to the customers' beer. On the holidays, they go back in the bush and set up camp. They'll party there for several days and you never know when you are going to run into one of their parties in the bush. It was on one of those holiday weekends that I had a group of Amish hunters in camp. I dropped off an Amish boy at his bait. When I went back out to pick him up with my ATV, it was pouring down rain. I walked into the bait area and he didn't come out. I called for him and he still didn't respond, so I walked back to his stand to find him. It was still pouring—a real heavy thunderstorm. When he finally came out, I asked whether he'd seen anything. He said he saw a bear and I asked him why he didn't shoot it. He said, "I couldn't because there were Indians all over the place. A couple of them were lying under the tree stand and more were between me and the bear. I couldn't shoot." I thought this kid was nuts. I wondered if he was on drugs. He said, "There were Indians all over the place and they had white buckets over their heads." I thought this boy was going crazy. I told him to get on the back of my ATV. We were getting out of there. All I wanted to do was get him back to the pick-up.

When we got back to the truck, four of his Amish friends and the leader were in the pick-up. I told the leader to get out of the truck with me that I wanted to talk to him. I told him there was something wrong with that young man. He told me the youngster didn't use drugs, and in fact, he was a businessman and a realtor. "He buys and sells farms." I couldn't believe it. I never had Indians around my baits. The boy got back into the pick-up, and as we started down the road, he began telling his buddies what he had seen. He kept talking about Indians. He said they had their faces painted and were lying around on the ground with beer cans all over the place and they were smoking dope. When we got back to camp, I called the group leader off to the side again and questioned him about the young man. He said he never saw him acting like that. The next morning, after it stopped raining,

I went back out to the bait site. I figured if he had seen what he told me he did, I'd see tracks in the mud, beer cans and cigarette butts. I didn't see any of those things. I'm sure he didn't see what he'd told me he saw. To this day, I am still trying to figure this out.

Bear hunting is challenging, enjoyable and fun; it also can be dangerous, especially if you're not being careful. When I am out in the bush, I'm probably within 50 yards of numerous bears each day. One of the most dangerous times is when I'm trying to chase a bear off a bait site. Once a bear has been feeding on a site for a while, it considers that site to be his territory. The older the bear the meaner they are. After 40 years of hunting and guiding, I've had a number of close calls, usually it was my own fault—something I did wrong.

One of those times when I did something stupid I picked up a hunter and went back with him to his bait site to pick up the bear he told me he'd killed. He told me it was a big bear and where it was lying. I told him we'd walk back in, because I couldn't get my ATV into the bait site. We had to walk in on a real narrow trail through the brush. I asked him, "Should I take my gun or are you sure the bear is dead?" He was sure the bear was dead, so we went in without guns. By this time, it was after dusk and pitch black. We walked in and I shined my flashlight around to look for the dead bear. I found it and it wasn't big, it was a small cub. I could hear the cub's mother in the bush growling and snapping her teeth. I picked up the little bear and we began backing out of the area. I could hear the mother bear following us. Finally, we got out of the narrow trail and the hunter turned around and ran. I wasn't far behind him carrying his bear. Going back to that kill site without a rifle was one of the stupidest things I have ever done. I should have waited and gone back the next day with a rifle to get that bear.

Another stupid thing I did while hunting happened when I was photographing bears at a bait site. Dozens of bears were hitting one of my baits regularly. I didn't have any customers in camp at that time, so I went to the site to take videos of the bears. I had to walk past the bait, then go back in the woods to reach my tree stand. I didn't give it any thought at the time. As I sat in the stand, one bear came out, then another one, then another and, finally four more big bears. I was shooting video of seven bears at the bait at one time. It's very unusual to have seven bears on the bait at the same time. I was so involved in what I was doing and seeing, I wasn't thinking. It was getting darker, and, finally, I realized I couldn't take any more video. Then it hit me. I would have to climb out of the tree stand, walk right past the bait and chase those bears off the bait. I didn't have a knife or a gun or anything to protect me. As I mentioned before, bears don't like to be chased off their bait. At nighttime, it's even worse; but I didn't have a choice, I didn't want to stay in the stand all night. I came out of my stand yelling at the bears trying to chase them off. By then, it was so dark I couldn't see most of the bears. I still don't know if they ran off or just watched me walk by. I had to walk about an eighth of a mile to where my ATV was parked. When I got it started, I took off down the trail. When I reached the main road, I stopped for a while and just sat there shaking.

Some baits attract more bears than others. If I put out ninety baits, two or three of them will be more active than the others. I won't put any of my hunters on those baits and save them for a hunter who is unsuccessful and I will put him on it the last night of the hunt. One year, when I was taking my hunters out to their baits, I made the mistake of telling them about the active sites. I knew at least six bears were hitting on one of the active baits. Of course, all of them wanted to be assigned to the hot sites. Some of the guys offered me big tips if they could hunt those sites.

One of those sites was just off the main dirt road we were on and only a couple hundred yards back in. I told them I would stop, and I would show them the bait and we could walk in and check it out. On that site, I had a 50-gallon drum full of cookies. On the bottom of the drum, I had an 8-inch hole the bears could reach in and pull out cookies. That way, only one bear could feed at a time and the other bears had to wait their turns. When we reached the site, I pulled out a bunch of cookies and piled them up right in front of the hole. I told my hunters I'd prove to them that most animals don't mind the smell of urine. I said, "I want each of you guys to take turns and urinate on top of these cookies." By the time we left there, the cookies were soaked with urine. I told my customers it wouldn't take 45 minutes and all those cookies would be gone. I took four of them out to other sites and dropped them off. After that, I took one of the hunters back with me to check out the urine site. When we got back to that site, all of the cookies were gone.

If you're hunting bear, I'll give you some advice. If you go in the Spring, get a good bug suit or a head net along with gloves and duct tape. Put on your head net and gloves and then duct tape your gloves to your coat and your pant legs to your shoes. The black flies and mosquitoes, at this time of year, can be unbearable. If you tape yourself like this, you won't have to use any type of bug repellent since repellent has a tendency to alert the bears to your location. In fact, any kind of coverup scent, other than vanilla, is something you don't want to use. Bears have a really good sense of smell, even better than that of a white-tail deer. I've had hunters in my camp who brought along earth coverup scent. The scent is supposed to smell like leaves. When the hunters jumped into the front seat of my pick-up, I told them, "Get out, go back into the camp and change your clothes or we won't go hunting."

A lot of my customers bring their own lures with them. If the lures you bring smell like something the bears aren't used to, you do more harm than good. Your outfitter or guide has probably been baiting with the same type of bait for years and the bears are used to it. Now, the market has come out with something called a bear bomb. It's in canisters and it's supposed to emit a smell the bears like. I've tried it and it doesn't work.

Over the years, I've tested many types of baits and different methods of baiting. Several times I took 5-gallon buckets of different baits out to see which ones the bears hit and which ones they didn't. I tried a bucket of oats and corn, which a lot of outfitters use; a bucket of molasses; a bucket of chocolate; and one containing fresh horse meat. I also tried a bucket of cookies. When I'm conducting a test like this, I check the baits twice a day, sometimes more. In every test, the cookies were gone first and the meat buckets were upset; but the bears didn't eat a lot of the meat, because they were full of cookies. After the cookies and horse meat were gone, the bears upset the bucket of hard chocolate and dug around in it but didn't eat much of it. The last items on their menu would be the oats and molasses. Some outfitters say the rankest meats are the best. The more it stinks; the more it attracts bears. Nothing could be farther from the truth. A lot of outfitters will tell you this, because they don't have a place to buy donuts and cookies or they don't want to spend the money.

The best bait is beaver, but they are hard to get. If I can get my hands on beaver, I'll guarantee that bait will be hit on the first day it's out. If trappers drop a couple beavers off at my camp, I tie them behind my ATV and drag them up and down the road, as much as a mile, before dragging them back to my bait site. As soon as a bear picks up the scent from the drag, he'll follow it right to the bait site. Actually, they do this same kind of thing in Africa when they're hunting for leopards and lions. They shoot an animal and drag it up and down roads for miles. As soon as a leopard or lion picks up the scent, it follows it to the bait.

When I leave the blacktop road from La Tuque, Quebec, heading for our bear camp, I drive on a gravel road that's pretty smooth. Bear hunters coming into camp drive about 40 miles per hour on that same gravel road. Guides usually drive between 60 to 75 miles per hour on it, but you need to be careful going into corners because you can slide. Traveling that road, you see a lot of cars and trucks down over the bank. Most of them are cars that were driven by drunken Indians. When they roll a car over, they don't want to pay for a tow truck to come from town, so they just let it sit there and rust. Another thing to watch for on this road are logging trucks. They often run right down the center of the road and run you into a ditch. One time, I had four Pennsylvania policemen in my bear camp—two of them were state policemen and two were city cops. I knew one of the cops pretty well. When I took the four guys out hunting the first night, I thought this was my chance to give the cops a joy ride. I ran this road everyday for years, so I knew it pretty well. We were coming up on a corner and right at the end of it was a stop sign. I picked up speed, close to 70 mph, went into the corner and started to slide through it. I knew where to look through the trees to make sure no other cars were coming. I slid into the corner and went through the stop sign at 70 miles per hour. I looked around and said to them, "Who is going to arrest me?" They all looked at each other and I didn't know if they were going to laugh or give me a hard time. The one policeman I knew, who was sitting in the front seat, said, "Well, Kenny, all I have to say is you're crazy."

Cooper Camp

The outfitter I'm working with today is probably the last one I'll ever work with. His name is Henri and, at one time, he owned Safari Nordik caribou hunts. Now he owns Cooper Camp, a bear camp. He asked me if I would come and work for him. He said he would open up a camp for my customers and I would be the camp manager. One of the reasons I chose to work with Henri was the size of his hunting area—2,500 square miles. I knew with all that land, I didn't have to argue with other outfitters in the area about hunting on their property. In fact, they would probably be coming over to my area. It's always a big issue when one outfitter trespasses on another outfitter's

Cooper Bear Camp

hunting area. Another reason I enjoyed working with Henri was the experience I had, working with him in the past selling and guiding for caribou hunts. He was honest and a good boss. He knew I didn't want to have to complain about not having enough bait.

It turns out, Cooper Camp was actually two bear camps. The main camp is called Cooper and the camp I manage is called Belplaze. The camps are about 40 miles apart. That Spring, when I got to Belplaze for the first time, Henri, had two guides there setting up the camp. When I pulled into camp, I recognized both of them. They were French Canadians who had guided with me on Safari Nordik caribou hunts. The next morning, they told me that Henri instructed them to show me 50 of the 90 bait sites I was going to be using for my hunters.

We left the next morning on our ATV's. They were always out in front of me. I didn't know where I was going, but I was behind them all day eating their dust; I had trouble seeing where I was going. Every time they came to a "T" or a crossroad and I caught up to them, they'd take off again. They tried to make my job as miserable as possible. When they showed me a bait site, they would just drive by and point to the trail that led to the site. They never gave me enough time to make a map or record directions so I would have an idea where I was going the next day when I had to go out and bait the sites. If I would have had a GPS it would have been easy but I didn't. We were out all day and they showed me all of the 50 bait sites I'd be using for my customers the rest of the season.

The next morning they told me that I could go out and start baiting my sites. One of the guides put 50 handfuls of Oreo cookies into three buckets, added two buckets of horse meat, and told me that should be enough for all 50 baits. Then they asked, "Do you think you can find all of your bait sites?" I said, "We will see." They just smiled and walked away. That evening when I returned, they asked, "How many of your bait sites did you find?" I told them I found 48 of them but couldn't find the other two. They were just as surprised as I was. I had thought I would be lucky if I could find half of them. I knew at this point it was going to be a long season but I decided to make the best of it.

A couple days later, they told me to drive up to Cooper Camp, and pick up the supplies we needed for the following week, which included our bait, gas and groceries. When I got to Cooper Camp and went into the kitchen for the groceries, I got the shock of my life. I recognized a guide who also guided on caribou hunts for Safari Nordik. All of the five booking agents working with Safari Nordik had received more complaints about this guide than for all of the other guides combined. Every year, I'd have some customers tell me they would never book another hunt with Safari Nordik if that guide would be in the camp.

During the ten years I worked for Cooper Camp, I had a lot of complaints about that guide every year I knew I had to deal with him the whole season, plus work in my own camp with my customers. When the first group of hunters came into Belplaze camp, I had ten customers and the two other guides only had four. Those guides would not help me take my ten hunters out to the baits. We were supposed to work as a team and help each other out, but they didn't. By the end of the week, nine of my ten customers had shot bears; while the four customers of the other two guides only got three bears. The following week those two guides had six hunters and I had ten. A lot of the hunters bring ATV's to camp, so they can drive out to more remote locations. Many of my hunters were Amish who didn't drive or own ATV's, so it was much harder to get them out to the bait sites.

The two Frenchmen came over to me that first night and said they were going to take six of their hunters into my area, because they thought my area was a better hunting area. All six of their customers had ATV's and a couple of them had very loud racing bikes. All the baits in my area had been hit every time I checked them. They took all their ATV's and motorbikes into that area. I told them they were not going to kill a bear with all that noise. The bears were used to hearing only my ATV and, due to all that additional noise, those six hunters didn't see a bear. At the end of the week, nine of my ten hunters got bears and the customers of the French guides only got three.

The next year I told Henri I couldn't work with those guides and that he should find me two Frenchmen who don't know anything about bear hunting and I would teach them. I told him I wanted two tons of cookies and 50 buckets of meat or I wouldn't be back to work for him. That next year I got everything that I asked for and, a few weeks into the season, I taught the new guides about baiting. I soon found out I couldn't tell them anything. I had all of my baits numbered and I told the two new kids the numbers of the baits where I wanted them to take my customers. That evening, when they came back after hunting, the customers told me the guides took them to the baits that were the nearest and the easiest to get to. This really messed up my baiting system.

The two guides that had worked for me the previous year were now working in Cooper Camp. The next time I went up to that camp for supplies those guides teased me for using two tons of cookies. They said all I was doing was feeding chipmunks, squirrels and birds. The next year, I told Henri I wouldn't be back to guide unless I could bring up my own help. I also told him I needed five tons of cookies and I would bring up 60 customers. Again, Henri said, "OK."

That first year I brought up two young Amish brothers, Amos and Benuel Stoltzfus, to work and bait for me. That was one of the best moves I ever made. They were the best workers I ever had. They never complained and they cut brush and worked hard all day. That year my first group was a group of ten. My goal was to get each of them a bear the first night. We didn't get ten but we did get nine. I went to Cooper Camp the next morning to get some supplies I really didn't need. I wanted to rub their noses in my accomplishment. I got there around 6:00 in the morning and the guides were still in bed. The only person up was the cook, and he asked me how I did the night before. I told him we got nine bears with ten hunters, then I left. I knew he was going to tell those guides. It took me over one hour to get back to my camp. Before I even got back, the Cooper Camp manager called on the radio to ask my cook if we really got nine bears that first day. Those two Amish boys worked with me for a few years. Another year, I brought two of my friends, Al and Dennis, up with me. Al and Dennis were a real big help; they never complained and were good workers.

One of my goals had always been to kill a bear with a spear. As far as I knew, that's the way the Indians did it back in the old days. I had already tried and been successful with many different methods, so I thought I could accomplish this. If I speared a small bear, it would be much easier; but I had my goal set on a bigger adult bear. I finally figured out how to do it. I would put my tree stand about four feet

Dennis Scritchfield and Jim Schlessman digging a hole for bear carcasses.

Bear camp staff; man in center of picture died in farming accident.

off the ground, and place a bait right under my stand. Then, if the bear came into the bait right under the stand, I could spear him. To set this up, I took logs and built a funnel, so the bear would have no choice but to come in straight under the stand. I made my spear out of an 8-foot-long pipe. That way, when the bear was under my stand, I could ram the spear straight down through him. I had bears come into the bait funnel, but in the last foot or two, they'd get very cautious, turn around and leave. They smelled me or detected something wasn't right. I never did kill a bear with a spear.

For six years in a row, all of my hunters had an opportunity to kill a bear, but not all of them killed. Then, one year, I had a 100% kill rate and that was the first time that ever happened in the Cooper Camp.

In each of the following years I asked for nine tons of cookies for my camp for baiting; when I arrived at camp, they had the nine tons of cookies for me. I guess they finally thought if they couldn't beat me, then they'd join me. During this time, I lost one of my Amish boys, Amos, in a farming accident. His boss who was a dairy farmer in Virginia, had gone into a waste pit to fix a pump and was overcome by the fumes. Then his wife went to look for him and she was overcome by the fumes. Then, Amos went looking for both of them and was overcome by the fumes. Finally, two of the farmer's children went looking for their parents and they both fell into the waste pit and died. Five people died in that pit. Amos was an Old Order Amish. He was 24 years old, but at that time, he hadn't joined the Amish church, because of their doctrine. I had spent the entire season in camp working with Amos and shared my testimony with him. Before he left camp, he accepted Jesus as his Savior.

Every year, when I go to Canada to work at bear or caribou camps, they always detain me at customs for a couple of hours. Sometimes, they keep me there as long as five hours questioning me about what I'm doing in Canada. They go over all my records. Every time I show them my passport it raises a red flag, because I'm already listed on their computer. The last time I had the Amish boys haul my trailer into Canada with three ATV's, chain saws and tools. I told the boys not to tell the customs agents anymore than they had to. "If they ask, tell them you are going up bear hunting. Don't tell them more than they ask since I am giving you a free hunt in return for your work." The customs agents cornered them and asked them, "Why do have all these tools if you are only going to hunt?" After two hours of questioning, one of the Amish boys told the agents they were also going to do some work for Ken Gingrich.

The customs agents held my ATV's and trailer at customs and told the Amish boys they had to turn around and to go home, they couldn't enter Canada. When I went down to pick up my ATV's and take them back to the United States, they charged me a $2600.00 duty fee—and those items never made it into Canada. Over the years, I've had a lot of nightmares at the border with Canadian customs. My two Canadian bosses, who own the outfitting businesses I work for, one who is an attorney, over the years advised me not to get a green card to work in Canada. They told me that I am not doing anything wrong, I was not getting paid in Canada to work, I was making a commission on my hunters in the states. The Canadian customs did not see it this way. I tried to explain this to them every year and they always said, even if I was not getting paid I was taking the job of a Canadian. I told them I was bringing a half a million dollars worth of business into their country each year. The customs officials said this did not matter to them, their job was to catch people working in Canada. They always let me enter Canada after discussing this for hours, up until the last year, when the Amish said they were working for me. The Amish boys were getting paid by receiving a free bear hunt and not wages.

The Mountain Lions
and the Hounds

President Teddy Roosevelt held the world's record for taking nine mountain lions. Now, as far as I know, I hold that record because I've shot 14 mountain lions.

When I booked my first mountain lion hunt, there weren't many outdoor shows, booking agents or outfitters. After reading a copy of the *Outdoor Life* magazine, I decided to go with an outfitter from New Mexico. He was located in the southern part of the state in a town named Truth or Consequences. I flew into Albuquerque and the outfitter picked me up there. On the way to the hunting area, we stopped at a grocery store and picked up enough groceries for the week's hunt. Then we drove 200 miles south, not very far from the Mexican border. The last 50 miles to the camp were over dirt roads, and when we got there, it was an old cattle rancher's cabin. Cowboys stayed there in the one-room cabin, with a dirt floor, for six months and erected barbed wire fences for local cattle ranchers. They had about four horses in the corral in addition to 20 dogs, including plot dogs, blue ticks, and walkers.

On the first day one of the cowboys got up and made us pancakes for breakfast. We had the same breakfasts, lunches and dinners for the entire six days. After breakfast, we went outside and put tracker and shocker collars on all of the dogs. Often, when you're hunting lions, the dogs are out of sight and sound, especially when you're hunting areas with canyons and bluffs. You can't see or hear the dogs, so the tracking collars help guides and hunters locate them and the lions.

The tracking collars have radio antennas that can reach distances up to five miles. The shocking collars only reach a couple miles. If a dog got on a deer trail instead of a lion's, the guide would push a button to shock the dog and you'd hear the dog yelping way off in the distance. In the area where we were hunting, there were a lot of cacti, thorns and thistles; it was very hard on the dogs' feet. After a day of running over sharp stones and cactus, their feet would be all bloody. They would only run individual dogs every third or fourth day to give their feet a chance to heal.

Every night, while I was trying to sleep, an older cowboy would play all the old western songs on his fiddle. When he finished playing a song, he'd ask, "Kenny do you know what that song was? It was the

Fiddle player keeping me up all night.

Yellow Rose of Texas." Then he'd continue playing and wouldn't let me sleep.

During lion hunts, you ride all day on horseback until the lead dogs pick up the scent, then the guides turn all the dogs loose. They usually have six to ten dogs and they can identify individual dogs by their barks. This day we turned the dogs loose on a track and they took off. You can always tell by the way the dogs are barking if they are on a fresh track and if they have a lion treed or cornered on the ground. This day, the dogs all took off and before we knew it they were gone. In a couple of minutes, they were miles off and the barking grew fainter and fainter. After a while, we couldn't hear them barking at all and the tracking collars couldn't even locate them. So, all we could do was ride and call for the dogs. When it got dark, knowing we had a long ride back to camp, the guide just laid his coat down on the ground and we headed back. After a day or two, if the dogs were still alive and didn't get killed by the lion, they would come back to where the guide left his coat and stay right there until their master came back to get them.

When we went back a couple days later to look for the dogs, only five out of the six dogs were there waiting for us. One of his best dogs was missing. Often, the dogs will chase the lion and the lion will lose them. He'll jump down over the rocky edges of bluffs or canyons. A cat can jump 10 to 15 feet down over the bluffs; while a dog will have to work its way down, because it can't jump like a lion. Often the dogs will die out there if the guides can't find them. If only one or two dogs corner a lion by themselves and the whole pack isn't there, the lion will often kill the dog. We spent six days hunting on that trip and I didn't get a lion.

I went back with the same outfitter the following year, for another six-day hunt. Since this was only my second year hunting mountain lions I had a lot to learn. It didn't take long to figure out if an outfitter didn't have good dogs. The first morning of this hunt the dogs took off on a lion track and I thought my luck was changing and I might have my cat the first day of the hunt. The dogs took the track in the wrong direction, which is called back tracking. Then the guide will have a hard time catching his dogs and turning them around and heading them in the right direction. I felt this guide did not have the best dogs to track lions on bare ground. It's much easier to track lions if you have snow. In fact, most outfitters will only hunt lions when they have snow. Some outfitters won't even let you come out to hunt if there isn't a couple inches of snow. Most outfitters hunt out of their pick-ups. They drive the mountain roads for days until they find tracks in the snow and then they release the dogs. I also learned that many outfitters won't turn their dogs loose on small female lions. Outfitters usually won't turn their dogs loose unless it is an adult tom, unless they want to run the dogs for fun chasing a young lion, to give the young dogs training.

The following year, I booked another lion hunt, but this time in southern Utah. The terrain was similar to the area I hunted in New

Giving the dog with sore feet a ride.

Bluffs and canyons of Southern Nevada.

Mexico, hot and dry. However, when we were hunting up in the high country, we often had a couple inches of snow. This outfitter had real good dogs, but we couldn't find any big cats. One day the guide turned 20 dogs loose. Some were young dogs he ran with the older dogs to train them. When all those dogs got on a track, they made the most awesome sound—20 hounds barking at the same time in the canyons. It made chills run up my back. I hunted with this outfitter for five days. On the very last day, we turned the dogs out on a good tom cat and ran the lion for about a half day. The area had a lot of deep canyons and steep bluffs. We knew there was a chance we might lose his trail because mountain lions know where they are able to lose the dogs. There weren't many trees in the area for a cat to climb and that's usually what they do to get away from the dogs. As the dogs chased the lion, the guide kept saying that the dogs had a hot trail, and should tree him at any time. He said he would be able to tell by the dogs' bark when they had him treed. When we caught up with the dogs, they did have the lion treed in the only tree in the area—one that was 20 feet high that grew on the edge of a bluff and hung out over the canyon.

The guide said, "You can shoot him, but if you kill him, he'll fall out of the tree right into the canyon—about a 200-foot drop. Then, we'll have to ride the whole way around the canyon. It'll take about a full day's ride to get to the lion." It looked to me like the biggest lion I had ever taken, so I told the guide I was willing to take my chances of him falling into the canyon. There was only one branch coming out of the tree and it was shaped like a fork. When I shot the cat it fell right into the fork and hung up in the tree. The guide asked, "Are you going to climb up in the tree and get that cat down?" I told him that's what I was paying him for. He said, "I'll have to go back to the pick-up and get some rope." He did, then he tied the rope around his waist. I grabbed the other end of the rope, sat behind a rock and held it tight so the guide wouldn't fall into the canyon. He climbed out on the tree, fortunately, everything went well and the guide recovered the second biggest lion I ever harvested.

Lion guides like to be recognized and called houndsmen. It's all about their dogs and they all claim to have the best hounds. They try to develop their own bloodline of hounds by interbreeding them with different types of dogs. If a dog is known to be a real good lion dog, guides will ship them all over the country to breed them with other good hounds. Prices for these dogs can range from $5000.00 and up.

If you are lucky when you are hunting lions, you might find a fresh track the very first day. However, you can go an entire week before you find a track. Sometimes, when dogs are turned loose, they can tree a cat in a half hour, or they might have to trail the lion for the best part of a day. I always tell people a lion hunt can be the easiest hunt you've ever been on, or it can be one of the hardest hunts you've ever been on, especially in deep snow.

I hunted the next few years with a couple of different outfitters in Montana and Colorado, but never killed a lion. Then I booked with another outfitter and we ran into a lot of snow. He told me we were going to be hunting with snowmobiles and pulling sleds behind us with dog boxes on them. He asked me if I ever rode one, I said, "Yes. In fact, I own a couple of snowmobiles." He said, "I'll give you this one to ride. It's really fast. Take it for a test run." I did and when I was going around a tight corner, I hit a rock right under the snow, flipped the sled, and broke my foot.

They took me to a hospital which was about a half day's drive. Another guy in camp said he wanted to ride along with me to the hospital. When we arrived, my friend sat in the waiting room and started talking to the nurse. After a short time, she asked him, "Are you okay, you look pale?" He told her he wasn't feeling well, so they checked him out. After the exam, they told him, "You are right on the verge of having a heart attack." Then, they performed some additional tests and found some of his arteries were 90% blocked. They offered him an option. They said, "We can operate on you here, or send you home, because you need to have a bypass." He elected to go home. The doctor then asked me whether I wanted them to operate on my foot or get it done when I got home. I told him I wanted to have it done at home.

Unloading dog boxes to pull behind skidoo.

Returning with my 1st mountain lion.

Getting home turned out to be an experience. First, my flight was rescheduled and I had to fly into Atlanta, Georgia; then the flight out of Georgia was cancelled, so I had to stay overnight in Atlanta. Imagine me limping around on one foot with crutches and getting on and off buses going and coming between the motel and the airport. I was in quite a bit of pain. Finally, I got back to the Philadelphia airport and my wife was there to pick me up. The day after I got home, a doctor put my foot in a cast for several weeks.

My hunting friend still calls me from time to time to say thanks for saving his life. If I had not broken my foot, we both would have been out in the mountains wading through deep snow. More than likely, he would have had a heart attack out in the wilderness and died.

The following year I booked with another outfitter. He kept bragging about the hounds he owned and I took him at his word. The first day of the hunt we had about four feet of snow and we walked through drifts up to five feet deep. It was tough to navigate. On the second day, we did see a lion track, so the guide released his hounds. Now, I thought, I'm going to see how well his pack of eight dogs perform. They took off and started yelping and chasing what we thought was the lion. After an hour, the dogs started howling and the guide said, "They have the lion treed and you definitely will get a shot at this lion." It took us another hour before we caught up with the dogs and the first thing I heard was the guide yelling and swearing at his hounds. Turned out, the hounds had surrounded a moose. That moose was the only animal we saw during the whole week.

Some outfitters will schedule your hunt with a phone call. When the outfitter calls, it usually means he has fresh snow and expects you to be there within a couple of days. Some outfitters scout for tracks before you arrive. Others will even tree the lion and keep a pack of hounds under the tree until you arrive. They'll take you right to the tree and you get to shoot the lion. This is what I consider a lazy man's hunt, if you can really call it a hunt at all.

Over the years, I've had enough bad experiences with outfitters that I've become more selective in making my choice. On one of my searches, I ran across an ad in an outdoor magazine. It advertised real mountain lion hunts and guaranteed "No kill, no pay." I placed a call and as a result, met Roger, one of the most interesting guys in my life. We became real good friends for a ten-year period. He lived in northern Nevada about two miles from the Idaho line. The town where he lives had a population of around 200, and Roger was the only non-Mormon in town. The Mormons always invited him and his family to their picnics. Roger would always explain to them what he believed was different than what they believed.

Roger was a God-fearing man, however, when he got mad at his dogs; he used some awfully foul language. When discussing his hunting experiences, he told me he decided he wanted to learn how to hunt mountain lions when he was only 16 years old. He bought an old car and drove a couple hundred miles to an old lion hunter's home. This lion hunter's name was Willis, who was known as one of the best lion hunters in his time. He was taught by Ben Lily who was a legend in the 1900's. Ben Lily hunted and taught Willis how to hunt lions and Willis was passing down the tradition of lion hunting to Roger. Roger walked up to the old timer's door and said, "I am here to learn about lion hunting." The response was, "Why do you think I'll take you in and teach you lion hunting?" Roger said, "I was hoping I would be able to hunt with you at least for a couple days. If you're not going to take me in, I'll have to borrow some money from you. I'm out of gas, hungry and don't have enough money to get back home." The expert hunter looked Roger up and down and finally said, "Ok, you can stay with me for a couple of days." Those couple days turned into a couple years during which Roger was schooled in lion hunting.

Roger had an interesting background. In his early years, he was known in the local bars for fighting and being an outlaw. Game wardens were after him all the time for breaking game laws. One night, when two game wardens pulled Roger and his friend over and questioned them, it turned into a brawl with Roger and his buddy beating up the wardens. Roger had a daughter and two sons, Earl and Roger Jr., with his first wife. I never got to know her because she died of cancer before I met Roger. His second wife Lois, was 20 years younger and a real outdoors woman. She ran a trap line and went lion hunting with us every day. His oldest boy, Roger Jr., also accompanied us on our hunts. Roger was trying to teach him everything he knew. Roger would yell at Junior all day, just like he yelled at his dogs. Then he would turn right around and tell the boy, "I love you awful bad." In fact, he'd say the same thing to his other kids and his wife. He loved all of them "awful bad."

Roger also worked for the federal trappers. There were quite a few sheep ranchers in the area who grazed their flocks in nearby mountains. Anytime the ranchers had problems with lions killing their sheep, they would call the feds. If the federal trappers couldn't get the lion, they would always call Roger, because he was known to have the best pack of hounds. Many times, one mountain lion will kill up to 25 sheep or more in a single night. It's not just for food. They do it mainly for fun and sport. They corner the sheep and kill as many as they can. While they may eat sheep, a lion's main diet is deer. Roger knew all of the sheep ranchers in his area. He had keys to their gates, so he could get onto their property. The sheep ranchers would leave him hunt anywhere he wanted, because they wanted as many lions killed as possible. Roger could get on the ranches and unlock gates to get into areas where even the game wardens couldn't go.

The first time I ever hunted with Roger, we got on a lion track and he turned his dogs loose. The dogs treed a female lion and we found she had four kittens. Roger looked at me and said, "Well Kenny, we don't like to do this, but I have to kill all the kittens." I asked, "Why?" He said, "If the rancher would find out I didn't kill them, I would never be allowed back on his land again. They want every lion killed." I was very opposed to him killing the kittens. Later that week we killed a tom cat.

The following year Roger and I came across a real fresh kill. A lion had just killed a deer and covered it with snow. The lion hadn't even started to eat the deer. Roger told me the lion would be back that night to feed. He said, "When a cat has a full stomach and a meal waiting, it won't usually run far. This should be an easy chase." We got up the next morning about 5:00 a.m. and released the hounds. The temperature was zero degrees. We went where the lion had buried his kill and found he had been feeding on it that night. The dogs took off, and we followed on foot, wading through about three feet of snow. We trailed that cat all day, trying to keep up with the hounds. The dogs finally treed him after dark. I had killed a lot of lions with a bow and a rifle, but this time I had Roger's pistol. I pointed it up at the lion in the tree, shot and hit the lion. It dropped out of the tree and took off running. The dogs took off running after it and Roger took

Dogs being rewarded by catching the lion.

off after the dogs. After a while, I heard the dogs yelping and carrying on and Roger was yelling at me, "Get down here, the cat is killing my dogs!" Roger jumped in among his dogs, grabbed the lion behind the neck, put his pistol to its head and shot him. A couple of his dogs were really torn up.

We skinned the cat right on the spot and began walking back to where our pick-up was parked. We had a three-hour walk ahead of us and it was late at night. I was already worn out and tired from walking through the deep snow all day and I was carrying camp gear and the lion's skin and head on my shoulders. I was so tired I told Roger I couldn't go anymore. He started yelling at me and calling me all kinds of names to get me upset so I would get mad. He knew that was the only way he could keep me going and it worked. If I had been alone, I would have given up, laid down in the snow and froze to death. By the time we reached the truck, we were soaking wet from sweat and the temperature was now 30 degrees below zero. That was the hardest hunt I have ever been on in my life.

Another year, when I was out in Nevada with Roger, he took me on sheep ranches and I killed a cat. On the back of his flatbed truck, Roger had eight dog boxes, usually one or two ATV's and a couple snowmobiles—it depended on the weather conditions. This time, after I killed my lion, he put it in one of his dog boxes. I asked him why he was putting my cat in a dog box. He said, "Never mind!" We hadn't gone down the road very far when we got pulled over by a game warden. He started to question Roger about where we'd been hunting. Roger didn't give him much information. Then the warden took his flashlight out and started shining it in the dog boxes. Roger told the warden, "Be careful with the dogs, a couple of them are really mean." I guess the warden knew that plot dogs are known to be fighters. Anyway, the game warden left us go. Roger said we were lucky again. I didn't know it at the time, but later I found out we'd killed that lion in an area where my permit was not valid.

Mule deer across the line.

Roger told me the game wardens harassed him all the time and they were always watching him. I told him that wasn't surprising. I said, "Anybody who beats up on a couple of game wardens can expect the wardens to be laying for them. It'll just be a matter of time until they catch you doing something illegal." He told me that fight with the wardens happened many years ago and they've forgotten about it. I said, "I don't think so."

I killed a nice tom early in this hunt then I asked if there was anywhere in the area I could hunt for mule deer. He said, "You can spend the rest of the week hunting mule deer up behind my house. There are a couple nice mule deer in that area." So, I went up there the following day and shot the second largest mule deer I ever killed. The next morning Roger and I rode back in on horseback to pack out my mule deer. When we got to the deer, Roger said, "It's a very good mule deer. The only trouble is you killed it in Idaho." Roger then told me that as soon as we got back into Nevada, it would be legal.

Another time when we were hunting together, the dogs cornered a cat in the rocks. That's the worst place to try to kill a cat. By the time I got there, the dogs were all over the cat. I had to shoot the lion while he was fighting with the dogs. Roger kept saying, "Don't kill my dogs." A couple of his dogs were lying there all torn up. I thought they were dead. After I killed the lion, Roger picked up one of the dogs and put the dog's intestines back in its body. He always carried a needle and thread with him to sew up his dogs. He stitched up the dog, then carried it back to the house. The dog did survive.

Often, when we rode horses up through the rocky canyons, Roger would yell, "Jesus I love you!" It would echo throughout the canyon. He just loved to talk about God and the Bible. I could never figure this man out. Sometimes, when we treed a cat, if it was a young cat or a female, and I chose not to kill it, he would climb up in the tree, grab its tail and yank it out of the tree so his dogs could trail the cat and get more training. He would yank cats out of trees two to three times, just so his dogs could practice tracking. One time, Roger showed me a picture of him in his younger years when he had chased a cat so long and hard that it was completely tired out. When he caught up with it, Roger took off his hat, reached over and put it on the cat's head. The cat was so tired it couldn't fight anymore. Roger hunted cats year round. He was in the mountains every day with his dogs. One time he told me, "Don't you ever tell my wife, but God is my number one priority; my dogs are second; my wife and kids come third." Roger spent 90% of his time with his dogs and the rest with his family. He told me that one night, when he and the dogs were stuck out overnight, all his dogs came up to him and laid around him to keep him warm. He said his dogs saved his life more than once.

Roger believed and claimed his dogs understood every word he spoke when he was talking to them, one on one. He told me a story. He said, "I had a pack of hounds and one of my dogs kept chasing deer. You know you can't have a dog in your pack that does that. He

Roger placing his hat on a live lion.

Roger speaking to his dogs as if they were humans.

wouldn't listen to me, so I called in all of my dogs and they made a circle around me. They were all sitting around me and I told them why this one dog was bad and wouldn't listen to me. Then I pulled out my pistol and shot that dog. "Every one of those dogs knew why I shot him." I just kind of smiled. This upset Roger again, and he said, "Don't you ever try to tell me my dogs didn't understand what I had just done."

Every evening, when we got back to his house, Roger would be on the phone for hours talking with other outfitters and houndsmen about their dogs and different breeds. His whole life was built around dogs. He refused to sell his puppies, because he didn't want any houndsman to have his bloodline. He thought he had the best pack of hounds and he didn't want anybody to have his dogs or their offspring. When one of his hounds had a litter of puppies, he would select the one out of the litter he thought was the best. He would put the rest of the puppies in a burlap bag and drown them in a creek. He could have made thousands of dollars selling them, but that was Roger.

After my sixth year of hunting with Roger, I had shot six lions and he wanted me to shoot more. He said when he died he wanted to be known as a legend. He wanted people to write books about him, so his goal was to have a customer kill more mountain lions than President Teddy Roosevelt. He asked me to agree to continue to hunt with him for the next six years. He promised it would cost me less to hunt with him each of the following years. He told me he'd lower his rates a couple of hundred dollars each year. It sounded good to me, so I took him up on his offer.

Sometimes lion hunting can take a long time, especially when you're hunting on bare ground, because the scent only stays on the ground a short time. Following tracks in the snow is much easier. On one of our hunts on bare ground, Roger and I came upon a set of tracks left by a big tom. He looked at the track and said it was a couple of days old. Usually, most hunters want a track to be a couple of hours old. Roger said, "I think if I turn my dogs loose on this line, they might be able to take the trail." So, he put his dogs on the track. We trailed that cat all day and never caught up to him. Finally we quit for the night. Then we went back the next morning and turned the dogs loose again. We trailed that cat all day and again that day we never caught up to that lion. The following day we turned the dogs loose on the track again. They trailed it until late afternoon, when the dogs finally treed the lion, I killed it. That performance was as good as any pack of hounds can do following a three-day-old track on bare ground.

Another time, when Roger and I were out hunting cats again, I killed a lion early in the hunt then I told Roger I'd like to kill a 6x6 bull elk. I asked whether he knew of an area where I might have an opportunity to harvest a nice bull. He said, "Let me think about it." The next morning he and his son were sitting in their living room talking. Roger was telling his boy where he should take me to hunt elk. The next day he dropped me and his son off at a site early in the morning before light. His son was only wearing Wrangler jeans and a light jacket. He told me we'd have a long walk ahead of us and we took off walking in a couple feet of snow. We climbed up a mountain checking for elk signs, but we didn't see any tracks or elk. Then when we came over a ridge and looked down into a valley, we saw a herd of 75 elk. There were four or five really good bulls in the herd. We carefully worked our way down toward them and I tried to pick out the best bull elk. When I did, I shot and killed a good 6x6. He only ran a short distance and died. I caped out the head and cut off the antlers.

By this time, it was getting darker and colder, and I was really sweating. We took the antlers and the cape and started back toward our pick-up area, which was about five miles away. We knew we'd be walking in deep snow for four to five hours. Roger's son started to complain to me that he was too cold. The temperature was near zero and he began shaking real bad. It was pitch black in the woods as we continued to slog through the snow. Finally, Roger Jr. said, "I can't go anymore." Then he remembered what his dad had told him to do if he was in really cold weather out in the woods. There is a pine tree in the forest where the sap drains to the bottom of the tree after it dies. When that happens, it's very easy to set fire to the tree to help you stay warm. Roger Jr. got out his matches and lit the tree. It burned like a torch. We stood next to it until we warmed up, then took off and walked another half mile or so before setting another tree on fire. As we kept walking, I looked back at the trees burning like torches—thankful we hadn't set the woods on fire.

By this time, it was around midnight and we still had a couple of miles ahead of us. Roger Jr. looked at me and said, "I'm lost," but we kept walking until we came to the edge of a steep drop-off. It dropped straight down and it was hard to judge how far it was to the bottom. It didn't look too bad and we thought we were moving in the right direction so Roger Jr. said to me, "I'm going to jump off. I don't think it's that big of a drop." I told him to go ahead and jump first and then I'd follow him. He threw the antlers down first, then the cape. We couldn't see where they landed, but we heard them hit the ground. So Roger Jr. jumped. I yelled, "Are you OK?" He said he was, so I followed him. It felt like it was a 100-foot drop; actually, I think it was more like 20 to 30 feet. We kept on walking—maybe limping would be more accurate—and jumped off two more drop-offs with Roger Jr. leading the way.

We had probably walked another half mile when we thought we heard people talking. We walked toward the sound and found ourselves in a boy scout camp. It was around 4:00 a.m. and most of them were sleeping. The two of us were so hungry and thirsty we just went into their cook tent and helped ourselves to their food and water. We left their camp around 5:00 in the morning and continued to walk on the dirt road where we found Roger Sr. waiting for us. He told us he had been driving up and down the road all night looking for us. Then he took us back to his home. I asked Roger when we could go back in to recover the meat. He said, "Forget about it. We are not going back in. You shot that elk in a game preserve area." I'm sure he had known from the beginning he was sending me into a forbidden area.

The last year I hunted with Roger I killed a very big lion. Roger roughly measured the skull and told me he thought it might be the

Biggest lion I had ever taken.

number one lion of all time, and it would definitely be in the top ten. (Roger holds the number two record for the biggest lion ever harvested.) He was making a big deal about the skull size, but to me, records are not that important, so I made the mistake of saying, "Who cares?" That made Roger so mad he told me if I didn't appreciate it, I was not going to take the lion skull home with me. He kept it and he never did tell me how high that lion ranked in the record books. I know it was the biggest cat I ever killed; from nose to tail, it was around nine feet long.

I did hunt a few years after that with a couple other outfitters, but I was getting older and it was getting harder for me to go on these hunts.

About four years after my last hunt with Roger, I got a knock on my door and answered it. I opened it and two guys were standing there. They introduced themselves as federal game wardens and showed me their identification. They asked me if I knew a lion outfitter named Roger. I told them I did. They asked if they could come in, because they had a lot of questions to ask me. I told them to come in.

Once they were in the house, they said they knew I had been hunting with Roger for a lot of years. They said, during those years, they had been following and watching us. I said, "I'll tell you everything I know about these hunts." They asked me what areas I killed my lions in. I said, "I honestly don't know." I just assumed that my outfitter, Roger, would only take me into legal areas. I answered all of their questions and they told me I would be getting a call to appear in a Nevada court to testify.

After they left my house, I called Roger and asked him what was going on. He said, "The feds had an undercover federal agent book a hunt with me, so they could catch me doing something illegal. I let the undercover game warden kill a bobcat that he didn't have a tag for. Then, I had one of my neighbors tag it for him and I shipped the bobcat back to the customer. That meant the bobcat crossed the state line making it a federal offense." He also told me the federal agents came into his house, took all of his paperwork and all the items I had given him and his kids over the years. That included videos, caps and jackets. They took everything, but I never got called to appear in court. However, they did charge Roger and he lost his outfitting license.

Caribou Migration
Over the Tundra

For many, many years I hunted bear in Quebec with a French Canadian named Ed. We became good friends and one year he asked me if I would be interested in going caribou hunting with him and nine other French Canadians. I thought this would be an interesting adventure on two levels. First, being I had never hunted caribou before; second, because my friend, Ed, and I were the only ones in the group who spoke English. I said, "Yes." There are two areas in Northern Quebec where you can hunt caribou. One is Sheffersville, a mining town about 700 miles from Montreal; the other is Ft. Chimo, now called Kuuqquaq, and it's 1000 miles north of Montreal. In both of these areas, you hunt on the tundra. There are no trees at all in the Kuuqquaq area, but there are some around Sheffersville. There are only two ways to get to Sheffersville, one is on a commercial jet and the other by train. The train only runs one time a week and it carries out iron ore from the local mines. We decided to fly into Sheffersville. It takes a 24-hour train ride to travel between Montreal and Sheffersville, it is quite an experience.

The passenger car on the train is usually filled with drunken

Indians. (If you miss your train on your return trip home, you sit in the train station for a week before the next train arrives.) Upon arrival at Sheffersville, there will be a bush plane on floats to fly you into your hunting camp. Going home, quite often the bush planes can't fly out on schedule due to fog or wind; so a lot of the hunters get stranded in camp for a couple extra days. When they finally fly out of the bush, they can end up on standby for their next flight; because the passengers who had tickets for that day always go first. There was only one flight a day out of the small airport. The airport was always packed full of hunters waiting to get out. A lot of them would be on standby; and they would have to wait a day or two to get a flight. There are a couple bars in town, so that's where the hunters spent their time while waiting for their flights. A lot of the hunters would be upset and mad because they were missing work back home, so they'd spend their time drinking and often they would get drunk.

Hauling hunters, along with their baggage, from the motel to the airport, and trying to please them was one of the hardest parts of my job. Fortunately, I only had to do that when I didn't have clients coming into camp to hunt. Sometimes I'd be stuck in town for as long as six days. During that period, when I went to the train station, I'd see this same hunter sitting in the corner by himself. I went over and asked him what happened. He said, "I got flown out of the bush late and missed the train going back to Montreal by one hour. So now, I have to sit here for a week until the next train is due."

To reach the caribou camps you usually have to fly about 150 miles from Sheffersville with a bush pilot. On my initial hunt, 10 Canadians and I went shopping in Sheffersville for enough groceries to last us a week. The cost was about 50% for groceries and 50% for hard liquor. I have been hunting caribou for 40 years, and I can tell you that this first trip was the worst caribou hunt I ever went on. We hunted for four days and no one even saw a caribou. We were on an unguided hunt which meant we didn't have a guide or a camp manager. All we had were two-way radios, so we could call back to the base camp in case of an emergency. The French Canadian hunters were so mad, they called back to the base camp and threatened the outfitter. They said, "If you don't send a plane back for us, and move us to another hunting area, we'll burn your camp down." There were planes flying over our camp, on the way to other camps, but none of them landed. Then the hunters called back again and said, "If you don't have one of your planes land and pick us up, we'll shoot down the next plane that flies over." All of this was being said in French, so my friend, Ed, was translating for me.

There was a lake in front of our camp, about one mile wide and five miles long, and a couple of us had fishing rods and lures with us so we got a chance to do some fishing. One of my lures caught most of the fish we landed. One was a large pike and it broke my line and my favorite lure was gone. The next day some of the other guys went fishing on the lake. When they came back to camp, they handed me my lure. They had caught a fish and it had my lure in its mouth. There was probably only a one in a million chance they'd catch that same fish in a lake that large. Finally, on the last day of our hunt, they sent a plane into camp to pick us up. My friend Ed went down to the beach and when the pilot pulled up on the sand, Ed walked out on the floats of the plane. When the pilot got out, Ed grabbed him and threw him up against the plane and said, "You're not leaving here until all our luggage, gear and hunters are on the plane."

One of the other Canadians and I decided to go back up again to that camp a couple weeks later. I thought my first trip there was was a disaster. The second trip was even worse. The weather conditions had changed a lot. It was much colder and we ran into a lot of snow when flying into camp. The first morning when we got up, it was blowing and snowing. It was a white-out. We had a camp manager this time, but that was all—the camp manager, my friend, and I. The manager wouldn't let us go out of camp, due to the weather conditions. You wouldn't have had to walk very far from camp to get lost. The visibility was very bad. I told the manager I had been hunting there a few weeks before and didn't see any caribou, so I was going out, but I wouldn't go far. I went out and some caribou walked right in front of me, maybe 50 yards off. When I went to look through my scope, I couldn't see a thing. Finally, I did pick up one bull in my scope. I pulled the trigger, but my gun wouldn't fire. I chambered another round, pulled the trigger, but the gun still wouldn't fire. The firing pin was frozen. The next morning the camp manager loaded us into a boat and told us we were going to try to cross the lake, if we could. It was still blowing hard and waves were crashing around us. We had only gone a short distance, when he said, "We're putting our lives at risk. We're going to go back." We were constantly baling water from the boat, just trying to stay afloat. We finally made it back to camp.

In the afternoon, we tried to cross a small body of water behind the camp. We made it to the other side, pulled the boat partway up on shore and went for a walk. We were only gone a couple of hours and the storm got worse. The wind was blowing 50 to 75 miles per hour and it was tough just walking. When we got back to the boat site, we found our boat was completely underwater. We had a small bucket in the boat, so we pulled the boat further up on shore so we could begin baling out the water. When we finally got rid of all the water, we tried to start the motor. It wouldn't start due to being underwater so long. The only choice we had was to put the boat in the water and pull it along the shoreline. Two of us were in the boat while the other one pulled us. We used the oars to keep the boat off the shore and we took turns pulling. It was dark at this point. There was ice on the lake and the water we were wading in came up past my waist.

After six hours, we finally made it back to camp. We were frozen and only had a small wood-burning stove. Our tent camp was set up on a wooden platform. That night the storm got worse and the wind blew so hard it lifted the platform off of the ground. We took our beds and belongings and propped them up against the tent wall, hoping that would stop the tent from blowing over. As we were lying in bed trying to secure the walls, we could feel the platform raising up a foot or two, then dropping back down. We took all the ropes we had in camp and tried to tie the tent and the platform down. During this period, there were hunters in other camps in the area and they were out in their boats. They couldn't make it back to their camps, so they were stuck out on the tundra for days. A couple of the boats sunk while trying to make it back to the camps and some of the hunters drowned. Several planes also flipped over during the storm. That was the worst storm on record they had ever had in the North Country.

A couple of days later, they flew in with a helicopter to get us out. After we climbed in the helicopter, they put all of our luggage, gear and the tent in a large bag and attached it to the bottom of the chopper. It was still real windy. When the chopper took off, the bag started blowing around in circles, so the pilot had to pull a lever to release the bag with all our gear. We lost our luggage, the tent and our guns. We never did get back into that area to retrieve all of our gear, but we felt very fortunate that we reached the base camp alive.

The following year, I put a party of 10 guys together from my local area to go on the same type of hunt—hoping things would go better. This time, we took our own food and did our own cooking. This was called a drop-camp hunt. I had one strict rule for this group, no alcohol allowed. We had a good hunt and everyone killed a caribou. On the last day of the hunt, when we were supposed to fly out, it was a nice clear, calm day with no wind. Then we got a call from the base camp, located 75 miles away, telling us the bush plane could not fly out because it had to fly over a 3,000-foot mountain and the weather was bad with a lot of fog. Weather conditions often vary from one side of a mountain to the other. We had already packed our bags, so we had to unpack them all.

The next day we repacked all our bags, carried them to the

Mustard on bread, marking day 10. Our plane was five days overdue to pick us up.

shore of the lake and waited all day for the plane to arrive. It didn't show up. We tried to call the base camp, but we had lost radio contact. The following day there was still no plane. We were running out of food, so we started rationing it. We only had a couple eggs, a couple loaves of bread, some peanut butter and a small bag of apples left. Then, the guys started fighting over the food. The next day, we went back down to the shore and no plane again. To put it mildly, the guys were getting uneasy and started to argue a lot, and there was one fight. I was really glad we didn't have any alcohol in camp, that would have made a bad situation worse. Finally on the fifth day, they came to pick us up.

When we got back to Montreal with our trophies, there was a group of anti-hunters protesting and giving us a hard time about killing caribou. A couple of the guys in our group were real big guys, so we weren't too concerned about the protesters pushing us around and trying to start a fight. They wanted to make the local news. We had enough guys in our group and we felt we could handle them. However, if we got in a fight here in a foreign country, they might lock us up. I suggested we load our trophies into our pick-ups and get out of there. One of our guys was an ex-Marine; and as he walked back into the motel where we were staying to go to the men's room, the biggest guy in the anti-hunting group was waiting for him. He grabbed him and threw him down. They were rolling around on the floor punching each other. The anti-hunter grabbed my friend, Butch, by the beard and yanked half of his beard out. Butch then grabbed him around his Adam's apple and the guy turned white and passed out. A couple of us pulled Butch off the guy. By this time, somebody in the motel had called the police. When the police arrived, they asked us if we wanted to press charges. I told them to just keep those anti-hunters locked up in their cars until we got all of our gear loaded, then, we'd get out of there.

Despite the problems, I kept bringing more men up with me for caribou hunting in Canada. I'd bring up 50 clients a year. I'd stay in the caribou camp for six weeks and then come home with my last group of hunters. When my final group and I arrived back in Montreal, a couple of my customers parked their brand new four-wheel drive pick-up in the motel lot. Their trucks were stolen. This was happening every year and finally the company I was working for erected a high fence around the motel lot to protect customers' vehicles. This cut down on the theft of trucks. The police told me there is one vehicle stolen every three minutes in Montreal.

There was a total of 14 outfitters in the Sheffersville area, and four outfitters in the Kuuqquaq area. Since I was bringing more customers up every year, different outfitters would offer me a free hunt and a commission if I would promote their businesses. I chose to work for a company called Tuktu. At that time, they were the largest caribou outfitter in Quebec. Tuktu also offered to pay me to promote

One of my many sportsman shows.

them in outdoor shows in the United States. The first year with them I did four shows, including the Harrisburg Sportsman Show which is the second largest sportsman show in the United States. Within a couple of years, I was doing 15 shows a year, all up and down the East coast.

The most hunters I booked in one year included 240 for caribou hunts and 60 for bear. I was booking as many as 300 hunters a year. During the year, I averaged between 12 and 16 hunters at my camp at one time. The hardest thing for me was remembering all the hunters' names during that one-week period. I concentrated on remembering only their first names; but by the time I had memorized those names, their hunting was over and they'd leave camp. Then I'd have to start all over again with my next group. When I couldn't remember a name, I'd call the hunter, "Buddy." Six months later I'd run into a lot of these customers at outdoor shows. Some of them I wouldn't see again for a couple of years. They'd come up to my booth and address me by name, but I couldn't remember theirs.

The owner of Safari Nordik told me, at one of the shows, he also meets a lot of people every year and has the same trouble remembering names. He said to me, "Let me teach you a trick. If someone comes up to you and you're embarrassed you can't remember their name, just tell them you're sorry but you forgot their name. They'll usually only give you their first or last name. If they tell you their first name, then say, I know your first name is so and so, but I forgot your last name. If they give you their last name, use the same method in reverse. This always gets you out of an embarrassing situation."

I worked for Tuktu in Sheffersville for a good number of years. After I left Tuktu, I worked for several other outfitters in the Sheffersville area. The only reason I left one outfitter and moved to another was to get better results for my customers. One of the biggest problems I faced was getting my hunters in and out of camp on floatplanes.

At one point, I worked for Ft. Chimo Outfitters in Kuuqquaq. Years later, I went to work for the biggest outfitter in Canada, Safari Nordik. With Safari Nordik, over a six-week period, we had as many as 1,200 hunters in a single year. At the time, we had 30 camps set up out in the bush. When I was working for the Ft. Chimo Outfitters, a lot of our camps were on the Caniapiscou River. The river ran into Ungava Bay, then out into the Atlantic Ocean. We would use 150-horsepower jet boats to run up and down the river, but we could only operate on the river during certain hours of the day, because the tide could change as much as 14 feet in a day. That's the second highest tide change in the world. When I was working in Sheffersville, all the people I worked with were French Canadians. During that time, I only learned one French word—"tabernacle." It's a swear word. They use it the same way Americans use the "F" word.

When I moved my customers to Kuuqqauq. It was about 400 miles further north, but it was only a one-hour flight from there, on a small plane, to the Arctic Circle. Most of the residents in this area spoke English with the exception of the Innuit Indians. They had their own language and I could not begin to understand it. The Innuits are very friendly people when they're sober, however, if there was any alcohol around, they would drink it. They didn't drink because they enjoyed the taste. They drank to get drunk. I had a lot of them working for me in my camps. Anytime I had trouble with them drinking, I'd tell them if they got drunk in camp, I would call my boss and have him fly into camp, pick them up and fly them out. I always told my customers not to give the Inuits any hard liquor. Some of the customers thought it was funny to get the Inuits drunk. I told those hunters they were only creating problems for themselves, because the Inuits were the guides that had to take them out to hunt.

Most of our guides and cooks came over from Newfoundland. We had 50 people from a town called Old Forge Bay working for us. The town only had a population of several hundred. When the caribou season started, a large percentage of that population would leave to serve as guides and cooks working for a lot of outfitters in the area. We had a number of husband and wife teams. These Newfoundlanders were good people.

Old Forge Bay sits right on the coast of Quebec and Newfoundland. Most of the guides, when they weren't guiding, worked on crab boats. We had three or four boats in each of our caribou camps. They were 16- to 18-foot wooden boats with 20-horsepower motors. Every camp was located on a lake, so floatplanes could land and drop off supplies. Most of the lakes were good size—about one mile wide and up to 30 miles long—but we did have one small lake that was only a half mile wide and four miles long. Wind storms would come up very fast on the large lakes and the water would get real rough in a short period of time, so it was very important to have guides who knew how to operate boats in rough water. Most of our hunts began on boats. We'd put four hunters in a boat and take them up rivers and across lakes, then we'd beach the boat on shore and go on foot from there. When the water was too rough to get back to camp, we had to wait until the wind died down. Often, that meant coming back at night.

I always held a meeting the first night my customers arrived in camp. I warned them, "If you are hunting by yourself without a guide and wander off and get lost and can't find your way back to the boat and I can't find you, plan on spending the night out on the tundra. I will be back to pick you up the next morning." (After dark, it's almost impossible to find someone on the tundra.) I also cautioned my customers about trying to walk back to camp. When they're lost, what often happens is they walk in the opposite direction and go farther away from camp. I said, "As soon as you admit to yourself you're lost, stay where you are and try to start a fire. Make sure you're wearing

Hunter who died of heart attack seconds after this picture was taken.

your orange vest. A plane will fly out the next day to search for you." The tough part about this for the customer is that it can be next to impossible to start a fire, because it rains nearly every day up there.

There's not a lot to be afraid of when you stay out on the tundra overnight; however, there are some black bears, a lot of wolves and once in a great while you might see a polar bear. Over a 40-year period, I have had only two customers who died and they both died from heart attacks. Both of them died out on the tundra and I had to ask other clients to help me carry them back to camp. We called back to base camp and reported the deaths as soon as they happened. They tried to get a plane into camp the same day the deaths occurred; but bad weather conditions often restricted flying, so we had to keep the bodies overnight.

In one of these cases, the customer who passed away had other family members in camp. One time, it was a father and his son. It was very windy, and the pilots from base camp tried seven different times to land a plane on the dirt airstrip behind our camp. Each time, they had to return back to base camp, and we had to keep the body another day. The other fatality involved two brothers who were hunting together. The two brothers were making a stalk on a caribou. They crawled on their hands and knees until they got within range and then one brother shot the caribou. They walked up to the caribou and congratulated each other. The shooter posed with the caribou and his brother took his picture, then turned around to make an adjustment to his camera. When he looked back, a couple seconds later, his brother was lying there dead.

At the end of every season, the camp staff had to tear down all the tents, pull out the water pumps from the lake, and pack the leftover groceries. The base camp would always tell us when the plane would be coming in to pick us up. It usually took a day to tear the camp down and we'd have to have everything ready when the plane arrived. (If the plane had to wait more than 15 minutes to load, our

Scraping ice off the wings.

company would get charged for it.) We were sitting on the airstrip and it was snowing and blowing very hard. We waited until it was almost dark, then assumed the plane wasn't coming because it wouldn't be able to land. We carried all of the luggage back down to camp and set up one small tent, where we could sleep that night.

The plane came in and landed and we didn't hear it. The pilot walked down to our camp and told us he was waiting for us up on the airstrip. So we tore down the tent real fast and carried our gear back to the airstrip. It was just about dark. The pilot was flying a Twin Otter on wheels, which can carry 12 people with all their gear. We were somewhat overweight with our groceries and generator. The pilot was getting ready to take off when, all of a sudden, he shut down the engines; then, he went and got up on the wings and started to scrape ice off with his fingernails. A couple of us got out of the plane wondering what was taking him so long. Then the pilot got back in the plane and started up the engines. Pretty soon the pilot shut down the engines again, got out and climbed back on the wings and began scraping more ice off. Finally, he started the plane up again and off we went. Ice on the wings causes a lot of plane crashes. So we were a little nervous not knowing if he scraped enough ice off the wings to stay in flight.

There are 14 outfitters in Sheffersville and they have a total of about 20 bush planes. Just about every year, there are one or two plane crashes. Fortunately, they are not always fatal. A couple years ago, one of the outfitters I knew very well was flying a floatplane. He got out on one of the floats and didn't pay attention to what he was doing. He walked into the prop and was cut up into pieces.

One of my bosses, who co-owned Safari Nordik, holds a Guinness World Record for the most hours flown in a bush plane. He is a legend in the North Country and he's known as Johnnie May. He lives in Kuuqqauq and is an Innuit Indian. The total hours Johnnie has flown is 42,000, this is more than most commercial pilots fly. I flew with Johnnie a lot. Sometimes, we'd be in the air all day trying to find the caribou herd. You are flying low, about 500 feet up, and looking down for caribou. If a caribou herd isn't moving around on the tundra, it is very hard to spot them from the air. As I was looking

Wife Judy and Johnnie May, the legendary pilot.

down all day sometimes it made me airsick. Johnnie is really cautious and he's only had a couple of accidents in his lifetime.

His plane is a Beaver aircraft usually on floats and during the winter on skis. When he is flying on floats and the water is rough, he cannot take off or land. I sat with him many times on a lake for hours waiting for the wind to calm down, so he could take off. The only times I feel a little uncomfortable flying with him is when he's been out partying the night before and doesn't get enough sleep, and we have to leave early in the morning on a flight. I asked him one time when the two of us were flying, "What do you do when you are out partying the night before and you're flying by yourself all day? Don't you have trouble staying awake?" He said sometimes he does have trouble. I asked him what happens when he falls asleep. He said he'd show me. He set his controls on automatic pilot, folded his arms, dropped his head and shut his eyes. I watched him and we flew that way for about 15 minutes. I asked, "John are you awake?" He said, "Yes!" He folded his arms again and dropped his head and we flew another 10 minutes this way. All of a sudden, the plane went into a dive. I hollered, "John!" He grabbed the controls and brought the plane out of its dive. Then he said, "That's what happens." I asked him what if he hadn't woken up. He said, "So far, I have every time." Then he laughed.

I was in caribou camp one day working when my two Safari Nordik bosses flew in. I walked down to the shore and grabbed the rope to pull the plane in. I tied the plane fast to the dock and then noticed my bosses, the Inuit from Kuuqqauq and the Frenchman from Montreal, were arguing about something. They came up to me and pointed up the hill behind the camp, where I was flying the Quebec flag. I always kept a flag on the high point behind the camp, so hunters out on the tundra could see the flag for miles. That would help them find their way back to camp.

Some years, we fly a Quebec Flag; other years, we fly a Canadian flag. The Innuit told me to get up there and take the Quebec flag down. The Frenchman told me to leave it up there. They kept going back and forth. I thought they were only kidding each other. Then I realized they were serious. What I didn't know at that time was that the province of Quebec was voting to separate itself from the rest of Canada. I realized later this was really a big issue in Quebec. My French boss wanted to separate from Canada and the Innuit didn't. Before I left to fly to Kuuqquaq, I went to a lot of shopping centers in Montreal and found that none of the stores sold the Canadian flag. The only flag you could buy was French Canadian. The entire city wanted to be separated from Canada that year and that's why I couldn't find a Canadian flag. I understand the separation issue vote takes place in Canada every four years.

When I first came to Kuuqquaq and was working for Ft. Chimo Outfitters I only had a couple of customers. We were flown in by Alan Stone in a Cessna airplane on floats. It was a pretty small plane for the North Country and landing it on big lakes when the water was rough was very scary. Alan's plane would only carry him, three passengers and their luggage. My two customers and I flew into a spike camp which was set up for no more than four hunters. I had to do all of the cooking and take care of all of the capes, butchering and guiding. I am definitely not a cook, but this is the way the camp was set up. We hunted there for a couple of days and then the base camp called me on the radio and told me a big storm was coming in that night. I didn't give it much thought, because these storms come and go.

That afternoon, Alan flew into my camp with his Cessna plane. He said he was ordered to pick us up and move us to another camp—one which was much larger, had a bigger staff and a lot of hunters. I told him we were fine and had everything we needed and I would prefer to stay where we were. He said he had orders to move us. I said, "Ok, give us a little bit of time until we can get our bags packed and then we can fly over to the next camp." By the time we were getting ready to take off, the lake had a lot of white caps; it was getting to the point where it was unsafe to take off. We took off anyway, flew about ten minutes, arrived at the lake by the new camp and dropped down to land. The lake was much bigger and the water was really rough.

Usually, accidents happen more often when you're landing than when you're taking off. We touched down on the lake, then bounced up in the air, dropped back down, then bounced up and down again. I remember Alan saying this was dangerous. When we finally touched down on the lake and taxied into shore, there were about 10 hunters standing taking pictures. Alan said he was told to drop me off and then fly a couple of my customers back to Kuuqquaq. The two customers tipped me and I put the tips in my shirt pocket and got out of the plane.

As I walked toward camp, Allen, the manager, came down to meet me and introduced himself. Right then, I heard the customers standing on the shore saying, "He's going, he's going, he's going." I turned around, looked over my shoulder, and saw the plane's wings flipping over. The plane flipped upside down and was sinking real fast. There were a couple of boats sitting on the shore but they were full of water due to the waves breaking over their sterns. A bunch of guys ran down with buckets and baled out the water as fast as they could. Other guys were trying to turn the boats around, so their bows would be facing into the waves. They pushed the boats off shore while others were trying to start the motors. The motors wouldn't start because the carburetors were full of water. They finally got one motor started and raced out to the plane as fast as they could. It was only about a quarter of a mile off shore. When they reached it, the only things holding it up were the floats.

One of my customers who was in the plane had done some deep-sea diving back home and that's what saved him. He knew how to hold his breath for a long period of time. The water pressure knocked the windshield out of the plane and he said he saw a small hole and worked his way out through it. The pilot and the other guy did not survive. At this time, the pilot who drowned was going through a divorce, and his wife saw this as an opportunity to sue the outfitter and make a small fortune. She filed a two-million dollar lawsuit against the Ft. Chimo Outfitters. It was settled years later.

The officials asked me questions since I was on the plane a couple minutes before it flipped over. I told them the pilot was wearing waders and that most of the bush plane pilots wear waders because they're often in the water. They felt that Alan's waders filled up with water and that extra weight stopped him from getting out. What I didn't tell them was that when we flew in we didn't have any seats in the back of the plane. We just threw all of the caribou meat and the baggage in the back of the plane and told the passengers to sit on top of their duffle bags. (It's a law that everyone has to be in a seat with their safety belts on.) When the plane flipped over, all the meat and baggage they were sitting on probably landed on top of them. Maybe that's what kept them pinned and kept them from getting out of the plane. While the others were out trying to rescue the men, I ran up to camp and called, "May Day, May Day" in to the main base camp and they answered right away. I told them what happened and where we were located. They said they'd send another plane in as soon as possible. They also knew it was unsafe to fly.

Finally, one of the bigger floatplanes, an Otter, flew in. The pilot was instructed to pick me up and fly me to one of the other spike camps where the owner of the company was with a couple of customers. I didn't know for sure where this camp was located, but I knew a week earlier we had dropped some guys off at this camp along the Caniapiscou River. We kept flying around looking for the camp and it kept getting darker. All at once, I saw the camp and told the pilot, "That's it." The pilot was French and we didn't communicate very well. Finally, he figured out what I was trying to tell him and we landed on the river, which wasn't nearly as rough as the lake. The father of my customer who had drowned was in this camp. I had to tell him his son had drowned. That night we flew back to Kuuqquaq. They used a rescue squad made up of deep-sea divers to get the two bodies out of the plane.

The next day they flew me into another camp by myself and told me to get it ready for a party of 14. The following week didn't go well. The hunting was poor and the 14 customers were upset and I was having a hard time after losing a good friend I had known for years. There was a doctor in camp and he told me to just get over it. It was only a death. I guess being a doctor he was used to dealing with death. I wasn't and I was taking it very hard and I still had three more weeks in camp. They were a rough three weeks.

A couple of years later, I had a group of 14 fly into my camp on a Twin Otter on wheels. When the plane reached the landing area, there were caribou all over the airstrip. The pilot had to buzz the field a number of times to chase the big herd of caribou off the strip. Finally, he got all the caribou off and landed the plane. By this time, the customers were all worked up. When I opened up the doors of the plane, they baled out as fast they could. While I was taking their baggage and gun cases off the plane, the hunters were grabbing their guns and digging into their duffle bags for ammo. I was still busy unloading the week's groceries and baggage when I heard shots going off all around me. I looked up and everybody was running after caribou and shooting. I yelled at them to stop. Finally, the caribou herd ran off and the shooting stopped. There were caribou lying all over the place, I told the shooters they better have tags for every caribou they'd killed. Each hunter was allowed two caribou. There were a couple of cows lying there dead and nobody wants to shoot cows, everyone wants bulls. I had trouble getting the hunters to tag the cows, so I told them if they didn't tag the cows, I'd have to call the game warden. They came up with tags after that, but I wouldn't have called the game commission.

Human skull found on the tundra.

My wife Judy with Georgian, my camp cook for 10 years.

We used the cows as camp meat and I gave the hunters their tags back, so they could tag a bull.

One time, I had a group of hunters in camp and two of them were New York City detectives. Both had GPS's. This was the first time I saw a GPS. I always used a compass. One day, the detectives were out hunting, when they came back to camp they told me they had something to show me. One of them reached into his backpack and pulled out a human skull. They said they found it lying on top of the tundra. They had marked the spot where they found it with their GPS's. The following day, the group flew back to Kuuqquaq and the detectives reported their finding to the authorities in Kuuqquaq. That night Nicolus, owner of Safari Nordik, called me on the radio to tell me a couple of Canadian Mounties would be coming into camp; they would have the same type of credentials as FBI agents do in the states.

My wife, was also coming into camp the next day. When she arrived, my female cook, Georgian, and I were the only ones there. The cook and I had decorated the camp for Judy's arrival. This was the first time my wife had visited my caribou camp and we hadn't seen each other for several weeks. We took four single beds and put them together to make one king-size bed for Judy and me. My wife was a little upset when she found out Georgian and I had spent many weeks together in camp by ourselves when we didn't have customers. I tried talking to her and explaining there was nothing going on between us. It was only a working relationship. Georgian tried to explain to Judy that we didn't have a choice. Sometimes, the staff has to wait a week or two before new customers arrive.

The two Canadian Mounties flew into camp the next day. They said they would be spending the next several days in camp with me I had to go out on the tundra with them everyday to look for more human remains where the detectives had found the skull. They said they had to see if foul play was involved. Three of us went out everyday looking for bones. They kept picking up bones and asking

My wife Judy helping out in caribou camp.

me if they were caribou bones. There were a lot of caribou bones lying all over the tundra—some from prior hunts and others from wolves. This went on for days and days. They kept asking me over and over again whether the bones they found were from caribou. After a while, I thought I'd play a little trick on them. They picked up a couple more bones and asked me the same question again. I told them I wasn't sure what kind of bones they were, but I did know for sure they weren't caribou bones. They looked at me and said, "Kenny are you sure or are you just giving us a hard time?" I told them I wasn't; the bones looked like human bones to me. They got out a plastic bag, put a tag on it and marked it. They said, "You better not be kidding us. We don't want to get back to Kuuqquaq and find out these are caribou bones." After that, they stayed in camp a few more days shooting lots of ptarmigans, which is in the grouse family.

My wife spent the rest of the week with me. She is the only person I had in camp who never saw a caribou. After a year went by, we got a report from the Canadian Mounties that the skull was from a young girl. They said they traced it back to a girl who had mental problems. She would often wander off from her home, and at times, be gone for a couple months. Our camp, where the skull was found, is 90 miles from Kuuqquaq. The girl would have had to been wandering around on the tundra for a long period of time. It would take nearly a month to walk from Kuuqquaq to our camp. There are a lot of lakes she would have had to walk around. More than likely, she starved to death or froze.

Another year, I had a group of hunters who were in the second to last day of their hunt and hadn't seen any caribou. My boss was flying around in his plane trying to locate a herd. Late that afternoon, he called me from his plane and said he saw one of the largest herds of caribou he'd ever seen in his lifetime. He said, "It looks like the front of the herd is about two miles wide and it's 10 to 15 miles deep." When a herd that big, with thousands of caribou, comes through camp, it lasts for days and days; it's a sight to behold. In over 40 years of hunting, I had only seen the large migration five times—where they came through the camp by the thousands, lasting for days. I told the hunters only one out of a hundred hunters would ever have the opportunity to see a large herd like this. My boss told me the herd was about 10 to 15 miles from camp, so we'd probably see them sometime the next day. A migrating caribou herd will travel up to 50 miles in a single day.

I woke up early the next morning, right before daylight, and when I went outside and looked around, I saw caribou everywhere. I yelled out to the hunters, "Get up, there are caribou all over the place." When they got up and looked outside, the caribou were coming right through the camp. They grabbed their rifles and began shooting. I told them to be careful, because they were only allowed two caribou each. One of the guys came walking up to me shaking his head. I said, "I know what you did. You shot three of them." Then another hunter came up and told me he'd done the same thing. Then a couple more owned up to making the same mistake. We spent the next couple of hours trying to straighten things out by deciding who was going to tag the extra caribou. We had plenty of camp meat for the next couple weeks.

One other time, there were only two hunters in my camp for a week—a doctor and his son from Philadelphia. My job was to cook, guide, pack out their caribou and take care of the capes and the meat. I would take them out in the morning and drop them off; come back to camp and do the chores; then go back out and pick them up in the evening. The young boy was only about 18 years old. His goal was to hunt all of the North American species, then go to Africa and get all of the species there. His father was very rich and every day he complained about my cooking. I had a little wood stove for heat and I used the same stove to cook on. I had a very small coffee pot and both of them were big coffee drinkers. Each of them carried a quart coffee thermos when they were out hunting. In the mornings, they would complain that the coffee wasn't ready on time. That's because I had to make three different pots on the stove, plus cook on top of the stove.

The boy told me he was a member of the North American Hunting Club and the SCI International Safari Club; and, when he got back home, he was going to write a story for the clubs' magazines about the bad hunt he and his father had with Safari Nordik. I had heard this type of complaining many times in the past when a hunter was dissatisfied. That morning I took them out in the boats and dropped them off. Then, all day back at camp, I thought about those two complaining the whole time. It was working on my nerves. I was planning what I would say to the young man when I picked him up. I was going to tell him, "If you think this is a bad hunt, you better give up hunting right now; I can tell you that you'll be on worse hunts than this." When I went out to pick them up and got out of the boat, the boy, who was about 6'4", came right up to me. He picked me up and threw me in a circle while jumping up and down. He said, "This

My friend Duke the orange pumpkin.

is the most wonderful hunt I have ever been on." Then he shook my hand and thanked me. He gave me all sorts of praise. That's how fast a hunt can turn around.

A lot of hunters feel they're having a bad hunt when they don't kill something. Then, as soon as they shoot something, everything is wonderful. I tell my young hunters there's more to hunting than killing. Just to be out in nature is a plus all by itself; when you harvest your game, that's an added bonus.

I had a customer named Duke from York County, Pennsylvania, not very far from my hometown. He hunted with me a number of times. Duke was an older gentleman. He was overweight and had a lot of trouble walking. I usually tried to set him up right around camp, so I could keep a eye on him. He was always afraid of getting lost, even when I took him out on an ATV and set him up only a quarter mile from camp. I always made sure he could see camp from where he was sitting, but he was still a very nervous person and afraid of getting lost. To make sure we could see him, he always came dressed in orange pants, coat, hat and gloves. When I sat him on the mountain, he looked like a pumpkin.

The cook I had in camp was 24 years old and lived in Old Forge Bay. She also cooked for me in my bear camp. We often spent a lot of time in camp alone when we didn't have customers. One day, when Duke was sitting on top of his knob, we went out for a walk and looked up on the hill at him. We could see there was a big herd of caribou right behind Duke. He didn't see them because he was looking the opposite way. I forgot to mention that Duke's eyesight was very bad. The caribou then walked on both sides of him and he still didn't see them. All at once, we saw him jump up and we both yelled, "Shoot, Duke, shoot!" He was pointing his rifle toward the caribou and pumping bullets out as fast as he could, but he never fired a shot. When I went up to talk to him, I asked, "Why didn't you shoot?" He said, "I thought I was shooting." Right there at his feet in front of him were five fully loaded bullets lying on the ground.

There were a lot of caribou in the area at that time and I told Duke I would go out with him the next day to make sure he got his caribou. When we went out the next morning, we ran into a group of eight really good bulls. I laid Duke's backpack on top of a large rock, took his rifle, and put it on top of his backpack. I looked through his scope and put the crosshairs right on the biggest bull in the herd. The caribou were only about 150 yards away. I told him to take his time, look through the scope and make sure the real big bull was right in the center of his crosshairs. He looked and looked and then he told me he couldn't see them. I checked and the crosshairs were still on the big bull. I said, "Look in there. All you have to do is pull the trigger." He said, "I can't see them." I knew at that point I was in big trouble. The bulls kept getting further and further away and now they were about 250 yards out. I checked again and the bulls were still right in the crosshairs. Duke said to me, "Shoot 'em for me." I said, "No

Duke you shoot 'em. They're all there in a group." Duke said I should shoot at the pile. I didn't shoot any of them for him and the small herd walked off. That was it for the day.

The next day I told one of my guides to take Duke out and to make sure he got two bulls. The guide said, "What do you mean by that?" I just told him to make sure Duke got two bulls and not to come back until he had two bulls. He took him out on the four-wheeler and not long after that I heard a shot, then a few minutes later I heard another shot. A couple hours later they arrived back in camp and Duke was all smiles. I asked, "Did you get your two bulls?" He told me he did. I walked over and looked at them, both of them had been killed with perfect shots. I shook Duke's hand, and said, "Nice shooting." I congratulated the guide on a job well done.

Over the years, I got to know Duke very well and found he had trouble with alcohol. In our camp, we offer to fly beverages in, but it's very costly to have beer flown into camp. Every year, Duke ordered a couple of cases of beer flown in for himself. At camp, the charge was $50 for a case of beer. We always told our customers that beverages could be flown into camp the same day they arrived, if the plane was not overloaded. The luggage and groceries had first priority on the plane. Oftentimes, the beer wouldn't get to camp until two or three days after the customers. Sometimes, Duke would order his beer but it wouldn't get loaded on the plane with him. It wouldn't even get there on the second or third day. Every time a plane would fly over our camp, Duke would say, "There goes my beer." If there was any beer remaining when the customers left camp, they left it for the staff.

One time, I had a couple of six-packs remaining from a prior group and I hid them under some of bushes outside camp. Duke kept fussing about his beer, so I told him where I had hidden the six-packs up on the hillside. His eyes lit up and he got a big smile on his face. He started to walk up the hill looking all around for the beer. He looked like a kid on an Easter egg hunt. He couldn't find it, so I went up and showed him where it was. He was in his glory when I gave it to him. Every year after that, he would always bring me a six-pack of beer to the Harrisburg Outdoor Show.

That evening, I had to pick up some of my caribou hunters from the other side of a lake near our camp. I reached the opposite shore a little bit before dark. There were five hunters waiting for me and all of them had killed a caribou and the meat was ready for me to load. I loaded the meat and the caribou antlers on the boat first. There was probably about 600 pounds of meat. I told the hunters to get in the boat very carefully because it was overloaded. It was a 16-foot wooden boat with a 20-horsepower motor. By the time all five hunters climbed aboard, the water was only a couple of inches from coming into the boat. I told my passengers to sit tight and don't move or rock the boat. I was going to try and get all of us back to camp in one trip. It was getting dark and I didn't want to have to make another trip across the half-mile lake. Fortunately, they were all scared, none of them moved and the water was calm. If anyone in that boat would have made a real fast move, the water would have come over the side and the boat would have sunk. The customers thought the lake water was real deep. I didn't tell them the lake was only three feet deep and they could have gotten out and walked.

Sometimes, we have hunters in camp who don't want guides. When that happens, the unguided hunters are responsible for quartering and packing out any caribou they kill. That means they'll have to carry about 80 pounds of meat out on the their backs. That's hard work, but that's our policy for unguided hunts. I tell the unguided customers to carry out the two hind quarters first and then to go back the next day for the front quarters and the head. The antlers won't go bad, but the meat will.

One day, when I was working around camp, a hunter came

back to camp carrying his two hind quarters. He was all excited telling me he had shot a bull. I said, "Calm down and I'll go back in with you to pack out the rest of the meat." Around the area where he shot the bull, there were a lot of bushes. I asked him, "Are you sure you know where the caribou is? Did you tie any fluorescent orange on the antlers or the bushes?" He said, "I think it's over there right under that bush." Then he walked over and said, "No it isn't." We looked all around and just kept walking in circles. All of a sudden, I yelled, "There he goes. Shoot him." He took his gun off his shoulder, and said, "Where is he?" He was so excited, he laughed and said to me, "His two quarters are back at camp." Eventually, we found the two front quarters and the head and packed it back to camp.

One time, when I was working around camp, I saw a white animal a couple of miles away out on the tundra. I just took for

The polar bear that never came back to the U.S.

Twin Otter testing my airstrip.

granted that it was a white wolf, so I didn't pay much attention to it. About an hour later, I looked out in that direction again and realized I was looking at a polar bear. I told Isaac, the Innuit Indian, working with me in camp, what I saw. I grabbed my rifle and Isaac went to get his rifle. I looked at his rifle and told him, "You can't take that rifle. It's only a 22 magnum." He kept saying in broken English, "I will kill." I told him I had another rifle and he could take it. I had a hard time convincing him to take my other gun. Finally, he did, and we both jumped on the three-wheeler and took off across the tundra. We caught up to the bear, shot it and it ran into the bay. We had to go back to our camp and get a boat, so we could tie the bear behind the boat and drag him back to camp. Fortunately, when a polar bear is shot and falls into the water it floats. This took place during the time when you weren't allowed to bring polar bears back into the United States. The U.S. was talking about opening up the polar bear season again, so you could bring hides into the states; but it wasn't open yet.

We caped the bear out, salted the hide, and I asked Isaac if he would keep the hide for me for a couple of years until I could bring it back into the states. I told him I'd give him several thousand dollars for the hide. He kept saying he wanted to make a pair of mittens and booties for his wife. The next day he wanted to go out and hunt seals. I said I'd go with him. To shoot seals, you need to go about five miles out. All Isaac had was two 18-foot canoes, so he fastened them together side-by-side and attached a 60-horsepower Mercury motor. The canoes were full of patches. I don't know how they stayed afloat. We went out and shot a large seal and brought it back to camp. Isaac cut a small two-inch slot in the belly of the seal and began pulling out its intestines. He told me that after he had removed all the intestines his wife would cut them into real small slices, cook them in water and make soup for us. I wasn't looking forward to supper.

When I was working in Quebec, I did more than just run a hunting camp. One time, I actually helped build an airstrip. Well, maybe build is not the right word. One day, my boss called me and told me to go for a walk out on the tundra and see if I could find a flat area where a Twin Otter plane with wheels could land. The Twin

Outdoor TV personality Jimmy Houston in center.

Otter is a very expensive plane that can carry two pilots and 14 passengers. He told me what the length of the airstrip would have to be. I didn't have a tape measure, so I went out and found a flat area and stepped off what he said the length should be. The flat area was a little bit shorter than what he told me it had to be, but it was the only flat area I could find near our camp. I took white paint and painted about 50 rocks. I put 25 of the white rocks on each side of the airstrip, so the pilot could see the strip from the air and know where to land.

The pilot flew in and landed with no problem, but flying out was another story. He had to transport 12 hunters, me, luggage and meat. The plane was already overloaded when Isaac's daughters came down to the airstrip to get a ride. These ladies were overweight. They told the pilot they weren't feeling well and needed to be flown into Kuuqquaq to see a doctor. The law in Kuuqquaq requires that pilots find room for nationals on their planes. The pilot told me he knew the women weren't sick. This was just an excuse for them to get into town, but he had to take them.

The pilot loaded up the plane then backed it up as far as he could. With all the extra weight, he needed a longer take-off area to get the airplane off the ground. At the far end of the airstrip was a 30-foot drop-off. We took off down the runway and kept going and going and going. I kept looking out the window thinking to myself we were running out of white rocks. I knew we were at the end of the airstrip and were still on the ground; but, at the last second, we lifted off and I breathed a sigh of relief. After we were airborne, the pilot called into the international airport in Kuuqquaq and told them he had just about wrecked their plane and would never fly another plane into that camp. That was the last time my airstrip was used.

Over the years I've had the opportunity to meet, hunt with and guide a number of celebrities. I had Jimmy Houston in my camp, and representatives from Browning and Mossy Oak. I've also had the Eastmans and Keith Warren in camp. Keith hunted out of our camp for six straight years. I'm also friends with Bob Falkrod. This past year, Oliver North invited me to go duck hunting with him in Virginia. Oliver North is a combat-decorated marine and has documentary series War Stories on the Fox News. I've been fortunate to have hunted with a lot of special people.

Out on the African Plains

After hunting deer, turkey, bear, mountain lions and caribou in the United States and Canada, I thought it would be great to visit Africa just to see the country. I also thought I'd have an opportunity to hunt four or five species of game on the African Plains. Friends of ours, Jack and Betty Buch, had a daughter, along with her husband, Chuck, living in Africa. They were missionaries with the Nazarene Church. We had met Chuck when he was on deputation and visited our church to talk about his mission work. He also showed us a photograph book of pictures he'd taken in Africa. Chuck was also a hunter.

We shared with Jack and Betty our interest in going to Africa. Then they told us maybe we could visit their daughter, Judy, and her husband and stay at their house. We made arrangements to stay with Chuck and Judy for a three-week vacation. While we were there, they took us to Kruger National Park, where we stayed for three days. We had one of the most memorable times we'd ever had. We saw practically every animal species that was in the park, including elephants, cape buffalo, lions, giraffes, and Plains game like baboons, warthogs and hyenas. We stayed in a rondoval—a round building with a thatched roof. It was pitch dark at night and we could hear elephants trumpeting and lions roaring all through the night. There were high fences built around the complex where we stayed. They'd lock the gates at 6:00 p.m. each night to protect the residents.

My son Kenny was thirteen years of age at the time we went on our South African Safari. Thirteen is a good age to teach a son to hunt, so that's what I did. He really enjoyed his African hunts and still talks about them today. He went out with Chuck and me to hunt. He killed an impala and a warthog. During this period of time, there was an uprising in Mozambique and a lot of terrorists were still in the country. You had to be very careful where you went. I was told before I went to Africa that I would not be allowed to wear camouflage clothing, because that clothing was associated with the terrorists. I did take a camouflage belt with me, but they would not let me wear it. Chuck, being a missionary, knew his way around the area and was familiar with the nationals.

Chuck and I went on a six-day safari with an outfitter to hunt Plains game. We camped out in the bush and slept in a tent. The outfitter and Chuck told me to always sleep with a loaded rifle next to me. That's because there were still a lot of terrorists in the area and a lot of killings. They told me that some of the native black people that are around you during the day, even those that are working for you as cappers or trackers, could be terrorists. You don't know who the terrorists are. Night is when they can sneak into your tent and cut your throat. I was really scared. I kept my rifle in my hands all night and tried to sleep with one eye open.

Ultimately, this hunt was very successful. I killed five species of Plains game, including a very rare animal, a Tsessebe. After I shot it, my trackers had to track this animal for several miles. Anybody who has hunted in Africa will tell you how amazing these African trackers are. This wounded Tsessebe left only a single drop of blood about every 20 to 30 yards. The trackers got on this trail and followed it like they had a heavy blood trail. When tracking blood

Ken Jr. with his impala.

Ken Jr., Judy and Judy Gates and daughter at leopard preserve.

trails, their eyes are so much better than ours it's astounding; and they look for a lot more than just blood. They look for pebbles that are overturned and blades of grass that are bent or broken off. On this trail, the trackers got to an area and four of them were standing in a circle pointing to the ground and making a real big fuss. I couldn't understand what they were saying, so I asked my PH what they were saying. (The trackers call the guides PH's which stands for professional hunter.) He told me the trackers were saying the Tsessebe laid down right there where there was a lot of blood. I looked in the sand where they were pointing and couldn't see any blood at all. I asked, "Where?" and they kept pointing. Finally, I had to put my finger in the sand where they were pointing and I got a little bit of blood on my finger. They tracked that Tsessebe another quarter of a mile and found it lying there dead.

Leopard kitten.

While Chuck was out hunting, his wife, Judy, and her family invited, my wife, my son, and I to a leopard preserve. There was a high fence around the preserve and it housed 39 leopards. Visitors were given a chance to pet some of the leopards. There was also a female leopard there with her kittens. The owner of the preserve showed us around and we found it very exciting. He told us not to make any fast moves while we were inside the fenced-in area. The owner asked where the other husband, and Chuck's little girl said, "Daddy is out hunting." This raised the owner's eyebrows. We got to take some very interesting pictures while we were there.

During our stay, Chuck took us to a lot of the villages in the area, but he wouldn't let us get out of the car, because the villagers were going through their rituals. In this area, they circumcise their young boys at the age of twelve and then send them out in the bush for a month. If the boys don't die and they make it back to their villages after that month, they can claim their manhood. Chuck explained to us that the witchdoctors had demons in them and it wasn't safe to be around them.

I learned another thing about the culture in this area. Every white household had several black people working for them. If you were a white homeowner, you'd usually have about four blacks working for you as maids, gardeners, or cooks, as full-time employees. They'd receive a small wage. I had difficulty accepting this lifestyle. I'm not prejudiced and I feel the way the blacks are treated there is very unfair. That would never be accepted in America.

On the last day of our hunt, I got ready to tip my PH, my black trackers and cappers. We had about five blacks with us at all times and they worked very hard. I started to give them what I thought was a fair tip. My white PH saw what I was doing and came over, grabbed my money and said, "You don't tip them. You give the money to me and I'll tip them what I think is fair." The PH was getting paid well over a $100.00 a day, plus tips. The blacks were making less than one dollar a day. The guide said, "You Americans always tip the blacks too much." He told me a nice tip for the black trackers would be a ball cap. The men like it if you give them money because a lot of them are saving money to purchase a wife. After they save a certain amount, they go to a girl's father and offer him a price for his daughter.

Years later, before I went to Africa again, I went to a flea market near my home and bought about six watches to take with me. I also took a lot of caribou hats and a whole duffle bag of used dresses that I had purchased at a Goodwill store. When I passed these items out to my black helpers, they gave me a lot of praise and acted like I gave them the world. They were very happy and they showed their friends their watches. The PH told me we should treat them like slaves and not let them get ahead. He said, "We want them to know white people are more superior." This hunt took place before apartheid was abolished.

The PH did not want me to call them by their names. He always addressed them with the "N" word. The cooks in camp would pack a nice lunch for the PH and me and put ice in the cooler so our drinks would stay cold. When we took lunch breaks, during the hottest time of the day, we'd usually get out of the land rovers and settle in a shady spot under a tree. We'd sit in the shade and the five trackers would sit several yards away. The whites and blacks didn't mix together at all in Africa. In the villages, you would never see a white woman with a black man, or vice a versa. If you were seen with a black girl, your own people would have nothing to do with you.

Our lunch usually consisted of a couple of sandwiches, oranges, and cold drinks. The blacks had a white meal, called Meali Meali. In my lunch, there was always more than I could eat. One day I went over to where the black trackers were sitting, reached into my lunch bag, got some food out, and passed it around. I gave one of the blacks half of my cold soda that I couldn't finish and my PH guide yelled at me, "What are you doing? You don't give those guys anything." He came over, grabbed all of the food and took my soda and dumped it out right in front of them. That was hard for me to accept. After that, I learned to go behind his back and share with them every chance I got.

I went back to Zimbabwe for a 28-day hunt. I was trying to get two of the five dangerous game animals. The big five in Africa include the rhino, elephant, leopard, cape buffalo and the lion. Out of the big five, I was trying to harvest the leopard and the cape buffalo. My PH's name was Claude. Claude had started baiting for leopards a couple of weeks before I got there. One of the better baits for leopards and lions is zebra meat. You pay for every animal they put out for bait and the zebra is one of the higher priced baits. You can also use impala and warthogs because they cost less. They usually put out six baits. Sometimes they'll put out as many as ten or more and that can be very costly. They can get enough meat out of one zebra to make several different baits. Before putting the bait out, they drag the zebra behind a Land Rover for miles to lay a scent trail. When leopards cross over this trail, they'll follow the scent to the bait.

They hunt lions this way, too. The trackers build a blind out of high dry grass. They build it in a circle and weave it so tight you can't see out and animals can't see in. They leave one small hole and that's where you place your rifle. They lay blankets on the floor of the blind and have a chair for you to sit on. If you are planning on staying in there for the night, you can lay down on the blankets and pillows. It's quite comfortable. However, you try to get most of your sleep during the day, because the game usually shows up at night. During the day you can also hunt for Plains game or shoot more animals for bait.

That year I shot so many animals for bait, I was running out of bullets. I told my guide I didn't want to shoot anymore and he had to shoot them. When you're hunting at night and it's pitch black, it's hard to know when a leopard is feeding on your bait. To solve this problem, they tie a fishing line onto your bait and tie the other end of the line to a limb next to your blind. You spend your night watching that limb. When the limb shakes, you know there's something pulling on your bait. Before they had high-powered batteries and strong flashlights, they'd use a 12-volt car battery with a spotlight wired to it in the blind.

They had two strict rules. One was you couldn't fall asleep and snore and the other rule was no talking or even whispering. I've sat in blinds with guides for up to twelve hours at a stretch without saying a word. If your guide sees the limb shaking, he'll tap you on the shoulder three times. That means there's a leopard on the bait and you're supposed to sit up, get your rifle ready and look through your scope toward the bait. It's too dark to see the bait. A couple of seconds later, the guide taps you on the shoulder two more times. That means get ready. A couple of seconds after that, he'll tap you on the shoulder again and that means he's ready to turn on the spotlight. You practice this tapping over and over again before it gets dark. The guide explains you have six seconds to shoot the leopard after the spotlight is turned on. That doesn't give you very much time to get the leopard in your scope. The baits are hung in a tree and the leopard has to climb up in the tree to reach the bait. As soon as the light goes on, the leopard jumps out of the tree and is gone.

I sat in a blind for 12 nights and never saw a leopard. Then, on the 13th night, a leopard came in and I shot him. He fell out of the tree and ran off. Usually, they go out looking for the wounded leopard the next morning, because it's too dangerous to look for him at night. That night, we waited for a couple of hours listening and trying to hear him dying in the brush. There were a lot of hyenas in the area and my guide was concerned. If the leopard was dead, the hyenas might come in and eat him that night. The hyena's worst enemy is the leopard. If hyenas find a dead leopard, they will tear it up and eat it in a short period of time. The guide told me he does not like going after leopards at night, but we didn't have a choice in this case. By morning there wouldn't be much left of the leopard. He told me I had to carry the car battery and he'd take his sawed off-shotgun. As we were walking through the brush, the wires between the battery and the spotlight would get caught in the brush and tear loose and our light would go out. This happened over and over again. Finally, the guide said, "We must be crazy. This is very dangerous. Let's get out of here and look for him in the morning."

The next day, when it got light, we went back in with our trackers for a couple hours but couldn't find the leopard. The PH said, "I guess you missed him." I was really disappointed. The leopard is one of the hardest of the big five animals to harvest. Just about that time, one tracker yelled that he found the leopard. When I got over to him, he held the leopard up. The head and the front shoulders were the only parts remaining. We hunted a couple more nights in that area, then moved on.

The next day we drove all day to another area to hunt cape buffalo. We were driving down a dirt road when one of the trackers yelled, "Stop, there are buffalo tracks on the road." We could see where a herd of buffalo had crossed the road. We had three or four trackers riding around with us all the time. They were always looking for game and tracks. The tracker told us, "The tracks are less than a half day old. If we get on the tracks right away, we might be able to catch up to the herd." We followed the tracks for the best part of the morning and finally caught up to the herd. There were 30 or more cows and one monster bull in the herd. My PH told me it was the biggest buffalo he'd seen in years, but it was going to be hard to get into the herd to get a good shot at it.

We waited for a long time and the bull always stayed in the center of the herd where I couldn't get a good shot at him. Finally, he jumped on a cow to breed her and I told the PH I would be able to get a shot at him. The PH said, "Let nature take its course. It wouldn't be fair to the bull if you don't let him enjoy the last couple seconds of his life." Just then, the bull slid off the cow and I took my shot. The cows all ran off and we waited about a half hour until my PH felt comfortable for us to walk over and see if the bull was dead. They are

Remains of leopard after hyenas got to it first.

My first cape buffalo.

considered dangerous animals. When we got to the bull, the PH said it was probably the biggest bull killed in this area during the last six years, and he thought it might place in the top ten in the record book. The horns measured 45" across.

The trackers and capers dressed out the bull. They took out the stomach, cut off a small piece of it and poured a little bit of water over it to clean it. It is customary when a hunter shoots his first cape buffalo for him to eat a piece of it. I said, "No way!" but my guide told me the trackers would be offended if I didn't eat it. So, I held my nose, chewed it and swallowed it as fast as I could. Then, I grabbed a Coke and washed it down.

During this 28-day safari, I was also hunting other Plains game, including sable, eland, kudu and other species. We also went out spotting at night to shoot several small cats. During this period, my guide, Claude, was in his late twenties. He had served in the armed services for his country. Every white man in his country had to enlist in the service at the age of 18. Claude fought in the war for several years. When he got out of the service, he got a job as a game warden. His main job was hunting for poachers. He told me a number of stories in which he had to kill a lot of poachers. During this particular hunt, we were in an area where Claude said there were a number of poachers. He told me if we run into them, we have to open fire on them. That was the last thing I wanted to do. I came to Africa to hunt animals, not to shoot poachers. After that, I felt very uncomfortable hunting in that area. I asked him, "Why not just capture them?" He said, "That is impossible; because they won't let themselves be captured. They know if they are caught they'll be tortured until they tell the truth about who they're working for and who's buying the ivory and the horns. After giving up that information, they would be killed." Then he told me the poachers carry guns and will fight to the death. I only hunted in that area for a couple of days, and I was never so glad to leave an area. The poachers kill elephants and rhinos for the elephant's ivory and the rhino's horn. Those items are worth a lot of money on the black market.

When there are too many of a certain species of game in a designated area, it was Claude's job as a game warden to go out and kill a number of them. One of the species that create problems are elephants. Oftentimes, a herd of elephants will go into a small village, destroy the village and kill a number of people. When a group of game wardens go after a herd of elephants, they surround them. Six game wardens walk into the herd from six different directions and shoot a number of elephants on the outer edges of the herd; then they keep working their way into the center of the herd shooting until all the elephants are down. They kill bulls, females and calves. A couple of months before I arrived in Africa, the wardens killed 150 elephants in this area.

During our 28-day hunt, Claude and I became good friends. He guides hunters from all over the world and works for almost twelve months out of the year. He told me our hunt was one of the most enjoyable hunts he had been on for a long time. He had a custom gun case made out of buffalo hide and I kept remarking how nice I thought it was and asked him if he would be interested in selling it. He said he didn't want to sell it because he had made it for himself. At the end of our hunt, he came up to me with his gun case and said, "This is yours to keep." I was shocked because I knew how much this gun case meant to him. When the outfitter took me to the airport to fly home, he asked me what I was doing with Claude's gun case. I told him he gave it to me. He said that doesn't happen. He said he never heard of a guide giving one of his customers a gift. That made me appreciate him even more as a good friend. Claude wrote to me several times after I got back home. It's nice to know when you have friends in different parts of the world.

On my next safari trip to Africa, my wife went with me again. She really enjoyed herself over there. The locals catered to us and made the trip enjoyable. We had great meals, but you don't have to do a lot to satisfy my wife. She can enjoy herself by just sitting around reading. She'll go out hunting with me when I am hunting for Plains game, but not when I am after dangerous game. The primary objective of this hunt was for me to get a male lion. The lion was one of the animals included in the big five I wanted to harvest. We flew into Johannesburg and from there it took us a day to drive to Kruger National Park. The park is the size of the state of New Jersey and my outfitter's area was situated along the edge of the state park's boundaries. We baited this

My wife Judy in Africa.

area for lions and leopards. We put baits along the edge of the park boundary to try to draw lions and leopards out of the park. (You can't hunt in the park.) I sat in a blind for eight nights on this hunt and never saw a leopard or a lion.

One night, when we were staying in the blind all night, the PH was lying down next to me. The blind was so small we were touching each other. During the night, I felt him leaning over toward me, just about on top of me. I thought to myself what is this guy doing? I hope he's not one of those funny guys. The next morning, when it got light, and we left the blind, I asked him what he was doing last night lying on top of me. He said a big snake crawled right by him and he leaned over, so it wouldn't crawl up on him. He said it was too dark for him to see what kind of snake it was. (A large majority of the snakes in Africa are poisonous.)

Several nights later, when we were in the blind, a lot of hyenas were howling right near us. As usual, the guide had two guns with him in the blind—his rifle and a sawed-off shotgun. It was so dark it was hard to see the guide lying next to me, but there was enough light for me to see him when he sat up. I heard him putting a shell in his shotgun. Then I saw him lay back down again. He did this several times during the night. In the morning, I asked him what he was doing last night getting up and down. He said, "Four different times a hyena came in right behind you. The last time he was too close to you for comfort. I wanted to shoot him, but I would have had to shoot right over top of you."

That morning as we were walking out from our blind, I was praying and thanking God for looking over us and taking care of us that night. When we got back to where the Land Rover was parked, my guide said to me, "I heard you talking to God as we were coming out." I didn't remember praying out loud. After that, he had a lot of questions for me, and I had the opportunity to share with him the salvation message. He told me that I was the only one of all the hunters he'd guided from all over the world who shared the Gospel with him. It amazes me how God opens doors. We all have the opportunity to share our beliefs everyday if we are obedient, the Bible teaches this is our purpose here on earth to share the Gospel.

When you hunt dangerous game, like the big five, you need to have a .375H&H caliber or larger gun. I had a .375 for the big game and I was using my .280 for Plains game. I felt more comfortable with my .280 than I did with the .375H&H. I asked the PH's over and over again if I could use my .280 when we went hunting for lions, because I felt more comfortable with that rifle. The last couple days of the lion hunt, we came across a track they thought might be that of a black-mane lion, so they put out several baits. When they located that lion in one of the bait areas, he was feeding on one of the baits. The night before we were going to sit on this bait, they told me if I definitely felt more comfortable with my .280, I could use it.

Remington .280 did the job.

The next morning, when we got to the bait, the lion was lying down next to it. Prior to the hunt, we had practiced a lot about what we'd do if a lion charged us. Anytime you walk through the bush, everybody walks in line behind each other. If we'd see a lion, the two PH's would step off to the side and all of us would drop to our knees and shoot into the charging lion. They also told me over and over again where to shoot the lion to kill it with one shot. The lion on the bait was only 50 yards away and looking right at us. I was aiming for his shoulder and just about the time I was ready to pull the trigger, he dropped his head and turned it a little bit. I shot him right behind his ear. If I had tried, I couldn't have placed my shot any better. He dropped on the spot. As usual, to be cautious, we waited a while before walking over to the lion. When we got there, the guide checked and said, "He's dead!" Acting the fool, I ran over and jumped on top of the lion. When I jumped on him, he was full of air and when the air came out of his lungs he left out a loud roar. I jumped up and took off running. The PH's stood there and laughed at me for a long time.

During this hunt, we were staying at the outfitter's house located on the side of a mountain. His house was a mansion. Down in the valley there was a small village of grass huts where the black people lived. One night, I was sitting out on the porch and heard singing coming from the village. The singing went on for about an hour. I thought some of the singing and music sounded familiar, but I couldn't understand the words because they were in another language. One song I recognized was a hymn we sang in our churches back home. The next morning when the black maids and cooks came up to our house to work, I was trying to tell one of them, as I was sitting out on the porch listening to their singing; I recognized a couple of the songs. She didn't understand what I was saying. Then I made motions and pointed toward heaven trying to make her understand that I had heard the songs they were singing to Jesus. All at once, a real big smile came over her face and she understood what I was trying to say. She went over to one of the other black girls who could speak a little bit of English and got her to translate what I was saying; then they invited me to come down to their village the following Wednesday night, when they had their church service.

On that night, I told my outfitter and PH that I wouldn't be having supper with them, because I was going down to the village for supper and the church service. They said, "No white person has ever been invited down to their village for any occasion." I asked them if they would drive me down to the village. They kept asking me whether I was sure I was invited. I told them I was sure. When I got down to the village, the natives were waiting for me. We went into one of the grass huts and a little fire was burning in the center of the room. There were benches lined up along the circular wall. It was so dark you couldn't recognize faces.

The pastor was a black native. First he spoke to his congregation; then he interpreted for me. At the end of the service, they passed around a little tin cup and I could hear them dropping coins into it. When the offering cup made its way to me, the pastor told me they were taking collections for him to buy a motorcycle—so he could travel from village to village holding church services. I asked the pastor how much money they were trying to raise. I knew with their currency it wouldn't be a lot in U.S. dollars. He told me how much they needed, and I had enough money in my pocket to pay the total cost, so I gave it to the pastor. He then explained to the people what I had done. It wasn't a hard choice for me, because it wasn't a lot of money in U.S. currency. When I thought about how lucky I was to go on this hunt, and how much I was spending to do it, I felt what I was giving them was a pittance. The pastor asked me if I would share with them some of my thoughts. I did and he translated. The black people in Africa think all Americans who come over to hunt are very rich. I told them that's not quite true, and I thought it was really neat that we could all serve the same Lord.

Most people who hunt in Africa for the first time book their trip to South Africa. South Africa is known for its Plains game and not so much for dangerous game. Most of the Plains game hunting in South Africa takes place inside fenced-in areas in game preserves. Almost all of the hunts are in large high-fenced areas that cover up to ten miles. You can be hunting in these reserves and hardly ever see the fences. Most hunters in South Africa, on their first safari, will kill three to five different species. When you are on a safari in Africa, you pay a real low daily rate that covers costs for room, board, and guides. There's an additional fee for each animal you kill and this is called a trophy fee. The bigger the animal you shoot, the more you pay. For example, some of the cheaper trophy fees are for animals like warthogs, impalas and jackals, which are dogs much like our coyotes. These trophy fees run from $50 to $150 per animal.

Larger Plains game includes sable, kudu and eland. These

trophies cost between $500 and $1500 each. Dangerous game costs much more. For instance, three of the big five—lions, leopards and cape buffalo—cost between $10,000 and $20,000 each; plus the daily rate goes up. The trophy fee for an elephant depends on the weight of the bull elephant's tusks and runs between $30,000 and $60,000. The highest-priced animal is the rhino. A couple years ago, the trophy fee was $30,000 per rhino. I was looking to book a rhino hunt and I talked to several outfitters. They quoted me a trophy fee of $30,000 per rhino. My wife and I talked this over and we both decided that money could be put to better use, so I didn't book the hunt. The following year, I was still thinking about going on this hunt, I talked to the same outfitters again at the Harrisburg Sportsman Show. They told me I should have gone on the hunt the previous year. The rhino trophy fee was now $60,000. Now, I knew I would never kill the big five. I could have chosen to dart a rhino with a tranquilizer gun, that cost would have been about $15,000. You shoot the rhino with a dart which tranquilizes it and then you can pose with it and have your picture taken. After that, I would've been given credit for killing a rhino and received an award for taking the "Big Five." I chose not to take this hunt because the award wasn't that important to me.

Later, I did book an elephant hunt; so I could take four out of the big five. I scheduled my elephant hunt in Zimbabwe. It was several years since I had hunted in Zimbabwe and at that time it was fairly safe. Now, the country was very unsafe. There are about 50 blacks to every one white person in Zimbabwe. Originally, all of the land and businesses in the country were owned by white people. A couple years before my latest trip, the blacks took over the country and took almost all of the businesses, properties and houses from the whites and made them get out of the country.

I have a real good friend, named Dudley, who had been coming to the Harrisburg Sportsman Show for years. One Sunday morning, when we were holding church services at the show, he told us he had found out that the blacks had come into his house and told his wife and family members they had 24 hours to get out. They took his oldest son and put him in jail. Dudley told us the blacks told his family that when he returned from the United States they would leave his son out and put him in jail to take his place. He shared with us that he had no bitterness toward the blacks at all. He said his father had owned the property—thousands of acres—before he did. Before that, his ancestors owned it. It had been passed down through generations of his family. He said, "God gave it to us and He can take it away." It was hard for me to understand how anyone could go through something like that and have no bitterness. I wasn't sure I wanted to go on this hunt, knowing a lot of the area was very unsafe. The outfitter explained to me it is not all that bad, if you give the blacks whatever they ask for. The worst thing that could happen is they'll put up roadblocks, stop you and take your gas and food.

A friend of mine, Mike Brown, wanted to go with me on this hunt to take photographs. I said, "I think I can get the outfit-

Mike Brown spent his budget on this sable.

ter to take you at the rate of a non-hunter and that's only a couple hundred dollars a day." I told Mike if he wanted to shoot a couple of Plains animals under my license, I thought that would be alright. His budget was very low and he knew how much the trophy fees would be if he killed certain species. One of the first animals he saw on this hunt was a sable, which had one of the highest-priced trophy fees for Plains game. Mike knew if he shot the sable it would take most of his budget. He couldn't pass up the temptation, so he shot it. That left him with a little bit of money, so he could still shoot a couple of the smaller Plains game.

When I booked the hunt, I knew nothing about hunting elephants; but I learned fast. Looking back on all of the hunts I've had in my lifetime, I'd say the elephant hunt was the most dangerous. You spend a lot of time driving up and down dirt roads looking for elephant tracks. When you come upon a track, your PH will try to figure out if it's a big bull elephant. If they think it is a bull worth going after, then you go into the bush tracking it. The bush is about eight to ten feet high; there are game trails running all through this bush; and it's only wide enough for a person to walk on. When you're following them, you can hear elephants breaking limbs and pushing over trees a long distance off. When you hear them trumpeting in there, it makes chills run up and down your spine.

Your PH tries to get you within 15 to 20 yards of them before you shoot. There's only one small area on the elephant's head, right behind the eye, that you aim at. If you hit this spot, you can usually put him down with one shot. If you miss that spot, the elephant will often charge you. In the first group of elephants we saw, one of the bulls came charging toward us. The trackers behind me took off running. When I saw the trackers running, I turned to run too, but my PH grabbed me and said, "Don't move!" The elephant came within 20 yards of us and then stopped. I asked my guide how close he would let him get to us before we shot. He told me he could tell when a bull was really mad and when he was going to charge and wouldn't stop. He said, "If a bull elephant shakes his head from side to side, that's a sign that he is really mad and you better be ready to shoot." Pretty soon, two other bulls in the group began fighting and they pushed each other back and forth. We were standing behind a small tree. They pushed right by us and the guide grabbed me again saying, "Don't move!" There wasn't a tree in the area big enough to really hide us.

What's really dangerous is when you're involved with a big herd and it takes off running and you don't know if they're running away from you or toward you. Later in that week, we got into a small herd of elephants that included three adult bulls. We tried to work ourselves within 20 yards of them for a shot, but they kept moving around in the bush. I couldn't get a bead on the one I wanted to take. Finally, I found a little opening in the bush where I could see the head of the bull I wanted to shoot. I thought I could hit the spot they told me to aim at. So, I shot the elephant and it dropped right down. The PH reached over, grabbed me and said, "Nice shot." Just about that time, the elephant got back up and started to run off. I fired another shot and so did my PH. Then, we both shot again and the elephant disappeared from our view. The trackers picked up his trail and we caught up with him a couple of times and the PH and I got off more shots. We trailed him for a couple more hours. I was hoping we would be able to find that elephant. In Africa, if you wound an animal and can't find it, you still have to pay the trophy fee. That meant I owed $30,000 if we weren't able to find this elephant.

Eventually, we caught up to the elephant again and I fired a couple of more shots and he went down. When we checked, he had a total of 14 bullets in him. The villagers in the area were very happy. They're always glad when hunters come to hunt elephants. The whole village comes out in the bush to help butcher the elephant. This takes a couple of days and nothing goes to waste. There's plenty of food for the villagers. Most of the money paid for trophy fees goes to support

My largest trophy ever.

local schools and roads. It's like our property taxes. The black people in the area don't own property and they don't have any income to pay for their schools or road repairs.

When I got home, the local newspaper in our area wrote a story on my elephant hunt. The following week, on the editorial page of the paper, there were several articles from PETA, the anti-hunting group. They claimed there's a shortage of elephants and they didn't appreciate the story about me killing one. A few days later, someone wrote an article wondering why we weren't concerned about the millions of children being aborted each year, but got upset about the death of one elephant. For those who think there is a shortage of elephants, I'd suggest they read the October 2012 issue of the *National Geographic* magazine. In that article, they pointed out that poachers had killed 25,000 elephants in Africa. Then, in Kenya, the game wardens killed 23 of the poachers and the poachers killed six of the game wardens. That type of thing happens often in Africa.

This past year South Africa poachers killed 668 White African rhino. They are selling the tusks on the Black Market for over a million dollars a horn. They use them to cure diseases, especially cancer. This is the Asian people's belief.

A couple of years ago I booked a small group of hunters from Tampa, Florida. The group included doctors and lawyers. They asked me to go along with them on the hunt. Doug Mohney, an attorney, and his friend, Dr. Rick, brought their father with them to videotape their hunts. I told them there wasn't anything over there I wanted to kill. I had gotten everything I was after on my previous four trips. I just wasn't looking forward to the 18-hour flight to Johannesburg. However, after a little bit of coaxing, I decided to go along with them. It was scheduled to be a 14-day Plains game hunt. This was their first trip to Africa.

When we arrived in Africa, I asked them what species they were planning on taking. They each had a list of the animals they wanted to harvest. I told them, "If you definitely have your minds set on those species, don't let your guide talk you into shooting anything else." On this hunt, our PH was also our outfitter. He was making a commission on everything they shot. The outfitter was also working with Safari Nordik. I was selling his hunts to Africa at the Harrisburg Show and spending a lot of time with him. He always told me he didn't make enough money on hunters who came over and only shot four or five species; so, to enrich his commission, he always tried to get them to shoot a lot more animals. That's where he made his profit.

These guys had a lot of money and by the time the hunt was over each of them had shot 10 species. However, it was a nightmare getting their trophies back to the United States. A couple years went by and they still hadn't received their trophies from Africa. (This had also happened to me a few times. In fact, some of my trophies I never got back.) Since these guys were lawyers, they knew what to do and they worked hard to get their trophies back. They succeeded and had their taxidermist here in the states do the mounting.

I consider myself very fortunate to have had the opportunity to go on so many hunting trips in my life and to have harvested so many trophies in so many countries. To house my trophies, I built an addition onto my house. It's 1000-square-feet with a 26-foot cathedral ceiling. I have over 200 mounts and most of them are life size. I've had this trophy room for 20 years and every year we have an open house for the public over the Christmas holidays. The room is also used when I have perspective hunters come to my house to book a hunt. I have a lot of money invested in the hunts and taxidermy work, but the government allows me to use this expense as a tax deduction. Over the past twenty years, I only can remember going in that room one time to reflect on my hunting experiences. Since my occupation, through all those years, was selling and guiding hunts, that's the last place I want to spend my time relaxing. After being in the hunting business that many years, it's easy to burn yourself out just talking about hunting 99% of the time.

The three questions I am asked most often about hunting:

1. What is the most dangerous game to hunt?
First it is the polar bear, second is the elephant.

2. What do you enjoy hunting the most?
Turkey is my favorite hunt.

3. When and where are you planning your next trip?
I don't know when. If you want to come along with me, it is free. and it will be the biggest trip I ever took "To Heaven."

Changes of a Lifetime

I entered into this world, in the year of 1941. This has allowed me to see and experience many changes during my lifetime. I have done a lot of reflecting on the past 71 years and often ask the question, "What about these changes?" In the remainder of this chapter I am going to share my observations and thoughts about these changes. These opinions and concerns are shared from my perspective and I am not saying I am right. I am not the judge of what is right and wrong, God alone has that place of authority. I am sharing them for your thought and consideration. I am using the format of asking "What About" questions, covering various subjects. I hope it will assist you in reflecting on the past era and to ponder what we may be losing in our journey of progression, as we move into the future.

WHAT ABOUT COMMON SENSE AND SIMPLICITY?

As a child, we needed to use our creativity and common sense to build our own toys. There was no playroom filled with store-bought toys. I remember the excitement of making our own kites, guns, and go-carts. The few toys that were bought, were not tossed away as soon as they broke. We found a way to repair them and that was part of the fun. Many children are so involved in sports and other activities, I wonder if they are experiencing the simple joys of childhood.

Our parents were not financially able to give their children thousands of dollars to send us to college. Nor did they encourage us to attend college and then graduate with a huge debt, without a guarantee of a job. Obviously, I was not college material, but I believed I could be successful in life without having higher education. Many of my friends lived successful lives as they found good jobs and applied themselves, with hard work and integrity. Most success in life comes from using common sense; by following the simple good principles our parents taught us, and by learning from their life's experiences.

WHAT ABOUT ALL THOSE RULES?

While traveling, I am frequently asked, where I am from. I usually get a response when I say, "I live in Lancaster County, about four miles from Intercourse, Pa." Most people have heard about this town and the Amish people. They often ask about the differences within the Mennonite people. Lancaster County has various groups of Mennonites including Amish, Horse & Buggy Mennonites, Black Bumper Mennonites and less conservative Mennonites. The differences are many, but the common ground includes their historic ties as Anabaptists and pacifists. This means they do not practice infant baptism. They practice adult baptism, as a symbol of a personal decision made as an adult, to follow and identify with Christ. People are surprised to hear I was raised Mennonite. In my early years, when someone called me a Mennonite, I would deny it as long as I could. My identity was revealed when I was seen with my mother, dressed in Mennonite style. I was then taunted by my friends, and even to this day I am teased about being Mennonite. As an adult I am proud of my heritage, and thankful for my Christian parents; who desired to live their lives in obedience to the Bible.

The conservative churches are known for their many rules and guidelines. These guidelines are used as protection, to help keep their people from the ways of the world. They look to the Bible as their source and follow the scripture, "Do not be conformed to this world, but be transformed, by the renewing of your mind."

The Amish are the most conservative and use horse and buggies for their transportation, and also use horses for farming. As pacifists, they do not serve in the military, take oaths, or hold public office. Their clothes consists of black hats for men, bonnets for women, and handmade clothing made without buttons or zippers. I didn't have to struggle with the temptation of looking and lusting at a conservative Christian woman with their modest dress.

The Horse & Buggy Mennonites are also called Joe Wengers by the locals, named after their founder, Joseph Wenger. They are allowed to use tractors with steel wheels for their farming. The ladies wear handmade, long, loose-fitting dresses, for the purpose of modesty. The women do not cut their hair and wear a white prayer covering on their heads. They take a strong stand against divorce and remarriage, abortion and birth control. My aunt and uncle who were blessed with 21 children, were part of this church.

When I grew up in the Mennonite Church there were a lot of rules that are no longer observed. I remember my older sisters were not allowed to wear white shoes, jewelry or make up. When my sisters became a member of the church, they needed to wear their hair in a bob and place a white covering on their head. This was in accordance with the belief that women should have their head covered when they pray. In the last decade my mother was one of the few women in her church who continued to wear a covering. My parents wanted me to date Mennonite girls and stay away from the "gay girls." Back in those days the word gay was used without any sexual connotation. "Gay girls" was the way a non-Mennonite girl was described or they were called "worldly or fancy." Much to my parents' disapproval, I dated a lot of "gay girls."

The men were encouraged to wear a plain suit when they became a member of the church. This suit was purchased at a special store and had a different collar than store-bought suits. My father wore a plain coat all of his life and was one of the few men that continued to wear a plain suit. I remember many sermons about dress and staying separate from the world. Over the years the rules have become less restrictive for outward appearance. The prayer coverings became increasingly smaller and eventually were only worn for church services and most women cut their hair. The radio and TV my parents protested against me bringing into their home, are no longer issues. Remarriage was not permitted, and if someone divorced and remarried they were not accepted as a member of the church. The church no longer takes a strong stand on these issues and emphasize the importance of a relationship with Jesus, allowing the Holy Spirit to lead and guide in every aspect of life. Today the only resemblance to the Mennonite Church I grew up in, would be the sign outside the church, saying Goodville Mennonite Church.

Goodville Mennonite Church where I went to church as a young person

The conservative Mennonites continue to take a strong stand on many of these issues which other churches have left behind. One statistic states, 50% of young adults are leaving the church and their faith. In the conservative churches most of their young people stay in the church. Few of their youth leave the area for a higher education. Family ties and traditions are highly valued and seen as important to maintain. I recently asked a leader of a conservative Mennonite Church, why they continue to take a strong stand on many issues. He told me, history shows when you start to compromise on principles, you start down a slippery slope and there is no way to get stopped.

The leaders of these conservative Mennonites who serve as deacons, preachers, and bishops, consider their ordination as a lifetime calling. They don't take an early retirement or receive a salary from the church for their ministry. These leaders have never attended a Bible College or seminary, but depend on the Holy Spirit to be their teacher and guide.

WHAT ABOUT THE IMPACT OF CHURCH SERVICES?

From the age of five until fourteen years old, I attended Summer Bible School every year for two weeks, and another two weeks at a neighboring church. During this time I was taught many Bible stories, in addition to memorizing the Lord's Prayer, the books of the Bible and the Ten Commandments. What I learned at Bible School, remained with me all of my life. Today they call it Vacation Bible School, which typically lasts for only five days and in most cases is only for children, with no classes for the teenagers to attend. Today, families are so busy with sports, vacations, and other commitments, I wonder if they are missing the most important activity of the summer?

We also had Revival Meetings which lasted for two weeks at our church and in addition we would attend neighboring churches for their revival meetings. This gave a specified time and opportunity to hear from God and to respond to the Holy Spirit's conviction. We were given the invitation to ask for and receive forgiveness and to make a commitment to Jesus, as Lord and Savior. Many churches no longer have revival and renewal meetings and I wonder if people are missing out on the opportunity to commit and rededicate their lives to Christ.

As a youth I was required to attend Young People's Meeting every Saturday night. If my parents found out I didn't attend, I wasn't allowed to use their car the following weekend. We also had weekly Wednesday night prayer meetings, and frequently had a Sunday night service as well. Today it is uncommon to see churches open on Sunday nights. I realize being in a church doesn't make you a Christian anymore than being in a garage makes you a car but I do believe we are missing an opportunity to grow in our Christian walk.

Some churches have stopped church services on Sunday nights and started small home groups. Churches promote this as a setting where relationships and discipleship can take place. I have attended some of these small groups and they were very good and spiritually beneficial. Some of the small groups consisted of a brief devotional and the majority of the time was for social interaction and refreshments. A friend told me his small group serves beer on tap for their refreshments. I wonder if more, or less, discipleship is happening in these small groups?

The biggest outdoor show I did in Harrisburg, I always missed two Sunday morning church services. I didn't feel God wanted me to miss church, I wanted to be sure I honored the Lord's day. In several smaller shows some of the outfitters were Christians and we would get together and have a small church service. At the Harrisburg Show there were 100's of outfitters and vendors. My wife and I along with two other outfitters formed a church service for the two Sunday mornings we were at this show. We went to the management of the show and asked if they would announce we were holding a church service.

They said they could not because this was a public building, so we decided to pass out flyers. My wife and I and seven other people passed out flyers. My wife had the most time to spare, so she passed out most of the flyers. To cover the building complex took her several hours. When my wife laid these flyers on the tables a lot of outfitters would give them a quick glance. There were some smart remarks made to my wife, but she just kept smiling. This church service has continued over the years.

WHAT ABOUT RESPECT FOR OUR PLACES OF WORSHIP?

Guidelines pertaining to dress seem to be an antiquated issue in most churches, and no one wants to bring it to our attention. I want to share with you some things I have seen, that concern me. Some parents allow their sons to wear baseball caps during the church service. It amazes me the way a lot of the men dress up during the week for their jobs, and on Sunday go into God's house wearing casual shirts and jeans. This appears to be a trend pastors are buying into as well. Again I am not saying what is right or wrong, I just wonder if God is pleased with what is happening in His house, designated for His purposes.

I have seen a group of teenage girls standing in front of the church singing. All were wearing short, shorts. Several people felt it was so inappropriate, they walked out. A girl in her early twenties stood in front of me during worship. Her shorts were so short, I was seeing part of her cheeks and I am not talking about the cheeks on her face. I moved to another part of the church so I wouldn't have to deal with this distraction as I was there to focus on God. A couple Sundays before this, the pastor's message was on dressing modestly. He told us some of the men in the church came to him, and asked him to preach on this. The men said they have to fight this in the world, and they don't want to have to fight this temptation in God's house.

One Sunday, our pastor announced that a lady in the church was sending inappropriate emails to another man in the church. She was asked to step down from her position as worship leader. In back of the church there was a loud "Boo," protesting and opposing the decision of the pastor. In our church we had Super Bowl Sunday in place of a regular church service. The advertisements that came across the screen were inappropriate and certainly not to be seen in His house, meant for worship and prayer. I attended a church-sponsored, "Wild Game Dinner" and numerous hunts were auctioned over the pulpit. It seemed odd to have an auctioneer behind the pulpit instead of a preacher. At our church they added a strobe light to flash over the walls. In my past, I have been in nightclubs where strobe lights were used but it isn't something I am accustomed to seeing in church. There is a church in my local area I attended as a teenager that now the senior members of the church are having card parties. We know a lady who brings her dog with her every Sunday and holds it during the service and it isn't a seeing-eye dog. Sometimes I wonder if we are letting some things "go to the dogs."

Recently a new church building was built in our area. The first Sunday it was opened I drove by and saw the parking lot was so full they were having a problem knowing where to park all the cars. I observed an old church across the street that has been there for over a hundred years, with only ten cars in their big parking lot. Several Sunday's later, I went to see why they draw a crowd, while other churches are closing their doors. I arrived early, so I sat in my car, watching the people enter the church. I noticed none of them were wearing suits and ties, so I took my suit coat and tie off, not wanting to look out of place. I wasn't seeing anybody carrying Bibles into the church so I left my Bible in the car. Upon entering the worship hall, it didn't take long to figure out why people weren't carrying their Bibles. It was so dark you couldn't see to read them. I couldn't see where I was going and was bumping into people. An usher with a flashlight came to my rescue and guided me to my seat. When I went to sit down I almost sat on top of another person, I could barely see what was around me. There were no windows in the church allowing for natural light. The worship band came onto the lighted stage and it reminded me of the days I frequented the nightclubs. The music was so loud, I couldn't hear and understand the words of the songs. When the band went off stage, the movie screen came down and the pastor appeared on the screen to deliver the message. He wasn't there in person, but technology sure did a good job of making it appear as though he was. This way he could deliver his message to 13,000 people, meeting in various locations and buildings. It was one of the best and most powerful sermons I have heard in years. I couldn't believe what I was hearing, he was preaching on heaven and hell, a topic I haven't heard discussed for a long time. I know their vision and focus is to reach the unsaved people in the community and to invite them to enter into a relationship with Jesus.

I was anticipating the time when the pastor would offer an invitation, giving the thousands of people an opportunity to accept Christ into their lives. When he stopped preaching, the band came back on stage and ended the service with a song, then everybody got up and walked out. It was a huge disappointment for me as I watched the people leaving without having an invitation to say yes to heaven and no to hell. I wanted to stand up and ask if anybody wanted to accept the free gift of eternal life. I don't know why an invitation wasn't given but I do know many people heard the truth about heaven and hell that morning.

Perhaps I didn't see people carrying their Bibles into church because they had a copy of the Bible on their electronic iPods, Kindles, or smartphones. These new devices are convenient to carry and you have them with you nonstop, which is a plus. Our Sunday School teacher uses this technology to find Bible passages, but it amuses me that we usually find the verses faster the old-fashioned way. I don't have a problem with using these modern devices because all ways to read the Word are good. I do wonder if it is a temptation to check emails, catch up on the sports scores, or text someone during the time set apart to give your undivided attention to God. You could even play games or watch a movie while sitting in church. If these devices were available when I was a teenager, I wonder how I would have used them. I never would have carried a *Playboy* magazine into church but now the possibility is there, to view pornography while sitting in church.

WHAT ABOUT KEEPING THE LORD'S DAY HOLY?

During Bible School, I memorized the Ten Commandments including, "Thou shall keep the Lord's Day holy." The community we lived in was corporately involved in practicing this commandment. Stores, gas stations, and restaurants were closed on Sunday. People believed working on Sunday was not part of keeping the Lord's Day holy. You didn't see people working in their yards or washing their cars or shopping. This work was generally done on Saturday, so you would be able to honor the Lord's Day. Some of our neighbors who didn't attend church, respected those who did and refrained from doing things that would be offensive to their neighbors. When my mother invited company for a Sunday meal, she did all she could do on Saturday, so she wouldn't have to do more work than necessary on Sunday. The church discouraged us from playing baseball on Sundays. We boys definitely did not see baseball as work but rather as fun and play. There have been many changes in our culture over the years when it comes to accepted activities for Sundays. Christians have differing interpretations on what keeping the Lord's Day Holy looks like in our present day. God gave mankind His commandments for our good and well being and has lovingly provided us with one day to rest from our labors. I wonder if we are only hurting ourselves when we neglect God's wisdom in setting aside this day, to experience a time of refreshment.

WHAT ABOUT THE KING JAMES VERSION?

The conservative Mennonites continue to use the King James Version of the Bible, written in 1611. For hundreds of years this was the version used by Christians, to live out their beliefs and convictions. Today there are many versions, paraphrases, and translations of the Bible. Some of these newer Bibles are translated differently from what they said for so many years. In wanting to be gender sensitive, some of the meaning was altered. One new translation mentions God has prepared for us a "room in heaven," while KJV uses the word "mansion." Now we are told we will have a room in heaven instead of a mansion; giving a different mental image. Either way I am sure it will be good, since God isn't limited by the word we use. I also appreciate the KJV because this is the version my father used for his daily Bible reading. When I went to him for advice he would often say, "Let's see what the Bible has to say about that." When my father passed away there was only one of his earthly possessions I really wanted and that was his Bible. I knew he had a lot of the verses marked in his Bible that were special to him. I am now using his Bible and every time I come across an underlined verse, it is meaningful to me, knowing it was meaningful to him.

WHAT ABOUT WOMEN IN LEADERSHIP?

As a boy, most leadership positions were filled by men. The men were instructed to take the role of leadership and responsibility, as head of the home. God's desire was for a husband to be a loving protector of his wife and children. Today I see a lot of women filling the leadership roles men once held. Sadly, many women are forced into this position because the husband/father has left the family. Some husbands choose to sit back and allow their wives to run the home instead of finding a way to work through the inevitable conflict that comes with close relationships. When men are complacent in the church, the women rise up to fill the need. In the past 30 years I have seen many women fill positions as teachers, song leaders, pastors, serving on the church board, etc. I am not denying the fact that God gives gifts to women to use to enrich others. I wonder what we are losing as a church and a society when men fail to take their rightful place of responsibility and leadership, while women are left to pick up the slack.

WHAT ABOUT THOSE OLD HYMNS?

During my childhood I recall the words of hymns, sung at church, going over and over in my head. I learned to know many of these hymns by memory and to this day remember most of the words. I have the precious memory of my mother and sisters singing hymns while they worked in the kitchen and of men whistling and singing hymns while they worked. Recently, a Bluegrass Band was playing mostly hymns on a Sunday night, at a local church. The ushers needed to set up chairs to facilitate the crowd. I haven't seen the need for extra chairs in a church service for many years. I realized I am not the only one that continues to find the hymns of old, meaningful and relevant for today.

Fifteen years ago, several larger churches in our area switched to all praise songs for their corporate worship times. Many of the smaller churches followed suit and also went to all contemporary praise songs. For the seniors in these churches, transitioning from hymns to praise songs, became a difficult adjustment. One Sunday morning our pastor announced that the church board made a decision to use all contemporary Christian music. A couple of days later the hymn books were found in the dumpster. He went on to say, if you didn't agree with this decision there were other churches down the road you can attend. The worship team formed a band with bass guitars and sets of drums. For those of us with hearing aids, we found the music so loud we could no longer hear the words of the songs. We could see the words on the screen but found it difficult to sing along. When I mentioned to an usher that the music was so loud it was hurting my ears, he offered me ear plugs if I needed them. Most of the hymn books were soon discarded in the dumpster and some of the older members did end up leaving. I wonder if the younger generation is missing out on a valuable part of their Christian heritage as they no longer have exposure to hymns which have influenced many lives over the past years.

For fifteen years I have been trying to learn and sing the new praise songs. Unfortunately, I haven't been successful. It is an ongoing problem for me to hear the majority of the words or to sing these songs by memory. Occasionally, a hymn will be played without the band. It amazes me how many people enthusiastically join in with the singing of a hymn. The trend seems to be the introductions of new songs on a regular basis, making it difficult for anyone young or old to memorize these songs. I have asked several young people who have been singing praise songs most of their lives if they can sing these songs by memory. I wonder if young people will have songs stored in their memory to sing when they are my age? "When we all get to heaven," this will be a non issue as we join in harmony to worship the one true God.

WHAT ABOUT FINDING A PLACE OF WORSHIP?

The last several years I visited various churches trying to find where I fit into the Body of Christ. My biggest challenge was the style of praise and worship. In many places, I couldn't hear or understand the words of the songs. It was becoming an ongoing frustration to me and once again I found myself in the same scenario; I got up and walked out of the church service. This was the first time I ever walked out of a church service, although I did crawl out of one in my teenage years. Obviously, I didn't get to hear the pastor's message that morning. For some reason I went back to the same church a couple Sundays later. To this day, I don't know why I went back, except for the fact that God led me there. I stayed to hear the pastor and I felt his sermon was meant for me. At the end of his message, he gave an altar call and one eighth of the congregation went forward to recommit their lives to Christ. The next time I went back and the altar call was given, the whole front of the church was lined up with teenagers. I didn't see any teenagers seated in their pew, they were all up front. It was amazing to see seventy or more youth standing up front and to observe the Holy Spirit moving in a mighty way. For the next six months I ordered a CD of the pastor's message and listened to the message over and over. I passed the messages to my friends and family, as well. He is one of the most powerful preachers I have ever heard. I felt the messages were spirit filled and should be available for all. I wondered if some people were not able to afford the fee for the CD and were missing out. I felt so strongly about it, I wrote a letter to the church and offered to pay for the CD's, so everyone who wanted one, could pick it up free of charge. My offer was declined due to other arrangements, but I am blessed to be fed so well every Sunday. The challenge for me is to be a doer of the Word and not a hearer only.

I continue to attend this church but I usually walk in late, after the praise time is over. I can't hear the words of the praise songs but I want to be there to hear the words of the message. This church is large and as in most large churches you aren't held accountable for coming in late or for missing a Sunday or two. No one comes up to me and says they missed me last Sunday, because they noticed I wasn't there. I am not recommending walking in late to church and not taking part in the whole service, but this is what I am doing for now. In spite of trying, I have not been able to reconcile sitting through the praise time, consisting of praise bands that hurt my ears and listening to songs that I can't understand. I recognize the impact in my life of regularly hearing anointed teachings from the Word, so I believe this is where God has me now.

WHAT ABOUT HONESTY AND WHITE LIES?

My mother told me a story that has influenced me when it comes to honesty. She told me about a time she fell into a temptation to tell a lie. One Sunday she invited her sisters and their families over for dinner. She served a cake for dessert. Her sister remarked how nice it looked and how good it tasted. They asked my mother if she baked it, and she answered yes. The problem was, she didn't bake it. This lie haunted her for months until she went back to her sister and asked her to forgive her for lying. When tempted to lie, this story comes to my mind as I recall how seriously my mother took lying. God has commanded us not to lie, because He knows how a lie breaks trust and is detrimental to any relationship. God desires our relationships to be built on truth and honesty, knowing this is what works best. The Bible is very clear on where a liar will spend eternity.

I take telling the truth very seriously. My wife will tell you she never heard me tell a lie. If I get to the point where I am tempted to lie, I will say nothing at all. The biggest temptation I have is to stretch the truth when telling a hunting story. It is so easy to add a little something to make it more interesting. My friends would make fun of me because I believed every hunting story I heard. I took for granted if someone told me something—it was true. Unfortunately, I came to realize I can't believe everything I hear. I have heard my share of hunting and fishing stories that were stretched. I suppose this isn't a new problem, since the saying is cloned about, "the big fish that got away" or "that sounds fishy to me."

WHAT ABOUT ALCOHOL?

I have heard a lot of sermons, concerning the danger of drinking alcohol and the warning of gradually falling into the pit of alcoholism. I have Christian friends who don't think there is anything wrong with having alcohol with their meal or drinking a couple of beers at a party. I once heard a preacher say, "Alcohol might not hurt you, but the example you are passing down to your children and grandchildren will influence them." Children can easily conclude, if their parents and grandparents drink, it's ok for them to drink also. I wonder how adults can tell their teenager, to only have one or two drinks, when alcohol is available and flowing, and their friends are abusing it.

Up until a couple of years ago, when I traveled alone and went out for a meal I would often order a beer. For me, I felt one beer wouldn't destroy my Christian walk. I am now called Pop-Pop by my grandson and I thought about the answer I would give my grandson, when he asked, "Pop-Pop do you drink beer?" I made a decision never to drink another drop of alcohol, so I can truthfully give him the best answer, "No, I don't."

WHAT ABOUT THE INFLUENCE OF TV?

I have many good memories of my parents visiting my aunt and uncles, allowing me to play with my cousins. Every weekend we looked forward to visiting with someone or guests coming to our house to visit. As my parents spent hours visiting, I also had the joy of playing with my cousins. It is my opinion that TV has played a huge part in ending this era of visiting with family and friends. In the first year of our marriage we moved into the same area where my parents, brothers, and sisters lived. To this day, all seven of us siblings live within an 18-mile radius of each other. My wife didn't know many people in the area, so we regularly visited with my family. When the Mennonite church allowed its members to have TV, we noticed a change in the amount of time given to visiting. Families could now stay home and occupy themselves by watching TV. I have experienced this dynamic and its effect in our family. I wondered why my family didn't come to visit with us, without an invitation. I felt hurt but have forgiven them all. When my wife was diagnosed with Leukemia, my one sister and her husband came to visit us. Judy and I have always invited my siblings over on Christmas night. Our extended family has a planned annual Christmas Dinner for all of our children to attend. For close to 40 years we annually rent a large cabin where we gather together for a weekend of fun, food, and fellowship. The last several years of my parents' lives, the brothers and sisters would gather at their home on Sundays to visit with them and with each other. Now that they are gone we are taking turns, planning a date and place to meet and stay connected. Planning ahead is good, but I wonder what we are missing by no longer dropping in to visit with family and friends, without a preplanned invitation?

WHAT ABOUT DIVORCE AND REMARRIAGE?

Divorce and remarriage rates are high, both outside and within the church. Statistics show 50% of marriages end in divorce. This issue has affected many families including my own. Christians desire to follow the scriptures, but on this issue Christians have differing understandings. I was dealing with the questions, if attending a wedding shows my approval of divorce and remarriage. The first place I went for advice was to my father. He went to a Bible passage that speaks about divorce and remarriage in Matthew 19:9, "Whoever divorces his wife, except for sexual immorality, and marries another commits adultery: and whoever marries her who is divorced commits adultery." In my later years I came to highly respect and value my father's advice and his desire to value the scriptures. He told me that he could not attend this wedding by his interpretation of the Bible. He was a man of God who deeply respected the truth of the Bible and lived by it for 97 years. During this time of searching for the truth, I went to at least 25 other people to ask their understanding of this passage. I discussed this issue with several pastors and Bible scholars to receive their input. I shared my convictions with my family and the reason why I decided not to attend the wedding. It was difficult to stand alone, as other family members felt free to attend. I decided to stand by my personal convictions and understanding of Matthew 19:9. My ongoing desire is to live my life based on scriptures and to be an example to the next generation, just as their grandpa and grandma were.

WHAT ABOUT THE DIFFERENCE PRAYER MAKES?

As I look back over my life, I realize the impact the prayers of my family and friends had on my life. My parents regularly attended prayer meetings held every Wednesday night and prayed for me there. My parents and their church friends were praying for me year after year. I have experienced the power of prayer and saw how God answered the prayers of my mom and dad and others, on my behalf. I remember seeing my mom and dad kneeling by their bed, every night. I know they prayed daily for their wayward son, resulting in thousands of prayers for me.

As an adult, my parents invited me to come to their church, to listen to Martin, the guest speaker. At the end of the service, Martin gave an opportunity for people to share what God has done for them. I was one of the first ones to share and I had the privilege of thanking the older people in the church who faithfully prayed for me at my parents' request. Most of them were in their 80's and 90's, and it was a humbling and emotional experience for me to personally thank them. I also had the opportunity to stand up and testify following my father's burial during a shared meal with friends and family. I was honored to testify of my gratitude for having a praying father and the difference his prayers made in my life. I want to follow his example and be faithful in praying for others, for as many years as I am given. I also want to encourage all to continue praying for others. As a member of the older generation, I see various trends that cause me concern for future generations. One vital way I can make a difference is to take my concerns and turn them into prayers. I know from personal experience that prayers will make a difference in the lives of others.

WHAT ABOUT MATERIAL POSESSIONS?

In my life I have everything that should make a man happy. I have lots of friends, we took many vacations and hunting trips. I have owned snowmobiles, ATV's, motorcycles, and boats. I have lots of motorcycle trophies, big game animal trophies, and more than enough money. All of my motorcycle trophies are packed away in boxes, and I have not looked at them in 40 years. In my house where I have lived for over 21 years, I have a trophy room with over 150 mounts. The door leading to my trophy room is off of the kitchen but I often forget the trophy room is even there. I don't spend time in my trophy room, mulling over or looking at my accomplishments. I generally go into this room during an open house we have in December or if friends come over to see the animals. I only remember going in one time in all those years to reflect on my accomplishments. Trophies and other material possessions only satisfy for a short period of time. I still like to hunt and get out in the woods to enjoy nature. I don't need to kill something every time I go out hunting, but I won't pass up a big buck. What brings me true satisfaction and fulfillment is that I have been blessed with a steady income that is sufficient to supply my family's needs as well as to reach out and help others who are in need. When I leave this earth, I know I will leave empty handed, I won't be taking my possessions with me. I totally agree with a motto hanging in my parents' home, which said, "Only one life will soon be past, only what's done for Christ will last."

WHAT ABOUT BEING A GOOD STEWARD?

After my apartments were sold, I had a major decision to make. Should I take the money I made from selling the apartments and go into debt to make another large investment in buying a townhouse complex? Businesswise this looked like the right thing to do. My accountant urged me to buy more units to avoid paying property gains. I could have bought these units and had my tenants pay them off for me in a 20-year period and died a rich man, leaving a large inheritance for my son. Another choice was to put the money into the stock market, and take a chance that when I go into full retirement, I could live in a very comfortable retirement home and spend the rest of my life there. As I pondered these decisions, I considered what the Bible says about wealth. We are asked to be good stewards of the possessions and money, He has given us to manage, while living on planet earth. We can use it to bring glory to God by giving money to spread the Good News of the Gospel throughout the world and to give to the poor and needy.

My son and I had a discussion about the decision before me. I explained to him, I would not be doing him a favor by leaving him a large inheritance. In my own life I had a lot less stress while going through the years of struggling to pay my bills, rather then now when I have decisions to make about a surplus of money. My son, being a Christian, told me he understands and doesn't have a problem with not getting a large inheritance.

I chose not to invest in more property. By not tying my money up for the next 20 years, it gives me the freedom to use money for different types of ministries. I want to help people who are struggling in this bad economy and there is always a need for money in missions.

Some of my Christian friends have shared with me the amount of money they saved over their lifetime, and how they are looking forward to living in a nice retirement home. These decisions need to be made by each individual to the best of their understanding. We all will be held accountable, for the way we used the wealth God blessed us with. All the money is His anyway and He allows us to be a steward of it. In the latter years of my life, I want to use His money for His purposes. Money can be used for the most important job, of helping others hear the Good News and impacting their lives for eternity.

Throughout my life I have given thought about the Bible verse that says, "The love of money is the root of all evil." I have asked myself, am I guilty of this." I have come to the conclusion that money is good because it can be used to expand His kingdom. The verse does not say money is evil but the love of money is the root of all evil. There are people who don't have an abundance of money but love money. It isn't the amount of money you have but your attitude toward money. Some people gamble and play the lottery in hopes of gaining money by chance or luck, instead of following God's principle of working to obtain provision. Proverbs 12:11, "He who works his land will have abundant food, but he who chases fantasies lacks judgment." There are so many needs in our world and so many ways to use money to spread the Gospel. There are needs for Bibles and church buildings all over the world. I didn't write this book, to make a profit, but if it does, I will be happy to give any profit to missions.

Five years before my mother passed away, I was visiting alone with my parents. They told me when they both die and the will is read, I won't be in their will. They explained to me, I cost them a lot of money in my earlier years, because of the trouble I got into. They paid numerous fines for me, I lived at home until I was 29 years old, and never paid for room and board. They didn't feel it was fair to the rest of the family if I received an equal inheritance as my siblings. I told them I understood and I had no hard feelings concerning their decision. A year before my mother died, I was alone with my parents again and they told me I was back in their will. They changed their mind saying, God forgave me for my past and loves me unconditionally and they want to follow His example. A Bible story tells us about a prodigal son who left his home, leaving his father and brother behind. He went and squandered all the money his father gave him. When the son returned back home, his father forgave him and freely welcomed him back, sharing his blessings with both his sons.

After my dad died, and before the will was read, all of my brother and sisters were together on a Sunday afternoon. I told them I had something to share with them and told them about the conversations I had with my parents. I explained how I was removed from the will and then a couple years ago, put back into the will. They were all shocked hearing this for the first time. I said, if anyone feels I shouldn't take my share of the inheritance, I was willing to divide it up among them. If they desired to follow our parents' wishes, as written in the will, I would give my inheritance to missions. A discussion followed, as to whether the money belonged to the family or if it should go to charity. The consensus was, it was my decision, and I could do with the money what I wanted.

My brother-in-law, Nelson, is part of DOVE Christian Fellowship International and oversees several pastors in Haiti. He travels there several times a year to support these pastors in their vision to transform their community. The needs in Haiti were monumental, before the January 2010 earthquake and overwhelming after the devastation of the earthquake. Nelson introduced me to Pastor Precol, and he shared with me the challenge he faces on a daily basis. His church provides an education for the children, since the government charges a tuition, that most families can't afford. When financially possible they feed the students lunch, because this is often the only meal of their day. Precol said his teachers have been faithfully teaching without a salary. I have been so blessed, I was glad to help these six teachers and their families, by supplying them with an income. With my inheritance, I decided to give toward building the walls and a roof, for his church and school. The amazing part is how far our U.S. currency goes in Haiti. Percol comes to the States every year for a conference and this year he shared with me that the people of his church, pray for my wife and me every day. Haitians pray with intensity and more than just a few minutes. This year, more than ever, I needed prayer as I struggled to write this book. I realized God was orchestrating His work in amazing ways. The Haitians were spending hours on their knees praying for me, when I needed it most. I asked him to thank his people for their prayers on my behalf. He laughed when I told him, "This was the best investment I ever made."

THOUGHTS WHILE CRUISING?

Last year my wife and I took a cruise to Alaska with a group of sixteen people from our area. Our guide for the cruise was a Christian and we appreciated having this Christian influence during our cruise. Part of our group included two Mennonite bishops. The one was retired and the other one is still active as a bishop. One night we all decided to go see a movie offered on the cruise ship. I was a little surprised when the two bishops went along with the group. They, like me, grew up in the same era of the conservative Mennonite church, where movies were forbidden. During the movie there were certain scenes I thought some of the Christians may walk out of, but we all stayed until the movie was over. In the lobby, the two bishops were talking together and I went over and threw my arms around them. I said, "If someone would have told me, forty years ago, I was going to watch a movie with two Mennonite bishops, I would have called them a liar." The last day of the cruise the tour guide asked our small group to share the highlights of the cruise. When it was my turn to share, I said, "It was nice being on a cruise with over 2,000 Christians." My friends looked at me in confusion. The guide asked why I thought everyone was a Christian. I explained, "We are taught if we smile and are happy, the world will observe our life, see we are different and will be attracted to Christ through this testimony. Everybody on the cruise was smiling and laughing and having a good time, and that is what a Christian is supposed to look like." I said, "I saw three passengers on the ship that could be identified as Christians." Two wore a pin on their sweaters saying "Jesus, I Love You." One lady in our group wore a prayer covering on her head, showing she was taking a stand for her beliefs. This took me back to the days of my youth when the bishop of the Mennonite church set guidelines in hope its members would stand out as different from the world and could be a witness of their faith. I am not advocating we go back to all those rules but I wonder how Christians can stand out in a group, showing and then sharing the hope and truth we hold in our hearts?

WHAT ABOUT ETERNAL SECURITY?

The first church my wife and I attended together believed in the doctrine of eternal security, which means once saved always saved. They teach once you accept Christ, you can never lose your salvation, no matter if you chose a lifestyle of sin. My wife grew up in the Lutheran Church and came to accept this doctrine. This was opposite from what I was taught as a Mennonite and I never did accept this teaching.

Our Sunday School teacher was also a pastor. He left his wife and children and married another woman and has been married several times since this. If anybody challenges him, he tells them he knows what he did was wrong, but he continues to believe he is saved and going to heaven. If I believed this doctrine, my decision to make a change may have never happened. I would have believed the commitment I made at 15 years of age, would have been sufficient, in spite of my depraved lifestyle. I feel I never would have turned my life around, if I would have believed once saved always saved.

We attended this church for ten years until friends invited us to a revival service at their church. We accepted their invitation and listened as the pastor shared his understanding of scripture. He taught if you intentionally live a lifestyle of sin, you lose your salvation. When the pastor gave an altar call at the end of the service, my wife went forward. At the time, I didn't understand why she made this decision. When we arrived home, I questioned her why she responded to the altar call. I was not prepared for what she told me, it hit me like a ton of bricks. She said she was unfaithful to me and after that I don't remember what all was said. I lost control and physically attacked her. I knew what I did was wrong and there was nothing I could do to make it right at that point. The next several weeks I didn't know how to handle this crisis and lost my temper several times. She had to leave and get out of the house with our young son, until I could find a healthy way to deal with my emotions. I never imagined this would happen to me and that I would need to face this crisis, of saving our marriage.

We had Christian friends that were working with both of us, giving us Godly counsel as we walked through this difficult time. They played a large part in helping us through the issues we needed to face. The affair all started on Judy's job. As a husband I wasn't doing my part of paying attention to her needs as I was traveling a lot. She will tell you today, there isn't any excuse that makes it right for what she did. She shared with me, that her boss attended a church that taught the same doctrine as our church taught on eternal security. During the affair they admitted to each other, what they were doing was wrong, but they both thought they were still going to heaven. I wonder if there are people whose belief in eternal security is actually giving them a false security?

WHAT ABOUT HELL?

I heard many sermons on hell, which made a lasting impression on me. I know the fear of spending eternity in hell, had a huge impact on me making a recommitment to Christ. My wife, son, and I attended church services every Sunday morning and evening, as well as Wednesday night while our son was growing up. I thought it was important for my son to hear sermons on hell, like the ones which influenced me as a boy. Our son was becoming a teenager and he never heard a sermon preached on hell. I knew the word hell is mentioned more than the word heaven in the New Testament. I went to our pastor and asked him why he doesn't preach on hell. He proceeded to tell me, he believes, if you put the fear of hell into a person and they accept Christ for this reason, their Christian walk won't last. I didn't accept his answer, because I knew the difference the sermons on hell made in my life. We sent our son to a Christian college in Boston, MA. While home on spring break, he told me he didn't think God would send anybody to hell. This blew my mind and it was disconcerting to know I was paying to send our son to a Christian college, for this type of teaching.

While visiting in other churches where a sermon was preached on hell, I witnessed people, including young people, going to the altar to accept Christ. Today you hear an abundance of sermons on the love of God, but few on the wrath and justice of God. Some pastors refrain from talking about hell and speak of being separated from God for eternity. Christians know being separated from God, means spending eternity in hell, but the world doesn't know what it means. When hell is explained this way, most non-Christians don't care if they are separated from God for eternity. They are not faced with the reality of spending eternity in hell.

The purpose for my life is to glorify the one and only true God and to share His love and good plan with others. I have found, the hardest people to witness to are close friends. John 15:20 says, "The world hates us because the world hates Christ." Witnessing to a person who says they don't believe the Bible, limits them in receiving the truth they need. Sometimes, when I share my faith, people tell me they don't believe in an afterlife and don't have a fear of dying. I say to them, "If you are right, I have nothing to lose but if I am right, you will have the rest of eternity to regret the lie Satan tricked you into believing."

The Ultimate Choice

In 2011 at the Harrisburg Sportsman Show, I met Gerry Caillouet, a man who greatly influenced my decision to write my life story. He was a vendor, with a ministry called God's Great Outdoors. His booth had a selection of Christian DVDs and books. He passed out tracts and other Christian literature at the show. Someone gave him a copy of the tract I had written years earlier called, "The Ultimate Choice." He came to my booth and asked to talk with me that evening, when the show slowed down. I went over to talk with Gerry and there I met another gentleman, Dr. Tom Rakow. He has written several books and is the Founder and Executive Director of The Christian Deer Hunters Association. Gerry has a radio show that airs mainly on Saturday mornings. His show is aired over 250 times in the U.S. and Canada, and is available worldwide, through the internet @ www.ggoutdoors.org. God's Great Outdoors is available for ministry in churches, across the United States and Canada. They have videos and DVDs of interviews from Christian outdoor writers, sportsmen, as well as hunting and fishing celebrities. The vision is to share their life stories and how coming to Christ has influenced and impacted their lives. Dr. Tom Rakow shared that his story was aired on a radio program called, "Unshackled." He encouraged me to be open to recording a portion of my life story on this program. Gerry said he would like to interview me to share on his radio program. Both men encouraged me to consider writing a book. There were new opportunities in front of me, but I needed some time to process if I wanted to revisit my past and walk through this door. I certainly felt incapable and inadequate as I focused on my limitations.

Several weeks later, Gerry was putting on a Trail To Adventure Conference, teaching pastors and laymen how to do outdoor, outreach evangelism at their church. The conference was in Hagerstown, MD, which was close enough for me to drive there to meet with Gerry for the second time. Before the Sunday morning service, we took an hour in the pastor's office, to pray and share. In June of 2011, Gerry had a tour where he was scheduled to minister in churches during Sunday morning service as well as hold conferences. Gerry and his wife invited my wife and I to accompany them on this tour to Alaska. For various reasons, we decided not to join them, but this didn't stop Gerry from continuing to call and email me. I didn't return his calls and emails, due to a family issue I was consumed with. I was experiencing one of the deepest valleys in my life. My father passed away and I greatly missed relating to him. We were financially donating to God's Great Outdoors but that was the extent of my energy and time I had to give.

I continued to have interest in this ministry, knowing Gerry was doing a great job reaching a group of people I naturally related to. A year later, while hunting in Chestertown, MD, I received a call from my wife. She said Gerry from God's Great Outdoors emailed her and said one of the board members was resigning due to his wife's health issues. He asked if I would consider serving on the board of this organization. He said every time he prayed, as to who should take this board member's place, God always brought my name to his mind. He felt very strongly I was the one, God was calling. I told my wife to email him back and tell him I would pray about it.

That morning I went into the woods and climbed into my tree stand, an hour before daylight. This was when I had time alone with God, praying and praising Him. Sitting in the midst of nature was very peaceful, without the usual distractions. I also had a radio and earphones to listen to messages, via radio. Charles Stanley from In Touch Ministry, is one of my favorite preachers. This particular morning, he was saying there are millions of church members, who rarely witness about Jesus. He went on to say, "God can use you at any age, even when you are 70 years old." I felt God was personally talking to me because at that moment in time I was 70. When I came out of the woods, I called my wife and told her to email Gerry, and tell him I was willing to serve on the board.

God has now given me 70 years of life and I don't want to miss out on the purposes and plans He has for me in the remainder of my allotted days. I decided to take every opportunity and walk through the open doors God has placed before me. There were many days when my life was out of control, but now I have the desire to daily allow God to be in control of my life. I sensed God was asking me to share my story in book form in spite of the obstacles before me. Over the years, when I shared my life's experiences, many people told me I should write a book, but until now it seemed like an impossibility. Reading, writing and spelling were never a strength of mine, and as an adult I never read one book, cover to cover. I always believed if there is a will there is a way. I decided to tell my story, by speaking and recording my life's experiences, to the best of my remembrance and ability. I asked my wife and sister for their assistance. They knew my heart was to offer hope to others through my story. The encouraging truth is, with God's help anyone can change, and God is always willing to forgive our pasts. My wife was willing to type what I verbally spoke and my sister was willing to help organize my story into a readable form.

It took months to record my story and it has been a very emotional and difficult time for me. I didn't really want to revisit the many years I lived a sinful and depraved life. I knew I would have to think in detail about these stories and it would be painful recalling those days. I had many interrupted nights of sleep as well as sleepless nights. During the night, thoughts would come to my mind and I would get up to record them. I have shared a lot of stories that I am not proud of and struggled with knowing if they were worth repeating, for all to read. My purpose is not to glorify sin, to bring attention to myself, or to expose others. Life is relational, and it has been a challenge to know how to tell my story, as it involves many other's lives, as well. This has been the hardest thing I have ever done, however, if this book impacts one person, in light of eternity, I consider it to be worth it all.

Before Apostle Paul's conversion, he murdered many Christians, and he writes in, 1 Timothy 1:16, "But since I was worse than anyone else, God had mercy on me and let me be an example of the endless patience of Christ Jesus. He did this so that others would put their faith in Christ and have eternal life."

SAVING THE BEST FOR LAST

I have saved the best for last and want to share with you, the ultimate choice each person will make. Each individual will respond with a "yes" or a "no", to the offer of eternal life. I don't want to end this book without giving you as the reader an opportunity to hear and respond to God's invitation of forgiveness. Forgiveness is the central theme of Christianity, freedom from the penalty of our sin, as well as freedom to respond with forgiveness when others sin against us.

I have made a lot of enemies throughout my lifetime, especially in the first 30 years of my life. I am well aware of my need for forgiveness from God and others. God and other people have chosen to forgive me, for the ways I have hurt and failed them, for which I am very grateful. With all of the things I have done, of all the people I worked with and guided during hunting trips, I am aware of only a few people who hate me even to this day. I have told these people I was sorry, many times. Forgiveness is a gift and cannot be forced. I have chosen to apply the gift of forgiveness, towards myself, towards others, including those who see me as an enemy. It is freeing to not hold a grudge or to have hatred in my heart, toward anyone. The Bible teaches us to pray for our enemies. Almost every day, I pray for those who see me as their enemy, to have a good and safe day and to experience the gift of salvation.

The best news ever is the gift of forgiveness, offered by Jesus, when He went to the cross to die for our sins. Most people are familiar with John 3:16, "For God so loved the world, that He gave his only begotten Son, that whosoever believeth in Him should not perish, but have everlasting life." This tells us of God's unconditional love for all and of Jesus' willingness to take our punishment for sin.

Beginning with Adam and Eve, Satan entices all to sin. The bad and the good news is found in Romans 6:23, "For all have sinned, and fall short of the glory of God, but the gift of God is eternal life, through Jesus Christ our Lord." The bad news is the fact that sin separates us from God who is holy. The good news is the fact that Jesus paid the price for our sin on the cross and through this we are offered the gift of eternal life. No one can enter heaven by being good or by following rules, and there is only one way. Jesus says in John 14:6, "I am the truth the way and the life, no one comes to the Father, except through me."

God gives us freedom of choice and will not force anyone to accept His provision for sin. Each person makes this decision while on earth, effecting where they will spend eternity. God did not make hell for people but for Satan and demons. He has done everything He can do to provide forgiveness of sins and to give us a vital relationship with Him. He has given us the promise of heaven, where there is no death, sickness or tears, because there is no sin or evil. Hell will be totally opposite because everything that is Godly and good will be totally absent.

304 THE ULTIMATE CHOICE

Regardless of your past, good or bad, you are invited to ask God to forgive you of your sins and to have a new beginning, as you commit your life to Him. He wants to be your Heavenly Father and will accept you as His precious son or daughter. Romans 10:9 tells us how to enter into this relationship, "If you confess with your mouth the Lord Jesus, and believe in your heart that God hath raised him from the dead, you shall be saved." When you ask Him to forgive your sins and invite Him into your life, you will receive the Holy Spirit. The Holy Spirit will comfort, guide, and instruct you in His ways. Baptism is a step of obedience; Jesus showed us the importance of baptism, by His example of being water baptized, as the Son of God. The scripture commands us to, "Repent and be baptized every one of you in the name of Jesus Christ, for the forgiveness of your sins and you will receive the gift of the Holy Spirit." (Acts 2:38) Our daily walk with Him includes asking for forgiveness when we sin, talking with Him through prayer, growing in His ways through reading the Bible. God knows we need the encouragement and council of other Christians, we can experience this by participating in a good church. In life people hurt people, whether intentionally or unintentionally and God has provided a way of freedom as we forgive and release others. I am so grateful for God's provision of forgiveness, which has made all the difference in my life. Following this decision, we are not perfect, just forgiven. As good books often end, I will close by saying, "I will live happily ever after" and you can too!

I hope my life's story has impacted you for good and something you read, was helpful. I talked to others who have written their biographies and they said some people will find fault and have negative things to say about my story. I am well aware everyone will not agree with the way I shared my story or with my comments. The Bible is the only perfect book ever written, so I accept the fact, this book is not perfect.

After I am gone, I desire my legacy to be about the things that really count. I don't want to be remembered for the mischievous things I did, the races I won, the animals I harvested, or any other experiences I shared in this book. I want to be remembered as a man approved by God. I hope and pray my family, especially my son, daughter-in-law, and grandson will be blessed with a continued Godly heritage, that was passed down to me. I am endeavoring to live my life, in a way that is pleasing to God and brings glory to Him. My final goal and desire is to hear my Savior say, as I enter heaven's gates, "Well done, thou good and faithful servant, enter into the joy of the Lord."